D1825316

localities
class
and gender

Research in Planning and Design

Series editor Allen J Scott

1 **Place and placelessness** E Relph
2 **Environmentalism** T O'Riordan
3 **The 'new' urban economics** H W Richardson
4 **The automated architect** N Cross
5 **Meaning in the urban environment** M Krampen
6 **Feedback from tomorrow** A J Dakin
7 **Birds in egg/Eggs in bird** G Olsson
8 **The urban land nexus and the State** A J Scott
9 **Not on our street** M J Dear, S M Taylor
10 **Integrated urban models** S H Putman
11 **Explanation, prediction, and planning** M J Webber
12 **The evolution of spatial policy** P Lawless
13 **Localities, class, and gender** The Lancaster Regionalism Group
14 **Critical rationalism and planning methodology** A Faludi

p **Pion Limited, 207 Brondesbury Park, London NW2 5JN**

localities

class

and gender

The Lancaster
Regionalism group

Linda Murgatroyd Mike Savage
Dan Shapiro John Urry
Sylvia Walby Alan Warde
with Jane Mark-Lawson

Pion Limited, 207 Brondesbury Park, London NW2 5JN

© 1985 Pion Limited

ISBN 0 85086 115 2

Printed in Great Britain by Page Bros (Norwith) Limited

Preface

This book has been written by members of the Lancaster Regionalism Group. Their joint purpose is to explore some aspects of how class and gender relations intersect within different local areas, especially as those areas are subjected to various planning and policy instruments. A further intention is an exploration of the different policy and political outcomes, especially as they are mediated through local, spatially variable, processes.

We believe that this book will be of value both to planners interested in the context in which their work is undertaken, and more generally to a variety of researchers interested in developing a spatially sensitive social science.

We are very grateful to various groups within which some of our ideas have been developed. These include the Conference of Socialist Economists Regionalism Group, the Economic and Social Research Council Urban Change and Conflict Conference and other ESRC workshops, the ESRC Oil Panel, the Women's Studies Research Centre at Lancaster, and the Department of Sociology, University of Lancaster. We are particularly grateful to Maeve Conolly and Heather Salt for their work in typing and preparing this volume for publication.

Department of Sociology
Lancaster
December 1984

Contents

1   Introduction   1
    John Urry, Alan Warde

2   Deindustrialization, households, and politics   13
    John Urry

3   The class and gender restructuring of the Lancaster economy,   30
    1950–1980
    Linda Murgatroyd, John Urry

4   Comparable localities: some problems of method   54
    Alan Warde

5   Explaining peripheral change   77
    Dan Shapiro

6   Policy, planning, and peripheral development   96
    Dan Shapiro

7   Occupational stratification and gender   121
    Linda Murgatroyd

8   Theories of women, work, and unemployment   145
    Sylvia Walby

9   Spatial and historical variations in women's unemployment   161
    and employment
    Sylvia Walby

10 Capitalist and patriarchal relations at work: Preston cotton   177
    weaving, 1890–1940
    Mike Savage

11 Gender and local politics: struggles over welfare policies,   195
    1918–1939
    Jane Mark-Lawson, Mike Savage, Alan Warde

References   216

Author index   233

Subject index   235

Introduction

John Urry, Alan Warde

In this book we show first, that a number of important social and economic changes cannot be investigated satisfactorily without analysing how those processes are embedded within different distinct localities. This means, not merely that there are variations by localities in such processes, but that localities are themselves significant forms of social organisation which have been underexamined, or inappropriately examined, by the different social sciences. Second, we investigate the role that various planning, policy, and political processes play, both in the way in which different 'areas' are organised in terms of given policy outcomes, and in terms of the complex consequences of such policies for the restructuring of social relations within and between such 'areas'. And third, the particular social relations which we investigate in the context of different localities are those of class and gender. We seek to show both that the analysis of gender relations has been neglected in much social science, especially that in which 'localities' have been the object of study, and that this analysis challenges many conventional ways of understanding the structuring of social inequality and the planning and policy objectives designed to ameliorate such inequalities.

Analyses and policies concerning spatial inequalities in the United Kingdom have traditionally been organised around the concept of the 'region'. Awareness of what was known as the 'regional problem' arose in the interwar period when industrial stagnation obviously affected different regions unevenly. Since 1945, in the attempt to prevent such large regional disparities in prosperity recurring, regional policies of various kinds were implemented by successive governments with at least some positive effects. The consensus of opinion is that regional disparities decreased during the postwar period, indicators of regional difference suggesting some convergence in per-capita income, industrial structure, and employment opportunities, especially between 1965 and 1975. However, recession since the mid-1970s appears to have halted such a trend, with, once again, industrial contraction coinciding with greater regional inequality. Thus, for example, as table 1.1 shows, since 1976 the regions of the north and west have become relatively poorer and their official unemployment rates have increased more quickly than certain regions in the south and east of the country. This table, however, also shows substantial increases in the rates of unemployment in all regions, so much so that the relatively prosperous and very large South East Region contains, in absolute terms, more unemployed people than any other UK region.

Compared with the 1930s, however, the contemporary problem of spatially variable inequality should not be seen as simply that of decline brought about by the collapse of regionally organised staple industries, such as shipbuilding in the North East, cotton textiles in the North West, coal and steel in South Wales, and so on. This is for a number of reasons, partly connected with the structural shift from manufacturing to services in the economy since the mid-1960s. Thus, for instance, between 1974 and 1982, the number of jobs in manufacturing decreased by 22% in the South East, by 15% in East Anglia, by 30% in the North West, and by 34% in Wales; in the meantime, the number of jobs in services increased by 3%, 14%, 4%, and 9%, respectively (*Employment Gazette* February 1983).

As Murgatroyd and Urry show in chapter 3, these shifts in employment patterns must be understood as the complex product of the spatial restructuring of different manufacturing and service industries (see Massey and Meegan, 1982). One cause of this deindustrialisation of the UK economy has been the increased proportion of service workers within, especially, high productivity manufacturing firms, as well as the growth of specialist firms providing 'producer services' (see Gershuny, 1978) In the United Kingdom this has had a spatial effect, with professional, managerial, scientific, and technical workers being relatively concentrated in parts of the South East. This is partly because firms selling producer services flourish in the more encouraging economic circumstances in that region. But this shift is also the result of the reorganisation of the large multiplant corporations which have centralised their in-house functions of conception and control in the South East. This has created a virtuous circle for this region, one enhanced by the fact that the South East generates more innovations and has a higher rate of new firm formation (Goddard, 1983,

Table 1.1. Gross domestic product (GDP) per head and unemployment rates for UK regions, various years (source: *Employment Gazette* various; *Regional Trends* 1983).

Region	GDP per head at factor cost (UK = 100)		Unemployment rates, September (%)	
	1976	1981	1976	1984
North	96.3	94.3	8.2	19.1
Yorkshire and Humberside	94.6	93.0	5.9	15.1
East Midlands	96.6	100.0	5.2	12.6
East Anglia	93.7	97.3	5.0	10.2
South East	112.6	114.5	4.3	10.0
South West	90.9	95.9	6.6	11.8
West Midlands	98.1	90.6	6.4	15.9
North West	96.4	94.3	7.5	16.5
Wales	89.9	86.8	7.9	17.0
Scotland	97.9	98.7	7.4	15.5
Northern Ireland	75.0	72.2	11.4	21.9

limited and there was little development of an appropriate *balance* of locally available job opportunities; and that regional policy facilitated the growth of new forms of the spatial division of labour which have acted against the long-term interests of the 'peripheral' regions. More generally, it has been suggested that regional policy, though not significantly adding to the proportion of higher level managerial, marketing, and research and development jobs in the 'periphery', has increased the spatial separation between such jobs and the routine manual and service jobs which are increasingly exportable through the so-called 'new international division of labour' [see RSA, 1983, pages 11–12; and see *Financial Times*, 1983, on the 1983 White Paper on *Regional Industrial Development* (DoI, 1983)].

The positive aspects of Conservative policy since 1979 have involved a major shift towards local area-based initiatives and away from a more regionally focused planning policy (see RSA, 1983, chapter 1 for a useful discussion). Recent developments have included the establishment of Urban Development Corporations for the London and Merseyside docklands, the designation of twenty-two Enterprise Zones offering various tax and rates exemptions and reduced planning controls, the fairly widespread existence of Inner City Partnership Areas and Programme Authorities, the expansion of various promotion agencies to encourage inward investment, and the general shift in resources towards sectoral, rather than spatially delimited, industrial assistance. The most significant future planning change, as outlined in the 1983 White Paper on *Regional Industrial Development* will be one in which certain footloose service industries will be available for standard regional development grants (rather than selective financial assistance).

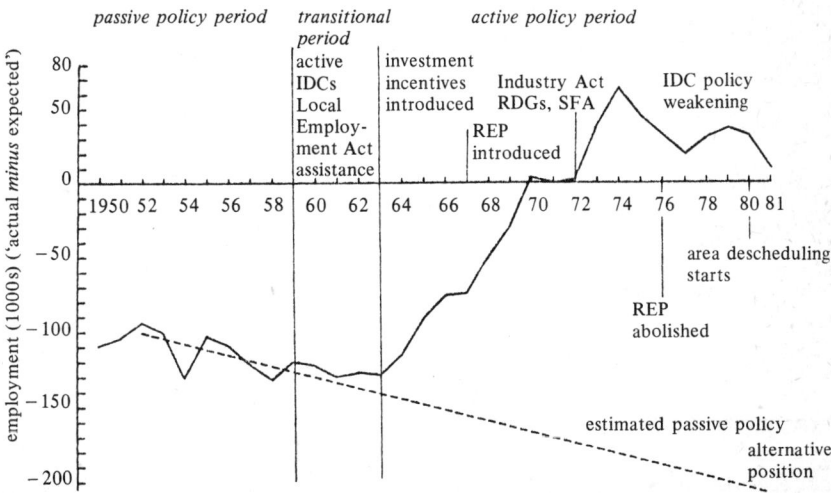

Figure 1. The growth of manufacturing employment in Scotland, Wales, the Northern Region, and Northern Ireland relative to the United Kingdom as a whole and after allowing for differences in industrial structure (source: CEPR, 1982). **Key** IDC: industrial development control; REP: regional employment premium; RDG: regional development grant; SFA: selective financial assistance.

There are connections between Conservative policies and important economic trends, particularly the increased emphasis upon the local area, upon the restructuring of industrial sectors, and upon the necessity to encourage service employment in Development Areas. The main problem with these initiatives is that they are ad hoc, contradictory, and unlikely to counteract the long-term structural changes currently taking place in the economy, which previous policies have, in part at least, brought about[1].

In the next chapter, Urry analyses certain social and political implications of the long-term structural process of deindustrialisation. He argues that there is no simple relationship within any area between manufacturing employment decline and service employment growth. Such observed changes are the consequence of complex forms of spatial restructuring within and between different geographical areas. Moreover, the very notion of a 'service' needs further examination. He distinguishes between service industries, service occupations, and service functions, agreeing with Gershuny that certain such functions are increasingly provided by the use of material commodities which enable household members to 'self-service' themselves (see Gershuny, 1978; Gershuny and Miles, 1983). It is argued that there is a widespread decline of opportunities in the 'formal economy', particularly for men; that various regional structures which had developed within and around certain male-employing manufacturing industries have collapsed; and that the growing acquisition of domestic production goods permits various forms of household and informal production. Because of the changing profile of capitalist social relations, Urry argues that there will be further decomposition of national social classes; the growth of nonclass social movements particularly focused around household and gender issues; and a heightened significance for 'local social movements', especially to recapitalise the 'locality'.

These last issues are discussed in chapter 3 by Murgatroyd and Urry in the context of the changing occupational and industrial structure of Lancaster during the period 1950–1980. They show that it would have been most misleading to have projected the City's industrial structure in the 1970s from its employment profile in the 1950s. The variation between localities within regions, measured in shift-share analysis as the 'differential component', far exceeded variation between regions. Murgatroyd and Urry demonstrate that spatial restructuring, nationally and internationally, in the manufacturing industries most important in Lancaster worked to the detriment of this particular local economy. From having had high potential for prosperity based on thriving manufacturing industries in the 1950s, Lancaster turned, rapidly and early, into a place dependent upon employment in services, particularly public services.

[1] Other policies, such as various local authority initiatives to encourage small firms, including cooperatives, and increases in the EEC Regional Development and Social Funds, might be subject to similar criticisms. Some aspects of local 'socialist initiatives' are discussed in the journal *Local Socialism*.

Moreover, this deindustrialisation of the local economy is shown to have been partly heightened by the regional planning practices employed in the United Kingdom, particularly between the mid-1960s and the mis-1970s. These policies caused considerable geographical movement of manufacturing plants, but those localities like Lancaster which failed to attract such mobile plants lost out directly, but also indirectly, as their capital stock became increasingly outdated. Murgatroyd and Urry further point out the relative weakness of the North West as a political force in the United Kingdom and hence its poor success in attracting regional aid. They also consider some of the political changes brought about by the restructuring of the local Lancaster economy, especially the increased role of women within the local labour force.

One implication of this chapter is that various national and international processes of industrial restructuring are producing new variations in local social structure. In chapter 4, Warde considers some of the problems involved in trying to specify what particular localities are like: how they compare with other localities, what the bases of comparison might be, and whether in recent years there has been a tendency for increased or decreased spatial differentiation between localities (also see Warde, 1984, on the last point). In this light, Warde examines several general taxonomies of localities to see whether they permit disciplined comparison. Each is described and submitted to evaluation on the basis of their profile of Lancaster and their usefulness in the analysis of contemporary social and economic trends. Warde argues that, though essential, existing classifications are of limited value for most purposes of social scientific explanation. This is because they generally lack any theoretical concern with spatial differentiation, with political processes, and with historical change. An adequate understanding of the impact of deindustrialisation in localities requires that the complexity of local social systems be better reflected in the construction of classificatory schemata; in particular, that attention is paid to the *comparative trajectories* of development of different towns and cities.

One particular classification of localities is explored in chapter 5, in which Shapiro discusses the problems involved in analysing the periphery of advanced economies. He considers some of the recent debates in a realist philosophy of social science, particularly as applied to the analysis of space and time (see Gregory and Urry, 1985, for a recent collection). This is then used to criticise the work of various writers, including Shapiro himself, who provide analyses of the periphery, either in class-reductionist terms or in terms of a dependent social formation. Shapiro considers how investigations of peripheral localities can avoid these errors and avoid unreconstructed notions such as 'community' or 'tradition'. He explores the applicability of the concept of civil society for mixed social formations. This notion is applied to the recent history of oil-related developments in the North of Scotland, an industrial sector with a distinct spatial division of labour and necessary relationships with given localities and with local states. Shapiro analyses the long-term effects on 'local civil society' of historical 'accidents' of policy. Gladstone's 'arbitrary' designation of Crofting Counties in 1886, in response to a short-term political expediency (votes on the Irish Question), can be argued to have produced a division in local social structure with at least a century of pertinent effects through the preservation of a 'semipeasantry'.

This issue of local planning is also explored in chapter 6, in which recent realist and neo–Gramscian theories of planning and spatial development are reviewed. Shapiro considers the relations between spatial location, local policies on development, local interests, and the response to development proposals. Examples from oil-related development proposals in peripheral areas of the North of Scotland are again used to explore the ways in which basically similar activities are defined and perceived in quite different ways in the context of different preexisting frameworks structuring local policy. Proposals for large-scale development starkly expose the implications of such policy environments, and the interests they may be seen to serve, and have the effect of unleashing complex and varying local struggles. The relative strengths of the parties to such struggles—major industrial corporations, local class and nonclass groupings, the local and the national state—are in turn affected by particularities of spatial location, and outcomes are also explored in these terms. Furthermore, these outcomes have marked effects on gender relations; for example, through the type of housing made available to incoming workers (temporary male work camps or specially provided 'family' units). The two chapters by Shapiro, then, particularly highlight the issues of resistance to planning and to the planning process, and of the effects of such resistance on eventual planning outcomes. The remaining chapters deal with these issues more generally in the context of gender relations and of their relationship to class in the determination of various policy and political developments.

One of the most striking social trends in the United Kingdom postwar has been a sharp increase in women's participation in the labour market. In 1951, 34.7% of women over 15 years of age were economically active, a proportion very like that of 1911 (35.3%). By 1981, however, the proportion had risen to 41.0%. This reflects in part a vast increase in the proportion of married women who do paid work, especially those returning to the labour market after the age of forty (see Hakim, 1979, on the bimodal pattern of women's employment). In the EEC, only Denmark has so high a participation rate for married women. Despite the extent of women's paid work (43% of the labour force are women), they are heavily concentrated in a relatively small number of occupations. Furthermore, where women and men work in occupations of the same name, women are crowded in the bottom strata of that occupation. These features have been described by Hakim (1979) as horizontal and vertical sex-segregation.

Murgatroyd, in chapter 7, explores vital theoretical defects of orthodox understandings of stratification with respect to sex-segregation in the labour market. She shows that there is so great a correlation between women workers, particular kinds of jobs, and poor rewards that serious doubt is cast upon the validity of the orthodox sociological distinction between 'places' and 'persons' in the division of labour. As a result, standard occupational class categories themselves become suspect tools, because they consider only occupational places without regard to the gender of the people who fill those places. Such a critique leads Murgatroyd to consider the origins of segregation and the relations between men and women at work.

Murgatroyd suggests that ultimately the basis of sex-segregation in the labour market is the conflict of interest between employers seeking to employ cheap female labour and groups of male workers trying to protect their own wages by excluding women. She also specifies some of the general conditions under which jobs for women are created. In fact, deindustrialisation has increased relative job opportunities for women, since much of women's employment is in the service sector. Some service sector jobs, however, tend to replicate tasks which in the domestic sphere usually fall to women (for example, nursing, cleaning), and others replicate typical male–female relationships outside of work (for instance, secretaries, whose hidden job content includes appropriately feminine and deferential behaviour towards a boss). That many of these jobs might be said to be distinctive by virtue of the social relations entailed in such work reinforces the point that a more discriminating occupational classification is necessary. However, Murgatroyd notes, at present too little is known about variations in the social relations of women's work.

In 1981, 47% of married women over 16 years of age were economically active. It is therefore a glaring omission, as Walby points out in chapter 8, that neither governments nor economic theorists have a coherent concept of married women's *un*employment. It is presumed that because married women have something useful to do when not in paid employment (that is, domestic labour) that they cannot be 'unemployed' as such. This procedure is encapsulated in contemporary UK policy, whereby married women are not counted as unemployed unless they are entitled to claim unemployment or supplementary benefit in their own right. Most married women are not so entitled, which, of course, minimises the official unemployment figures—the current official rate for women of 9.5% being a severe underestimate on any but the UK state's criteria. The appropriate criterion is, however, a matter of dispute, and Walby argues that the only satisfactory resolution is to consider all married women without jobs who would like paid work as unemployed (thus using the same criterion as for men or single women). To use such a notion, however, entails the development of a satisfactory empirical method of measuring women's unemployment in the United Kingdom.

Chapter 8 goes on to examine general explanations of the reason for, and the unfavourable conditions of, women's entry to and exit from employment. Existing accounts are shown to be in confusion. Many authors, despite divergent theoretical positions, attribute women's weak position in the labour market to their role in the family. Most other authors account for the position of female labour in terms of dual or segmented labour markets. Walby, however, argues that both explanations ignore patriarchal relations, and that attempts to explain the distinctive features of women's movement in and out of paid employment must analyse patriarchal relations within both the labour market and the household.

One important question arising from the study of women's participation in paid work is whether sex-segregation protects women from, or makes them more vulnerable to, unemployment. Walby concludes that the relationship between male and female rates of unemployment varies over time, and from place to place. This suggests systematic differences in the strength and interaction of capitalist and patriarchal principles. Her other chapter, chapter 9, demonstrates this with respect to changes in women's employment in various UK regions in the nineteenth and twentieth centuries.

It is a fundamental proposition of this book that consideration of spatial and historical variations in the interrelationship between class and gender is essential to social scientific analysis. The value of that proposition is made clear in Walby's analysis of women's paid work and unemployment in the United Kingdom. She separates out three processes which together account for uneven rates of employment decline for men and women: (1) industries and occupations with different sex-ratios may decline at different speeds; (2) more workers of one sex may be ejected from an occupation; and (3) new employment may be distributed unevenly between the sexes. These processes are interrelated and constitute the terrain upon which patriarchal and capitalist forces conflict. As Walby's several historical sketches illustrate, only with a conception of the gender restructuring of employment within different sectors can spatial and temporal variations in women's unemployment be explained. For instance, it was as a consequence of the way employment was sex-typed in the 1950s and 1960s, and of the pattern of industrial decline in the 1970s, that women do not appear to have suffered unemployment disproportionately to men in the current recession, although part-time women workers are especially vulnerable.

One hotly disputed issue in contemporary social theory is the relationship between class and gender divisions. The chapters by Murgatroyd and Walby demonstrate incontrovertibly that since work is undertaken on different terms by men and women, in the labour market and in the household, any adequate analysis of the social division of labour has to be able to explain and to incorporate gender differences. Patriarchal forces and capitalist imperatives combine and conflict in complex ways. What remains unclear is exactly how. The subordination of the working class in capitalist societies has had the well-organised consequence of political and industrial resistance to the bourgeoisie. The extent to which labour organisations themselves depend upon the systematic exclusion of women is, though, less frequently acknowledged. Moreover, the general assumption that capital seeks unequivocally to minimise labour costs is questioned by the fact that often employers will engage unnecessarily 'expensive' male labour. The final two chapters consider in historical detail the intricate ways in which, in specific localities, class and gender relations combine to produce distinctive political effects. The accounts are indeed complex, but they confirm the general methodological argument that temporal and spatial variation in class and gender structures are the sine qua non for analysing political and policy outcomes.

With such problems in mind, Savage, in chapter 10, explores one of the most interesting of interfaces between class and gender. He examines the development of control over the labour process in cotton weaving in Preston, North Lancashire, between 1890 and 1940. One of the principal features of weaving in Preston in the late nineteenth century was that most weavers were women, working under the supervision of male overlookers. The 'traditional' involvement of entire families in weaving, adapted for the large mills in the late nineteenth century, was exploited as the basis for a specifically patriarchal mode of control over the labour process. Patriarchal authority in the domestic sphere was invoked in the workplace in pursuance of labour discipline. In the absence of owners or managerial staffs with any functional concern with production, the overlooker had a considerable degree of importance. His autonomy vis-à-vis management was enhanced by effective unionisation in the 1890s; and his control over the mass of the labour force was maintained by control over hiring, output, and work discipline, not just through his patriarchal authority. Nonetheless he remained a manual worker, organised in a trade union, and heavily involved in labour and cooperative politics in Preston.

The ambivalence and precariousness of the overlooker's structural position is dissected in Savage's historical account of changes in control between the wars. A process beginning at the turn of the century, the power of the overlooker began to wane rapidly after 1914. A new stratum of managers, attendant on the (late) growth of the joint stock company in cotton manufacturing in the 1920s, usurped some of the powers of the overlooker. At the same time, certain of the familial–patriarchal bases of the prewar weaving factory were being eroded—largely as a result of changes in the Preston labour market. The implementation of Taylorist techniques in Preston was, thus, but a very late, and strenuously contested, step in a complex transfer of 'real' power over the labour process to a modern management. The growth of capitalist control at work is thus shown to be much more complicated than is often imagined. It is not, for instance, merely relevant to class relations, but also to gender relations. If levels of militancy be the criterion, the patriarchal mode of control appears to have been much more effective than Taylorism, for industrial conflict in Preston was muted until the 1930s. Moreover, forms of capitalist control vary not merely between industries but also between localities.

The final chapter of the book, by Mark-Lawson, Savage, and Warde, explores in detail the relationship between class, gender, and the politics of localities on the basis of a comparative analysis of urban politics and policies in three towns in the North West of England in the period 1918–1939. After some conceptual clarification about alternative ways of providing various kinds of services, they explain the reasons for sharp variations in the levels of provision by the local state of such services in Nelson, Preston, and Lancaster. Their study demonstrates the intricacies of the localised connections between gender and class divisions. They show that gender, routinely ignored in most inquiries into urban politics, is a critical determinant of the outcome of urban struggles. The strategies adopted by local labour movements depend upon the political strength of women. It is suggested that it is when women exert pressure that consumption issues take precedence over more narrowly defined economistic issues in the political demands of subordinate groups. This has important ramifications for the understanding of state welfare policies, for it implies that women have distinct interests in the public provision of services.

The question which this raises is under what conditions are women a politically effective force. Mark-Lawson et al show that the conditions are complex. It is necessary but not sufficient for women to participate widely in the local labour market. Rather, the nature of the social relations between men and women in paid work are critical. In the case of the town of Nelson the key variable was the fact that men and women in the textile industry typically worked in roughly equal numbers at broadly similar jobs. In that situation women had a significant impact upon the local state via the labour movement. By comparison, in Preston, with its history of patriarchal control in textiles and sharp horizontal and vertical sex-segregation in the labour market, the political interests of women went unrecognised and there was less generous provision by the local state.

These historical case studies illustrate the importance of the theoretical analyses of gender divisions and patriarchal relations discussed in earlier chapters. The sex-segmentation of labour markets and the patriarchal strategies available to male employers, supervisory workers, and trade unionists are shown to be essential to the understanding of various forms of policy and political outcome. The effects are usually to create and to reinforce women's subordination. However, there is significant local variation in that subordination and, under certain local structural conditions, women have been able to organise effectively to obtain some local policy outcomes which are fairly obviously in their interests. Clearly the relationship between women's organisations and the labour movement is highly controversial, but, without close attention being paid to the interrelationship of class and gender within different localities, the implications for politics and policy will remain obscure.

Deindustrialisation, households, and politics

John Urry

In this chapter, I shall consider the effects upon class relations and other forms of social struggle which follow from the processes by which the economy is becoming 'deindustrialised'. Broadly speaking I shall argue both against some of the claims of postindustrial theorists and their analysis of the service society, and against certain Marxist critics who reassert the enduring capitalist character of the United Kingdom today. It seems that, although it is not a 'postindustrial' society, there are important changes occurring within the United Kingdom which are transforming the interrelationship between capitalist social relations, on the one hand, and the other social institutions, practices, and forms of labour, on the other. In short, a new phase of capitalist development has recently been set in motion, at least within the United Kingdom, and in this phase there is a changed *profile* of capitalist social relations. What then was the old profile, and what is the new?

The old profile was dominant in the United Kingdom from the end of the nineteenth century until the 1960s. Under this pattern capitalist relations were relatively *widespread* and relatively *shallow*. By this is meant that there was a large number of relatively small capitalist manufacturing enterprises, these were located within distinct localities or regions, they employed particularly the male labour force, and they mostly sold the material commodities produced within that same region. Besides this capitalist industrial sector there were three others: a large but declining personal service sector; a moderate-sized capitalist agriculture; and a small but growing state sector. These sectors though clearly affected by market relations, were not directly subordinated to the power of capital. The effects of capitalist relations were relatively shallow, although those relations embraced a wide range of social practices and activities.

What then is the profile like now? Increasingly, capitalist relations of production in the United Kingdom are both relatively *concentrated* and relatively *deep*. The latter point is probably clear, and refers to the increasing concentration and centralisation of capital in the postwar period, and, in particular, since the later 1960s to the emergence of a declining number of phenomenally powerful transnational companies. The leading 100 UK companies now account for two-thirds of industrial output and they have the power to make or break particular localities or regions. National states compete amongst themselves to attract and to keep plants belonging to these companies. So capitalist relations are deep, and the remaining forms of noncapitalist labour and social activity are profoundly

affected by these vast conglomerations of capital. Yet there are also other
developments within the United Kingdom today which mean that within
this society, non directly capitalist forms of labour and practice are of
increasing significance. These developments include the large growth of
the state, especially as employer; the increasing tendency for manufacturing
investment and employment to be located abroad; the huge growth of
service employment, both public and private, with rather different labour
processes; the large increases in part-time work, underemployment, and
unemployment; and the apparently reduced importance of the so-called
formal economy. These developments suggest that, although capitalist
relations in the United Kingdom are increasingly deep, they are also
increasingly concentrated. In this chapter, I shall consider some
implications of these developments, and of the fact that, to put it simply,
most women and, increasingly, most men will not spend most of their
lives working full-time in capitalist enterprises producing mainly material
commodities. What are the political and social consequences of the fact that
the majority of people will not work full-time in such enterprises and that
for many people capitalism will be *indirectly* experienced as something
affecting their experiences within the sphere of circulation? How can we
make sense of these fundamentally significant changes in the structure of
capitalist Britain?

   In section 2.1, I shall consider one possible way of reconceptualising
contemporary developments, namely, the postindustrial society thesis.
Through consideration of the forms of service employment and the nature
of 'services' we shall see that this formulation is inadequate. I shall then
consider the relationship between manufacturing and service employment
more directly, and consider some resulting policy implications. In
section 2.2, I shall try to assess some of the effects that these changes are
having on the household, and, in section 2.3, on class composition and on
class relations and alternative forms of political struggle.

2.1 The service sector and service employment

I shall not consider the 'postindustrial' theses of Bell (1974), Fuchs (1968),
Gartner and Riessman (1974), Touraine (1974), and so on in detail here, or
more general issues concerned with the supposed centrality of theoretical
knowledge, or of the dominance of the scientific–technical elite, or of
how the universities are to be viewed as the 'primary institution'. As
Miller (1975, page 25) ironically remarks: "the post-industrial society was
a period of two or three years in the mid-sixties when GNP, social policy
programs, and social research and universities were flourishing. Things
have certainly changed".

   A central claim of the postindustrial society theory was that there had
been and will continue to be a shift from the concentration upon
capitalistically produced manufactured goods to the more socially conscious
provision of various kinds of services. Modern societies are seen as

becoming less and less 'capitalistic' and are increasingly involved in the provision of human services which are necessary given that basic material needs have been satisfied. As society gets richer, new needs develop which are more demanding of personal services, rather than manufactured goods, for their satisfaction.

However, there are major difficulties with this argument. As Gershuny (1978) points out: (a) those employed in the service sector may be as much involved in material production as in the provision of services to final consumers; (b) many service functions can be as or more effectively provided via material commodities, through *self*-servicing by individuals and household; and (c) there is no identity between the growth in service employment and the increase in the demand for, and provision of, services (also see Gershuny and Miles, 1983). Gershuny goes on to show that, although there have been very large increases in the proportions of the employed population working in 'services', there has not been in the United Kingdom anything like the same increase in the proportions of peoples' budgets spent on services (1978, pages 75–80). The proportion of the national income spent on services is less than half the proportion of the labour force employed in service production. Further, between 1954 and 1974, the category of personal expenditure showing the largest increases was that on 'domestic machines' (TVs, cars, domestic appliances) which enable people to 'self-service' themselves through entertainment, transport, producing food, and so on (see Gershuny, 1978, chapter 5). Substantial 'capital' investment takes place within the household and this enables service functions, once provided outside the household, to be provided within it.

A crucial difficulty which this analysis reveals in the postindustrial society writings is the considerable ambiguity in the very notion of a 'service' (see the discussion in Gershuny and Miles, 1983, chapter 2). Three distinct uses of the term can be identified: service *industries*— where the final product of the enterprise is a commodity which is in some sense intangible or immaterial, but which contains a labour force made up both of service and of nonservice occupations; service *occupations*—which involve forms of labour that are not directly productive of material commodities; and service *functions*—the specific uses (use-values) which consumers derive from the products both of service and of nonservice industries. The relationships between these can vary greatly, and much confusion in the literature stems from the failure to separate out these different notions. To examine this further, I shall briefly consider varying patterns of industrial change in the major Western economies during the twentieth century.

The main changes in France and the USA have been a major shift of employment out of extractive industry into service industry, the proportion in manufacturing increasing only a little over this century (see Rothwell and Zegweld, 1979, pages 38–39; Singelmann, 1978, chapter 5). However, the USA is also distinctive in that, along with Canada, its service industry sector has been proportionately larger than the manufacturing sector for all of this century, whereas in the European countries it is the manufacturing sector which has been larger until recently (on the USA, see Bluestone and Harrison, 1982; on Canada, see Walker, 1980). The experience of Japan is interesting in that its service industry sector has remained consistently larger than its manufacturing sector; and that although the latter is still growing proportionately, Japan became a leading industrial economy without a huge manufacturing sector (see Singelmann, 1978, pages 112–113). It has been able to do this by borrowing technology, which would also imply that newly industrialising countries will probably not develop very large manufacturing sectors. In other words, the Fisher–Clark thesis of a natural history of industrialisation, from primary to secondary to tertiary, as the leading and largest sector in turn, seems specific to Western Europe in the earlier years of this century (in general here, see Sabolo, 1975).

There is then no doubt that in all the major capitalist societies there has been a rapid and sustained increase in service industry employment; by 1975 it exceeded manufacturing industry employment in all European countries except the Federal Republic of Germany and Luxembourg (Marquand, 1980, page 27). However, the UK economy is relatively distinctive in the degree to which its manufacturing sector has shrunk. Manufacturing output has fallen from a peak in 1973, and manufacturing employment has fallen from 8.5 million in 1963 to 5.5 million in 1983 (for a general discussion of deindustrialisation, see Blackaby, 1978; Singh, 1977). Since 1970, while most economies have experienced jobless growth in manufacturing, the United Kingdom first experienced a period of job-destroying growth, then one of job-destroying zero-growth, and finally one of job-destroying industrial decline (see Marquand, 1980, pages 28–30 for the most accessible comparative material). Before considering some of the crucial consequences of this, I will make a number of comments on the service industry sector.

First, in most service industries, the service function is produced through there being some more or less direct interrelationship with the service industry producer, as is the case with many educational or health-care services (see Gershuny, 1978; Gershuny and Miles, 1983; Singelmann, 1978). In these cases, it is generally impossible to accumulate the service commodity, and there is nothing that can be termed commodity capital. Labour power has to be expended directly, when and sometimes where the consumer requires it. Labour power cannot generally be embodied in commodities whose value is realised at a later stage in the circulation of capital. There *are* exceptions to this—when the service involves material commodities such as dirty clothes, food, broken TV sets, educational courses, etc. In general it is more difficult to standardise the product, and hence to fragment the labour process, to the same degree as in manufacturing. There is a smaller separation of conception and execution, and a greater degree of control is maintained by many service industry workers over the nature of their work, even within distribution, clerical, and secretarial work. This is particularly marked in the case of those involved in so-called 'people-work' (see Stacey, 1981).

Second, because productivity growth is considerably slower in most service industries than in manufacturing ones, economising on labour costs principally occurs through the employment of sectors of the labour force who can be employed at less than the average wage of white males. In all the major capitalist economies (except the FRG), there have been much larger increases in the employment of women than of men in the growing service sector (see Marquand, 1980, pages 30–31). As a result, UK women are now five times more likely to be employed in service rather than in manufacturing industry (see Marquand, 1980, page 31; see Heath, 1981a, on the effects of this on social mobility).

Third, within manufacturing industry there has been a marked increase in the number of 'nonproductive' workers (service occupations), managers, professionals, clerks, scientific and technical workers, and sales and service workers. By 1971 these accounted for 34.6% of all workers in manufacturing industry (see Crum and Gudgin, 1977, page 5). Since the late 1950s the absolute number of direct production workers has fallen from 6.5 million to about 5.2 million in 1975 (Crum and Gudgin, 1977, page 5). Partly this reflects the changing industrial structure, so that roughly speaking the later the sector develops, the higher the proportion of nonproductive workers employed within it (66.1% in periodical publishing to 10.8% in miscellaneous wood and cork manufacture; see Crum and Gudgin, 1977, page 6). And it partly reflects the objective socialisation of nonproductive labour, of the differentiation of the functions of management between a large number of agents as conception is increasingly stripped from execution. Gershuny and Miles argue that the main cause of the growth in the number of service occupations is the changing organisational structures within each industrial sector (see 1983, page 65).

Fourth, even when we consider service employment outside manufacturing industry, we must not treat this as an undifferentiated category. The rise in service industry employment is undoubtedly a significant phenomenon— but we should regard the increase in the absolute and relative numbers as *an index of* underlying changes. This can be seen initially in the distinction between producer services and consumer services, where many of the former have been the most rapid to grow, whereas many of the latter have produced large job-losses. (UK employment in 'other business services' increased by 170% during the period 1960–1973, while laundries and dry cleaning accounted for a 43% job loss over the same period: see Marquand, 1980, pages 36–41; and Greenfield, 1956, more generally.)

Finally, it is necessary to consider the explanation of these various patterns of change; in particular, of the apparently homogeneous expansion of tertiary or service industry and of the number of service occupations. Gershuny and Miles (1983) provide a most effective criticism of the three-sector (primary, secondary, tertiary) model of economic and social change. They point to two particular deficiencies (see chapter 11): first, the model assumes unique linkages between particular economic sectors and specific sorts of human needs (for example, service industry meeting the need for service functions), which because of social innovation and technical change are not necessarily sustained; and, second, more specifically, it ignores how low-productivity growth in service industry may be met by providing the same service function through the purchase of manufactured commodities which enable the household to produce an equivalent service function for itself. Gershuny and Miles maintain that there are five interdependent processes which explain various changes in the economic structure. In the following, these changes have been incorporated into a further more complex explanation: (a) 'Engels's Law' changes whereby increasing wealth leads to the growth of demand for more varied, less 'basic' service functions (or use-values), and this produces some tendencies to socialising their provision; (b) changes in the mode of provision of particular service functions to households—first, through increased provision of services, and second, through increased self-servicing; (c) 'intermediate subcontracting' changes, in which activities once part of manufacturing production become separated off and become specialised 'producer services', particularly as a result of economies of scale and necessities implied by the falling rate of profit within manufacturing industry (see Heap, 1980, on the last point); (d) the productivity gap (and hence price gap) between labour-intensive service industry and capital-intensive manufacturing industry; (e) an occupational tertiarisation, which leads to an overall increase in the number of service occupations and within this to a decreasing ratio of clerical workers to the total; (f) the consequence of rising real incomes, which means that fewer people, particularly white males, are willing to provide a 'service' for others on a one-to-one basis; (g) political pressures which generate an expanded state, and hence an expanded formal service industry and an increase in the number of service occupations rather than informal, voluntary, or household provision of such service functions; (h) the development of new technologies within manufacturing industry— which can enable service industries to be socialised; and (i) the extension of commodity production to new product areas, such as computer software, where most are employed within service occupations.

Because this is such a complex process there is no simple relationship which can be posited between manufacturing and service industry. This poses particular difficulties for some versions of the deindustrialisation thesis which presume some simple relationship between manufacturing job-loss and changes in service industry and occupations. Some commentators maintain that there has been and will be necessary shift into so-called service employment or manufacturing employment contracts (what can be called the transfer thesis); others argue that if the industrial base declines then so too will service employment (on the industrial base thesis, see the discussion in CSELWG, 1980, page 69).

The main difficulty with the former view is that no mechanism is specified which would account for the transfer, except of course the availability of a larger number of unemployed workers to depress wage levels and to encourage especially secondary labour-market employment in various service industries. Furthermore, this supposed transfer partly conceals the fact that an increasing proportion of service employment is part-time, that the available work is in effect spread amongst a larger labour force. By 1976, for example, one third of all women workers in the UK service sector worked part-time (Marquand, 1980, page 31). The final difficulty with the transfer thesis is that it ignores the increasing way in which services are being replaced by domestic production goods, which ensure that the 'same' service function can be provided at a fraction of the labour time embodied in the conventional capitalist provision of such services. There are two important points about this: first, that this represents a further lowering of the costs of reproducing labour power, and hence raises the rate of exploitation to offset in part the empirical tendency for the rate of profit to fall (see Heap, 1980). And second, the decline in provision means that consumers are forced to provide themselves with material commodities produced by, what I earlier termed, relatively *deep* capitalist relations. We cannot avoid buying the capital goods necessary to service ourselves; the United Kingdom today is dominated by capitalistically produced material commodities—but *contra* the transfer thesis, not by capitalistic manufacturing and service employment.

There are three problems with the industrial base thesis. First, it ignores the fact that a great deal of service employment can be, and has been, generated within the state sector, in the United Kingdom, for example, between 1966 and 1978, or in the USA between 1975 and 1978 (see Gershuny, 1978; generally, see Sabolo, 1975). It is not clear why this could not be a relatively enduring pattern provided manufacturing *output* continued to rise. Second, it assumes that the spatial location of service employment will roughly mirror that of manufacturing employment. Yet this is not the case. Though 15% of the population of England and Wales lives in Greater London, 23% of service jobs are located there. Overall, 35% of the population live in the South East, but it contains 42% of service employment. In all other regions there is a location quotient, representing the proportion of service employment to population, of below 1.0 (see Marquand, 1980, page 69). Hence we cannot guarantee

that any particular form of the industrial base will 'generate' particular
levels of service employment, either within a locality or a region, or even,
to some extent, within a nation-state. And the third deficiency of the
industrial base thesis is that it presumes that service industries are less able
than manufacturing industries to generate output, growth, and welfare.
This is a very complex issue, but the evidence does suggest that at least
some service industries *can* generate increases in labour productivity,
output, and exports little worse than manufacturing industries, and can
produce increases greater than manufacturing industries in productivity
per unit of capital and in national and local income multipliers (see
Gershuny and Miles, 1983, chapter 3; Marquand, 1980, chapter 3).

Two related points follow from this discussion. First, within a given
locality or region, the planning authorities cannot guarantee that there will
be a viable relationship between manufacturing and service employment.
The main determinants of this are the decisions of large capital-units,
which are increasingly able to subdivide their economic activities, both being
able to locate offices and research in one area, and manufacturing activity
within another (see Buck, 1979), or to subdivide their manufacturing
activities within different areas in relationship to the pools of labour
variously available in different localities (see Massey and Meegan, 1982).
Second, at the level of the national economy, it does not seem that any
particular levels of manufacturing or service employment will be necessarily
sustained. For example, within manufacturing, the evidence suggests, at
least within inner cities, that job-loss has mainly resulted from the complete
'death' of existing plants, not from their relocation (see Keeble, 1980,
page 111). It might thus be concluded that the entire mainstream
production of material commodities could disappear from the United
Kingdom, leaving, as important exceptions, state-owned and state-financed
industry, industry related to geographically immobile resources like North
Sea oil, and the declining proportion of industry which has to be located
close to its market. And in terms of service employment we would
expect that the continual decline in manufacturing industry will have some
effect in reducing goods-related service production, which accounts for
about half of all service employment (see Gershuny, 1978, chapter 6).
And, at the same time, we cannot expect employment in consumer
services to increase substantially, since we have already noted the
tendency for the replacement of paid employment in service provision by
household labour using the 'capital goods' purchased from the deep but
concentrated capitalist sector. We can also expect some considerable
mechanisation of service work, given the generally high labour content and
hence high labour costs—this will be particularly true where some kind of
materialisation can be effected of the commodity in question (see CSEMG,
1980, chapter 5 on how the growth of micro-electronics is related to the

rising labour costs in service employment). Gershuny and Miles (1983, passim) argue that, even with the most optimistic scenario of the 1980s, a new information-based technological infrastructure, although generating some new jobs, "will actually accelerate the displacement of many categories of traditional service workers" (page 256).

The most obvious effect of these patterns of deindustrialisation is to produce very large increases in the levels of unemployment and under-employment. The following are some of the main points to note:
(a) The level of registered unemployed is over three and a quarter million and, according to the 1984 General Household Survey, we can add 25%–30% to this figure to indicate the number of nonregistered unemployed (see OPCS, 1979a, page 67; and see Showler and Sinfield, 1981, page 9 on the 'discouraged worker' effect).
(b) Most of the labour force is rarely unemployed, but a sizeable and growing proportion bears much of the impact (recently 3% have borne 70% of the weeks of unemployment in a single year; see Metcalf, 1980, pages 25–27; and see Daniel and Stilgoe, 1976, on how unemployment is especially concentrated amongst particularly weak sections of the labour force).
(c) There has been a very marked increase in the number of long-term unemployed (those unemployed six months or more rose from 930000 in January 1981 to 1750000 in January 1983; *Employment Gazette* June 1983, S 31).
(d) The supply of labour will continue to rise, with perhaps up to one million more in the labour force by the end of the 1980s—thus, without any decline in the demand for labour, there would need to be 800 new jobs created each day to maintain the present balance of demand and supply of jobs (see Showler and Sinfield, 1981, page 6).
(e) There is a considerable decline in the rate of economic activity in the United Kingdom—for example, between 1978 and 1982 the employed labour force fell from about 24.5 million to 22.5 million (*Employment Gazette* June 1983, page 57).
(f) There is a decline in the proportion of people employed on a full-time basis through the year—in the USA, for example, in most industries only about 60% of the employed population work full-time for the whole year (see Castells, 1980, page 182).
(g) Because of the positive correlation between increases in output and in labour productivity, there will be continuing long-term decline in the availability of work in the formal economy. This is because if UK output was to increase by 3%–4% per annum, this would raise labour productivity by 2%–3% per annum and hence produce very little increase in levels of employment (see Gershuny and Pahl, 1979, page 121 on how it is only if output increases by 6% per annum or more that output growth will generate employment growth).

There is, then, overwhelming evidence that the so-called formal economy in the United Kingdom is in long-term decline. In the next section, I shall consider the implications of this for the organisation of the household and of the forms of labour that exist within it.

2.2 Deindustrialisation and the household

In much political debate it is conventional to argue fairly directly from the analysis of the formal economy to certain sociopolitical consequences. This is obviously inadequate, however, if we seek to examine the increasingly significant area of gender politics which has developed around the division of labour in the household and around the patterns of male domestic violence. However, I want here to argue much more generally, that the analysis of the formal economy cannot provide an adequate understanding of the likely patterns of contemporary politics, and this is because such an analysis reflects an absolutely central dimension, namely, the characteristic social relations and social practices within and between households (what elsewhere I term 'civil society'; see Urry, 1984b). The following are three processes which are currently affecting households and which mediate the effects of the changes in the formal economy just discussed: first, the declining opportunities for regular paid employment within the formal economy, and the differential effects of this upon various household members, especially the gender differences (see chapters 7, 8, and 9 below); second, the decline in the community structures that had developed within and around male-employing manufacturing industries (such as steel, coal, fishing, railways, shipbuilding, merchant navy, etc); and third, the growing acquisition of domestic production goods by which households are able to service themselves.

The combination of these various processes has led many commentators to suggest that there is an increased importance of forms of work which are outside the formal economy (although these should not be lumped together as an 'informal economy').

The first set of evidence for the growth in a substantial informal sector in the 1970s comes from the divergence between the gross domestic products (GDPs) of income and expenditure. When the latter exceeds the former, this implies that there are fairly large amounts of income which are unrecorded. During the 1960s this difference was only 1% (of GDP of expenditure), but by the 1970s it had risen to 3% (see Macafee, 1980, pages 84–85), although it disappeared from 1979 onwards. We can take this as prima facie evidence for some increase in the forms of irregular or hidden sources of income (also see Macafee, 1980, page 87 on the rising value of notes and coins in circulation). A second set of evidence relates to changes in the taxation system. The introduction of value-added tax (VAT), and the fact that income tax is now paid by most income recipients, encourages numerous forms of tax avoidance and tax evasion.

Joel Barnett (Labour politician and former Chief Secretary to the Treasury) has suggested that the latter represents a loss of £3500 million in the financial year 1980–1981 (*The Guardian* 1981), and the Chairman of the Board of Inland Revenue calculates that income undeclared for tax may represent at least 7½% of GDP (Macafee, 1980, page 86). Matthews (1983, page 265) argues that the black economy has increased in size from 2.9% GDP in 1973 to 15.9% of GDP in 1980. There is no doubt that the effect of reasonably high *personal* taxation (note the shift away from company to personal taxation in recent years) is an inducement (a) to do the job required oneself; or (b) to pay someone 'under-the-counter'; or (c) to get someone to do it 'free' in exchange for some goods or service one can provide oneself; or (d) to pay for it with money acquired irregularly within the household economy. Burns (1977, page 163) says that the effect of high personal taxation is that initiative and incentive "reappear outside the market-place in the efforts of individuals and families to create for themselves that for which they once paid". Finally, we can anticipate that the growth of investment within the household enables many people, who are either not employed, or only irregularly employed within the formal economy, to engage in either monetised or nonmonetised irregular work. Especially with the relatively rising cost of services, there is much incentive to provide the service oneself, or to provide it for others on an informal basis. Burns suggests that even by 1966 in the USA the value of household property exceeded that of private capital, and that it becomes increasingly rational to work longer hours in the household economy and to use domestic capital goods to replace paid services (see 1977, pages 55 and 191). Some support for this comes from the United Kingdom, where there has been a 12% increase in the number of the recorded self-employed between 1979 and 1981 (*Economic Gazette* June 1983, page 258), but Matthews (1983, page 262) maintains that the true figure is considerably larger, especially because of the underreporting of part-time work in the service sector.

More generally, Pahl (1985; also see 1980) has recently and plausibly argued for the investigation of 'household work strategies', that is, the distinctive practices adopted by the members of a household collectively and individually to get work done. With respect to the 'informal' components of such strategies, Pahl argues that we should distinguish between (a) informal work within the formal economy, such undeclared and unrecorded 'shadow' work being most developed in Italy; (b) unpaid labour for self-consumption in the home, or what Tofler (1981) calls 'prosumption' (also see Pahl, 1985, pages 247–249), often using the sophisticated production goods referred to above, which in effect enable diverse forms of reskilling; and (c) informal reciprocal work outside the household, but in the locality, forms which depend upon knowledge of informal networks which are often more accessible to women than to men (see Gershuny and Pahl, 1979; 1980; Pahl, 1985, page 249).

In a given locality there will be a particular pattern established between these different forms of informal labour, depending in part upon the dimensions of the formal economy. Pahl maintains that different household work strategies emerge which are not related to variations in the man's social class as determined by his position within the formal economy. He also maintains that in his research on the Isle of Sheppey, types of work (a) and (c) above declined quite dramatically between 1978 and 1981 (no longer was steak and chips cheaper than fish and chips, for example). But his survey in 1981 did provide evidence of an "astonishing amount of work inside the household" (1985, page 260), although, roughly speaking, he argues that overall the decline in the formal economy has probably led to some decline in all other forms of work. However, for those households without much paid work, these forms of informal work, (a), (b), and (c) above, are particularly significant. Furthermore, although there is nothing new about these informal patterns of work, they are of particular importance because of their *scale,* the *sophistication* of the goods and services used and provided, and their *centrality* within the work strategies of some millions of households.

2.3 Deindustrialisation and politics

There are a number of important political consequences that follow from these changes, the effects of which are highly diverse. However, in assessing such changes it is important not to construct a misleading picture of economic and political struggles prior to 'deindustrialisation'. Roughly speaking the most significant form of oppositional struggle within the 'industrial' period of UK capitalism was economic militancy, combined with support for separate political struggle within the Labour Party. This pattern was found in the major industries—coal, steel, docks, railways, engineering, automobiles, etc. In each case there were a number of distinctive features: large numbers in each workplace, a high proportion of male workers, some development of an occupational community, and the centrality of that industry to the national economy. Yet, of course, at the same time, many industrial areas and sectors were not economically militant (such as Lancaster). What we now have to consider is not simply what are the forms of politics characteristic of deindustrialisation, but rather what are the variable effects the deindustrialising pattern will have on existing patterns of accumulation and struggle within each area. In other words, there is not a single form of politics which we can characterise as 'deindustrial', in the manner in which postindustrial theorists thought there was a 'postindustrial' pattern of politics. Our task is rather to illumine how the impact of new patterns of private accumulation and state activity are restructuring existing forms of economic and political struggle. We should not see these changes as simply undermining existing forms of struggle.

To illustrate this point, consider Massey's (1983) analysis of how industrial restructuring is a process of class restructuring. She considers in particular the differences between coalmining localities, especially in South Wales, and industry and politics in Cornwall. In the former case, it is not difficult to see how a number of conditions ensured the pattern of economic militance: a relatively undifferentiated working class; a single union; pride in the masculine character of mining and steel work; the relative lack of a new middle class or of a small entrepreneurial capital; and the lack of alternative forms of labour (Massey, 1983, pages 75–83; on masculinity and work, see Cockburn, 1981). However, the decline in the mining industry and the arrival of multinational plants and new forms of service employment threatens the power and dominance of especially the mineworkers. There are the following effects: first, to increase the size of the 'new middle class' and thus to blur lines of conflict between labour and capital; second, to increase 'external control' of the region and hence the difference between South Wales and more 'central' regions, and to heighten the demand for more top management and professional jobs *within* the region (rather than the regaining of the functions of conception and control); third, to decrease the average skill-level and to increase semi' and unskilled labour, especially for women, and hence to undermine the homogeneity, uniqueness, maleness, income, and status of the previous dominant forms of labour; and fourth, to introduce capitalist or state wage-relations to a relatively inexperienced and unorganised labour force.

Massey then considers the impact of similar industrial and occupational changes on Cornwall. Here she suggests the following opposite effects are to be found: first, to increase waged labour and not to depress wage levels; second, to produce a more homogeneous working class and other waged sectors; and third, to threaten traditional capital with competition both in the labour and in the commodity markets and hence to increase previously highly blurred lines of conflict between capital and labour (1983, pages 83–85). Hence the impact of a roughly similar pattern of accumulation and state activity seems to produce different effects because it is articulated with a quite different preexisting structure. Massey convincingly shows that to assess the significance of trends in de-industrialisation, we should not characterise regions in terms of *present* industrial, occupational, and class changes.

However, there are some issues raised by Massey's argument which need further exploration. In particular, she analyses fairly large areas or regions and does not explore the very important variations within them. Elsewhere I have argued for both the economic and sociopolitical importance of 'localities' (see Urry, 1981b), a view reinforced by Fothergill and Gudgin (1979, page 173), who argue that subregional variations in manufacturing and service activity are "truly enormous, with little if any consistency within any region. This massive variation

within regions brings into question the whole notion of 'regional' shifts
in activity" (also see Urry, 1984a).

One probable consequence will be to undermine the regional basis for
conventional working-class politics, to break up the 'radical regions' such
as South Wales (see Cooke, 1984b). Furthermore, especially while the
economy is being deindustrialised, this central importance of the local
labour market will heighten the significance of non-class-based politics
which are focused around the axis, the local social structure vis-à-vis
capital and the state. Clearly, the local basis of potential mobilisation will
vary, from being conurbation-wide (as in the case of the 'Save Merseyside'
Campaign) to being town- or city-specific (on the 'Save Consett' Campaign,
see *Local Socialism* February 1980, page 1). In either case, however,
there may well be disparate struggles directed against both or either large-
scale capital and/or the state because of perceived consequences of how
'external control' is undermining the strength of the local economy. As
stated in the 'Merseyside in Crisis' report (MSRG, 1980, page 41):
> "As the traditional industries continued to contract, the penetration of
> the multi-nationals created a further vulnerability. The future of
> Merseyside's workers was more often than not in the hands of companies
> whose power centres were continents away. And if not Detroit or
> Tokyo, then London".

In some places this has generated something of a 'local social movement'
based on protecting the locality (broadly defined, except in the case of
conurbations, in terms of the local labour market) against capital and the
state. This 'movement' may well be highly disparate, it will include a
number of distinct social forces which are on other issues opposed to each
other (local labour movement and local small capital), and it will employ
a variety of tactics (from marches, strikes, and sit-ins to lobbying
members of parliament, entertaining potential employers, etc; on recent
interlocality competition, see *The Guardian* 1983). Supposedly like 'urban
social movements', there is a "growing homogeneity in the interests of all
popular classes" (Castells, 1978, page 61). However, in this case it is an
homogeneity that does not transcend the locality, but is one which is
based on the specific differences between that and other localities. The
homogenisation is only local. So although there is often considerable
mobilisation of popular forces, and these may well provide much of the
original impetus for the local social movement, this mobilisation can do
little but to fragment social classes and to prioritise non-class-based
political movements (the journal *Local Socialism* is a very interesting
effort to prevent this). These local struggles are not generally intended to
abolish capitalist relations, but rather to increase the capitalisation of that
locality, so as, in effect, to sustain its reproduction. They are also intended
to increase, or at least to prevent any decrease in, the manufacturing base of
the local economy; that is, to counter its deindustrialisation and the growth
both of services and of the informal economy. However, paradoxically, the

struggles to sustain manufacturing employment will increase the likelihood that that locality will be further deskilled, and will be treated as a repository of secondary labour, perhaps on a par with many Third World economies (see the articles in Crick, 1981, for details of the deindustrialisation of various local and regional economies).

There are two other political consequences which in part follow on from processes of deindustrialisation. First, one of the effects of the relative cheapening of domestic capital goods is to encourage new or revised forms of household enterprise. In particular, there is an extension of petit bourgeois activity, resulting in part from the positive rejection of waged employment within the formal economy, whether by large corporations or by the state. Contrary to the arguments of Braverman (1974) or Mandel (1972) on the 'universal market', it would seem that there is a rotation by capital in and out of different departments and commodity sectors. As a result, profitable openings are available, in rotation within different sectors, to small-scale capital or to a kind of counter cultural petit bourgeoisie (see Gershuny and Pahl, 1980, on these developments). These are able to use relatively cheap household capital goods, they can save on overheads, they may be partly funded through the state (directly or through transfer payments), and they can serve local markets. These possibilities of extending the household and informal economies have potentially an important consequence in commodifying, individualising, and marginalising particular political struggles.

Second, this development can be seen as one aspect of the more general shift in political forms, partly away from the politics of production to the politics of consumption. Gartner and Riessman (1974, especially chapter 3) argue that (a) the industrial worker is no longer the leading force for social change and that this role is now played by youth, women, the minorities, and the 'educated affluents'; (b) the major movements now are related to consumer-oriented issues—the environment, participation, inflation, taxation, the quality of life; (c) a new dimension of politics has emerged which deemphasises electoralism and traditional organisations, and focuses instead upon movements, boycotts, publicity, legal actions, consciousness-raising, and community action; and (d) the basis for these politics is a new consumer consciousness which stems from the unique conjuncture by which individuals are consumers both of the sophisticated products of capitalist production and of the services especially of the state (also see the discussion in Miller, 1975). Two particular features of a progressively deindustrialised capitalism have contributed to this: on the one hand, because a considerable portion of the population will not have to work within the industrial work force, the population will be more open to a variety of alternative consumption and value orientations; and, on the other hand, the profitable production of capitalist commodities requires that consumers are constantly stimulated to feel dissatisfied with last year's product and to seek new forms of commodified satisfaction.

Exploitation has then in part shifted to the sphere of circulation and is expressed through rising taxation, inflation, faulty commodities, declining provision of services, and so on. Struggle shifts to this domain of consumption and is reflected both in the formation of specifically consumer bodies and, more generally, in what Dunleavy (1979) terms 'consumption sectors'. Saunders (1979, page 136) talks of the development of 'consumer trade unionism', namely, limited, piecemeal, reactive, and localised expressions of solidarism and dissent which may affect small shifts in resources, but which do not entail larger scale conflicts and struggle.

Cawson and Saunders (1983) have tried to systematise this distinction between production politics and consumption politics. They present this in terms of two ideal types. On the one hand, there is the sphere of the politics of production. Here capital and labour are directly represented as classes and they both negotiate with the state in the corporate sphere of the polity. Such politics are conducted mainly at the central and regional levels. And, on the other hand, there is the sphere of the politics of consumption. In this case a plurality of consumption sectors mobilise as non-class-based interest groups. They battle with each other over specific issues within the competitive sphere of the polity. These struggles are conducted in part at the central level but mainly at the more accessible local level. The latter struggles are fragmented by the diversity of consumption sectors, mobilisation is likely to vary greatly from issue to issue, and the possibilities of generating widely based local struggles, let alone national struggles, are highly limited. Local politics and regional and national politics are relatively separated.

There is, however, one particular difficulty with this formulation (see Harrington, 1983, for more general criticism). It is surely not the case that local struggles necessarily revolve around the politics of consumption. The deindustrialisation of an economy effects a substantial restructuring of the politics of production. This is partly because production is put back on the political agenda (if ever it went off), but in a manner in which struggles revolve around the recapitalisation of localities. Furthermore, various kinds of inter' and intraregional conflict are heightened, partly focused upon the unequal spatial distribution of industries and occupations. Struggles are oriented around the form taken by capitalist and state activity. The consequence of the imposition of new rounds of accumulation, with 'service' industry as the leading sector, will tend to disrupt working-class politics, partly because of the decline in the absolute and relative size of the traditional working class, and partly because of the increased local effectivity of employees in the service sector (for a rather different discussion, see Gorz, 1982). This thus means that there are local struggles focused on production, but often these will not take a directly class-structured form. However, at the same time, increasing numbers of UK workers will not be employed within capitalist enterprises. To the extent there is a growth of informal forms of economic organisation then there will be a further development both of consumption politics and of struggles to push back even further both capitalist and state forms of production. There is then an important realm of production struggles generated within the UK capitalist state, but these are progressively focused upon the optimal relationship between the formal and informal economies and between the state and private industry. We can anticipate that the growth of the household as a unit both of consumption, but more paticularly of material production, will further encourage struggles of a nonlabourist individualist kind. Certain of these struggles will involve opposition to capitalist relations, but often in a manner which involves opting out of regular, sustained, and full-time employment within capitalist enterprises or within the state (this has happened most amongst members of the Italian Communist Party in Emilia–Romagna; see Sabel, 1982, pages 220–222 on the 'high-technology cottage industry').

2.4 Conclusion

I have thus tried to detail some of the important political consequences of deindustrialisation—namely, that in certain regions conventional trade-union and labourist politics will be undermined, although perhaps developed elsewhere; that crucial importance is to be attached to localised disparate forms of struggle, especially to efforts to recapitalise the locality; that the household is an important determinant of political practice and *chaotic* that varieties of household economic and social relations will fundamentally affect political responses, especially of women; and that the growth in service employment, however related to capitalist production, will generate alternative forms of limited, transitory, and shifting struggles, particularly within the politics of consumption broadly conceived (that is, the 'fragments' as analysed by Rowbotham et al, 1979). We seem to be moving out of the heavily industrialised era of Western capitalism—but not into a postindustrial society. Neither the conceptual apparatus that sociologists employ for industrial capitalism, nor that generated in the optimism of 1960s postindustrialism, seem appropriate to the task of understanding the United Kingdom today, which appears more akin to a nonindustrialised country, but one with much of the structural and cultural heritage of a former industrial country—perhaps we will increasingly talk of FICs, 'former industrial countries', of which the United Kingdom is the leading example.

The class and gender restructuring of the Lancaster economy, 1950–1980

Linda Murgatroyd, John Urry

3.1 Introduction

In this chapter we shall consider how one particular local economy within the United Kingdom has been reorganised over the past thirty years. We shall suggest that this reorganisation, reflected in the apparently simple changes in the relative size of manufacturing and service employment, is in fact the product of complex relationships between the underlying 'restructuring' of the various industrial sectors pertinent in the locality. Thus changes in industrial location and employment are not to be viewed as the consequence of certain general processes which are merely developed to a lesser or greater extent in any particular local economy. Any such economy must rather be seen as a specific conjuncture, in both time and space, of the particular forms of capitalist and state restructuring within manufacturing and service industries. As Massey (1978a, page 116) argues, "the social and economic structure of any given local area will be a complex result of the combination of that area's succession of roles within the series of wider, national and international, spatial divisions of labour".

There are three important implications of this 'structural' approach for the analysis of industrial location and employment changes (see Storper, 1981, for a brief overview of this 'structural' analysis). First, the changing forms of the spatial division of labour, especially the shift away from a high degree of regional specialisation, derive from new patterns of capital accumulation, including the internationalisation of capitalist accumulation (see Fröbel et al, 1980).

Second, changes in the location of industry are not to be explained simply in terms of either 'economic' or 'political' factors. Location is rather to be understood in relation to those forms of economic restructuring within and between industrial sectors which are necessitated by the requirements of capital accumulation and state reorganisation (see Massey, 1977, for a critique of the conventional literature on industrial location). However, relations between classes, and other social forces, particularly gender groupings, also significantly affect patterns of economic restructuring, and the latter themselves influence social relations within particular localities to a substantial extent.

Third, problems of uneven development cannot be analysed simply in terms of 'regions' and of regional growth or decline. With the growth of national and international branch circuits of capital there has been a decrease in the degree to which productive systems are centred upon a particular region (see Lipietz, 1980; Massey, 1978a; 1978b). This has been related to the dispersal of new manufacturing employment on something of a 'periphery–centre' pattern and to some consequential decline in regional variations in unemployment and economic activity rates between the mid-1960s and the late 1970s (see Dunford et al, 1981, pages 12–13; Keeble, 1976, pages 71–85). This homogenisation amongst the peripheral regions has also been partly reinforced by the growing concentration of the functions of conception and control within the South East Region of the United Kingdom (amongst many sources, see Buck, 1979; Crum and Gudgin, 1977). Similarly, in terms of industrial change, Fothergill and Gudgin (1979, page 157) conclude that "there are much greater contrasts within any region than between the regions themselves" (more generally, see Urry, 1981b; 1983). One example of such contrasts may be seen in the North West Planning Region, in which Lancaster is situated. In 1966 this was one of only two regions said to possess a 'regional' industrial structure (see Fothergill and Gudgin, 1979, pages 170–172, and 174–176). Yet even in this case there have been considerable intraregional variations in patterns of employment in the recent period: (1) in the percentage change in male employment, 1960–1977, between −27.7% (Liverpool) and 15.6% (Crewe) (ignoring the new towns in the Region); (2) in the percentage change in female employment, 1960–1977, between −33.5% (Rossendale) and 58.7% (Northwich); (3) in the 1980 ratio of female to male employees, between 0.534 (Warrington) and 1.165 (Southport); and (4) in the unemployment rate, June 1980, between 5% (Crewe) and 13.7% (Liverpool) (Department of Employment, ERII[2]).

In this chapter we shall consider these three points in some detail, in particular in relationship to the deindustrialisation of the Lancaster subregion. This local economy is situated in the north of the North West Planning Region (north of Preston and Blackburn) and consists of the former Urban Districts of Lancaster and of Morecambe and Heysham, as well as extensive surrounding rural areas from the Fylde to the Lake District, and from Morecambe Bay in the west to the Pennines in the east. It constitutes a relatively self-contained labour market, with in 1971 only 7.6% of residents in the area travelling elsewhere to work and 8.7% of those working in it living outside [1971 Census of Population (see OPCS, various); for background details, see Murgatroyd, 1981].

Lancaster, like much of the rest of the United Kingdom, has been 'deindustrialised' in recent years. However, this change in the pattern of employment, consisting of a shift out of manufacturing both into service employment and into unemployment and underemployment, results from a number of underlying processes whose impact varies greatly in different regions and localities. Thus there is no simple 'deindustrialising' process

[2] Unpublished statistics from the Department of Employment (Caxton House, Tothill Street, London SW1). Most of these statistics are known as ERII but some referred to in this chapter are not, and can only be referred to via the Department.

by which national and subnational economies develop, with one kind of
economic activity automatically replacing another as dominant.

Hence, to say that a local, regional, or national economy has been
'deindustrialised' is merely a way of *describing* certain shifts in the structure
of employment—it does provide any kind of explanation. Thus, although
as a whole the United Kingdom has experienced 'deindustrialisation' in
recent years, this in fact results from highly diverse processes, affecting
different localities in different ways depending upon their location within
preexisting and new forms of the spatial division of labour (see chapter 1
above). Hence we shall demonstrate the inadequacy of notions both of
'deindustrialisation' and of the 'region' to characterise the diverse and
complex processes of economic class and gender restructuring that are
involved here.

In the following we shall show how the 'deindustrialisation' of Lancaster
has resulted from a combination of such processes. Although during the
1950s and early 1960s this subregion was an important site for private
manufacturing investment, the national and international reorganisation of
capital from the 1960s onwards (under the sway of UK regional policy)
produced a rapid decline in Lancaster's manufacturing base. We shall
focus on three manufacturing industries in greater detail, to show how
their particular forms of restructuring had the consequence that most of
the new employment that was generated was located outside Lancaster,
both abroad and elsewhere in the country. We shall also briefly consider
the restructuring of the service industries in the locality. We then turn to
some of the implications of the process of capitalist restructuring in
Lancaster for class and gender relations.

3.2 The deindustrialisation of Lancaster
Figure 3.1 indicates the major changes in the structure of employment
between 1951 and 1977 in the Lancaster economy. Overall, there has
been a major reduction in manufacturing employment, from around
17 000 jobs down to 9 000, with considerable job-loss being recorded in all
the industries with a substantial labour force. And at the same time there
have been major increases in the number of jobs in many of the service
industries, such that the overall numbers increased by 5 000 between 1951
and 1977. However, this overall change has not occurred smoothly
during this period. In the 1950s, both manufacturing and service
employment grew considerably, the former by 9.5% and the latter by
13.2%, both between 1952 and 1964 (Fulcher et al, 1966, page 2).
Overall, there was an increase in the size of the labour force of over 4000,
a rate of employment growth about equivalent to the UK average, but
faster than the average for the North West Region. The North West
Regional Council predicted that the Lancaster subregion would be a future
growth point both of population and of employment. With the development
of new science-based industries and extensive office employment, it

expected that the population would have grown to 140000 by 1981 (compared with 117000 in 1961) (see Fulcher et al, 1966, pages 1–2).

  These optimistic predictions for the 1960s and 1970s were based in part on the experiences of the 1950s. Within manufacturing, employment in a number of industries grew considerably: textiles by 32.3% (representing 1349 employees), engineering by 56.5% (360), clothing and footwear by 17% (124), and floorcoverings and coated fabrics etc by 25% (1002) (all between 1952 and 1964). Moreover, these increases involved considerable new building and machinery. Lancaster in fact attracted 7% more new industrial building than one might have expected on the basis of the size and structure of the manufacturing sector (compared with the North West as a whole, which attracted 21% less than 'expected'; see Fulcher et al, 1966, pages 10–11 and 22). Certain categories of service employment also showed very substantial rates of employment growth: distribution, 38%; insurance and banking, 35%; professional services, 42%; and public

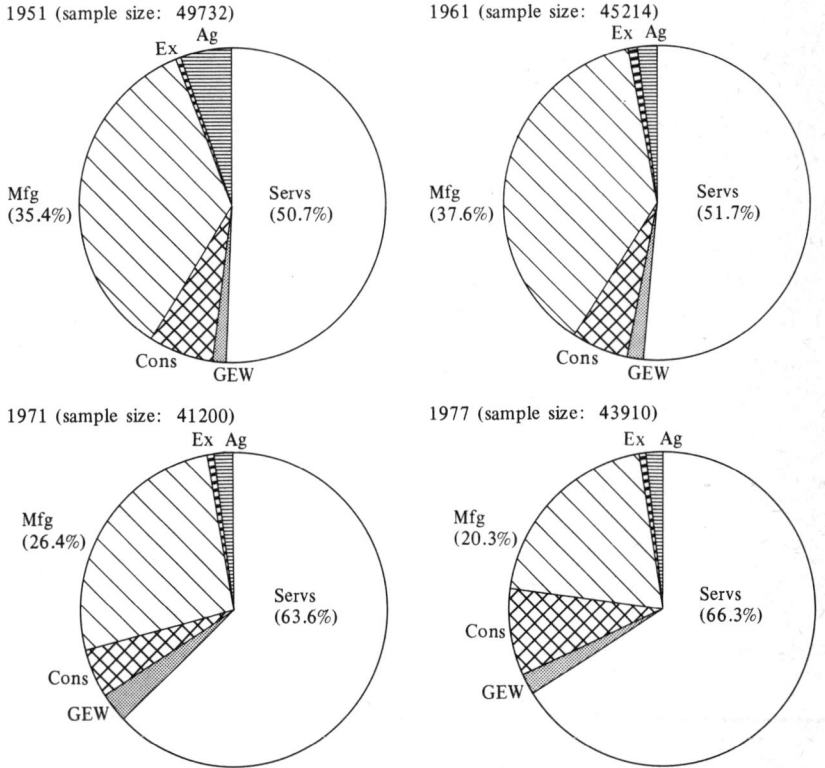

Figure 3.1. Sectoral composition of employment in Lancaster, 1951–1977.
Key Ag: agriculture [Industry Order (IO) I] ; cons: construction (IO XX); ex: extraction (IO II); GEW: gas, electricity, and water (IO XXI); mfg: manufacturing (IOs III–XIV); servs: services (IOs XXII–XXVII).
(Note: Industry Orders defined according to the 1968 Standard Industrial Classification.)

administration, 19%. The strong demand for labour was met by considerable migration into the subregion; between 1951 and 1964 there was net in-migration of 6845 people (1966, page 34). Moreover, even with this in-migration the rate of unemployment remained very low—the June unemployment figures, between 1954 and 1963, were lower than the national average in every year bar one (1966, page 38). This strong demand for labour was also reflected in considerable increases in female employment in the 1950s. The ratio of female employees to male employees increased from 57% to 61% (1952–1964), while the ratio for the North West remained more or less constant (Fulcher et al, 1966, page 37). Finally, even as late as 1964, local employers maintained that because there was more than full employment, they were unable to recruit the labour they required, and that labour had generally become much shorter in supply in recent years (1966, pages 40–41).

Over the next fifteen years this position was to alter quite dramatically. The significant feature of this period was the decline in manufacturing employment; at the beginning of the 1960s it accounted for about 35% of the labour force, by 1971 this was down to 26%, and by 1977 it had reached 20% (Department of Employment, ERII). The proportion of service employment has risen accordingly—by 1977 it accounted for two-thirds of local employment.

It is important to note, however, that this decline in manufacturing employment has not been accompanied by a corresponding decline in the size either of the population or of the economically active population, the latter has remained fairly stable, between about 44000 and 48000. However, this apparent stability conceals a number of divergent trends. Between 1951 and 1981, male employment fell by 5820, and the male economic activity rate fell from 81.4% to 71.9%; over the same period, female employment rose by 5400, or by just under 40% (1951 and 1981 Censuses of Population; see OPCS, various). This change was also reflected in the increase in the ratio of female to male workers in the subregion; by 1977 it had risen to 0.74, slightly higher than the mean for the North West, which has always had high female activity rates (Department of Employment). The general shift towards the service industries was related to the increased feminisation of the Lancaster labour force, since the proportion of women employed in these industries tends to be high. However, there was also a shift *within* the service sector towards increased feminisation (a 10% increase between 1971 and 1977).

Two further characteristics of the labour force should be noted here. First, there has been a considerable growth in declared part-time employment, especially during the 1970s, and, as elsewhere, women made up the majority of part-time employees (84.1% in Lancaster in 1977). Second, like elsewhere, there has been a long-term increase in the number of registered unemployed. The rates have been higher than the national average both for men and for women throughout the 1970s. The male rate doubled between the years 1980 and 1982 (8.5% to 17%), as did that for females (5.8% to 11.3%) (Department of Employment). Throughout this period there was a higher rate of confirmed redundancies in manufacturing than in services (average 66.6%). The year 1980 was the worst for redundancies in Lancaster (there were 1293), especially in manufacturing, and this mirrored the experience of the North West Region as a whole (Manpower Services Commission, personal communication, 1983).

Thus, up to the mid-1960s, Lancaster, with a considerable labour shortage, was a centre for investment. However, from 1965 this became less the case as investment took place elsewhere, and the local unemployment rate rose above the national average. The male rate in particular has increased steeply, there being a growing gap between the national and local rates, except during the 1972-1973 and 1978-1979 upturns in economic activity. One final point must be mentioned here. Although there has been a substantial rate of unemployment locally, the absolute numbers of unemployed have not until very recently been very large. Thus because of the relative isolation of Lancaster's labour market, Lancaster constituted a fairly small pool of labour, and this provides part of the explanation of why Lancaster failed to attract much major new manufacturing investment in the period 1966-1976—for many of the mobile plants a large pool of female labour was a prerequisite for accumulation (see Massey and Meagan, 1982, passim).

We have so far merely described the shift in Lancaster's recent history. An obvious explanation of this might simply be that this reflected the archaic industrial structure in the subregion. However, Fothergill and Gudgin's (1979; 1982) shift-share analysis of subregional employment change between 1959 and 1975 suggests that this was not the case (also see Keeble, 1976). Their analysis enables us to distinguish three components: first, employment change that would have resulted if employment had changed at exactly the national rate; second, change which would have resulted if each of the industries had changed its employment at the same rate as those industries had done nationally (minus the national component); and third, the differential growth caused by industrial movement into and out of the subregion and by indigenous performance. When applied to the Lancaster subregion we obtain the results presented in table 3.1. Thus we

Table 3.1. Different components of manufacturing employment change in Lancaster, 1959-1975 (source: Fothergill and Gudgin, 1979, pages 210-214).

National component[a]	Structural component		Differential component		Actual change[a]
	numbers	%[b]	numbers	%[b]	
−800	2900	19.5	−5400	−36	−3300

[a] In terms of numbers employed.
[b] Change in manufacturing employment, 1959-1975.

could have expected manufacturing employment to have increased by 2100 (2900 − 800) between 1959 and 1975. Indeed, the structural component for Lancaster was more favourable than for any of the other sixty-one UK subregions. By the late 1950s the industrial *structure* of Lancaster was exceedingly favourable. Fothergill and Gudgin note:

> "Expressed as a percentage of 1959 employment the worst subregional employment structure for *manufacturing* was North East Lancashire (−20.0%), reflecting its heavy dependence on the declining cotton industry, and the best was Lancaster (19.5%) ... dominated by a handful of firms in growing industries" (1979, page 169; the map on page 170 shows that only six subregions out of sixty-one had a structural component higher than 10%).

Hence the explanation of the decline in manufacturing employment (3300 between 1959 and 1975) rests with the differential component, with the fact that existing firms failed to grow and to expand employment, with their closure or shrinkage, and with their failure to attract the potentially mobile employment being generated in the 1960s and early 1970s. Indeed, Fothergill and Gudgin (1979, page 216) also show that the structural component remained positive throughout the 1960s, only becoming slightly negative in the period 1971–1975. However, in the same decade the differential component remained strongly negative; this then breaks down further in the period 1966–1971, as shown in table 3.2. In other words, in this period of considerable industrial restructuring there were no industrial moves into the subregion. The decline in manufacturing employment was wholly attributable to the 'poor' performance of the firms and plants located in Lancaster, although the industrial structure over the period 1959–1975 was, as we have seen, exceptionally favourable. Before considering how the pattern of accumulation in the 1960s had this dramatic effect, we will briefly consider service employment in this decade.

The results were almost exactly the converse of those for manufacturing employment (see table 3.3). The negative structural component for service employment was the highest for any of the UK subregions. The considerable growth in service employment in Lancaster was thus accounted for in terms of a very favourable 'performance' by service industries during the 1960s. The pattern in Lancaster was directly the

Table 3.2. Manufacturing employment in Lancaster, 1966–1971 (source: Fothergill and Gudgin, 1979, page 219).

Differential employment[a]	Net industrial movement[a]	Indigenous performance	
		numbers	%[b]
−2500	0	−2500	−17.7

[a] In terms of numbers employed.
[b] Change in manufacturing employment, 1966–1971.

opposite of that in most of the neighbouring subregions (see the maps in Fothergill and Gudgin, 1979, pages 170–171). In South Lancashire, Mid Lancashire, North East Lancashire, and West Yorkshire, the structural component for manufacturing was strongly negative, whereas that for services was positive. In Lancaster, as we have seen, there was a very favourable structural component for manufacturing, and a very unfavourable structural component for service employment.

Fothergill and Gudgin (1979, pages 178–180) thus argue that there was enormous variation *within* regions, in particular with regard to the indigenous performance of existing plants. In only three regions do all the subregions show an indigenous performance which is consistently in the same direction. Interestingly, even in the 1966–1971 period, which was particularly important in terms of industrial moves, indigenous performance was the main influence on manufacturing employment change. Fothergill and Gudgin argue that the main distinction in terms of employment change is between urban areas and semirural areas. It is in the former, and especially in the large conurbations, that manufacturing employment decline was most marked. This has resulted from the in situ contraction of employment and plant closures (1979, page 169). But it was in the less industrialised semirural areas that the most substantial increases both in manufacturing employment and in total employment were recorded (1979, page 189). This can be seen from table 3.4.

Table 3.3. Service employment in Lancaster, 1959–1971 (source: Fothergill and Gudgin, 1979, page 213).

National component [a]	Structural component		Differential component		Actual change [a]
	numbers	% [b]	numbers	% [b]	
2400	−1800	−8	2700	12.1	3300

[a] In terms of numbers employed.
[b] Change in service employment, 1959–1971

Table 3.4. Changes in manufacturing and total employment in different types of subregion, 1959–1975 (source: Fothergill and Gudgin, 1979, pages 183 and 184).

Type of subregion	% change in manufacturing employment	Total employment
London	−37.8	−11.4
Conurbations	−15.9	−4.7
Major free-standing cities	3.4	9.9
Smaller free-standing cities	17.9	17.0
Industrial noncity	16.3	22.0
Urban nonindustrial	38.8	18.8
Semirural	44.9	19.0
Rural	77.2	14.3

Fothergill and Gudgin classify Lancaster as 'urban nonindustrial', incorrectly we believe. However, even if it were reclassified, it would still fall into one or other of the categories *below* 'London' and the 'conurbations' in table 3.4. In other words, cities or localities similar to it in terms of its rural–urban characteristics showed very considerable growth of manufacturing employment in this period (between 16.3% and 17.9%). However, if we consider the category of 'urban nonindustrial' then their overall performance is truly outstanding—a mean increase in manufacturing employment from 1959–1975 of 38.8% compared with Lancaster's performance of −22%.

Furthermore, it should be noted that Fothergill and Gudgin show that the differences between the large urban and smaller semirural subregions still exist, even when the impact of regional policy is taken into account (see 1979, pages 189–192). The less-urban types of region show a differential growth over 30% better than the major urban centres, *both* in assisted and in nonassisted areas. The major difference made by regional policy is in relationship to net industrial movement, which, not surprisingly, greatly benefitted the assisted areas. However, indigenous performance and the growth of nonmanufacturing employment were no better in the assisted areas. The major difference, except then with regard to industrial movement, was that between the more urban and the more rural areas. Regional policy thus diverted movement towards the assisted areas; but it did *not* raise their indigenous performance. This further implies that so-called agglomeration economies are much less significant than has been previously estimated (see Fothergill and Gudgin, 1979, page 199; Townroe and Roberts, 1980).

Two conclusions can be drawn from this: first, according to Fothergill and Gudgin's analysis, Lancaster *should* have experienced some increases in manufacturing employment, given its industrial structure and the 'performance' of similar less heavily industrialised subregions. And, second, it is necessary to undertake more detailed analysis to explain the 'indigenous performance' of particular subregions, and hence to demonstrate the complex, interrelated, and spatially significant forms of capital restructuring involved here.

3.3 Lancaster and the restructuring of capital

Initially here we will summarise the main developments in the structure and ownership of the manufacturing sector. First, there was a significant increase in the numbers of establishments and of enterprises. In 1964 there were fifty-eight manufacturing 'firms' in the Lancaster subregion, whereas by 1979 there were 135 separate establishments. The size distribution has changed in the manner illustrated in table 3.5. There were very few small manufacturing firms in Lancaster in 1964, and this may have been connected with the tightness of the local labour market at the time; small firms found it hard to attract labour (Fulcher et al, 1966), and the abundance of jobs may have lessened the attractiveness of self-employment. Even allowing for some underreporting of smaller firms in 1964, though, there has been a substantial increase in the number of manufacturing firms in Lancaster, at the very same time that the subregion has been deindustrialised and manufacturing employment has dropped to about one-fifth. This increase is accounted for largely by the growth of small enterprises. Indeed, it is interesting to note how successful the subregion has been in establishing and attracting small manufacturing firms. Partly this may have resulted from the efforts of the City Council to encourage the establishment and growth of such firms, not simply because this is the only alternative, but also because of the perceived problems caused by dependence on 'externally controlled' capital. This problem was graphically highlighted in 1980 when the closure of the Lansil works owned by British Celanese (part of Courtaulds) caused more jobs to be lost than had been created by small firms during the whole of the 1970s.

We have already noted the local concern with the issue of external control. The local planning department has noted that:

"... it is significant that a very high proportion of closures and redundancies declared during recent periods of recession have been in firms who are under external control, i.e. 'pruning the branches to encourage growth'" (Lancaster City Council, 1977, Appendix IIIc).

Two interesting trends can be noted, though: first, an increase in the proportion of the labour force employed in 'externally controlled' enterprises over this period, but, second, a decline in the *proportion* of manufacturing firms that are in fact externally controlled (see Murgatroyd and Urry, 1983, table IV). A further point to note here is that *all* the large manufacturing firms in Lancaster are now externally controlled, whereas independent ownership is much more characteristic of the very small firms. Moreover, hardly any of the large plants were established by

Table 3.5. Size distribution of manufacturing firms in the Lancaster travel-to-work area, 1964 and 1979 (sources: Fulcher et al, 1966, page 14; Lancaster City Council, 1977, updated with figures from the City Planning Department and from *Who Owns Whom*, various years).

1964		1979	
Size of 'firm'[a]	Number of firms	Size of 'establishment'[a]	Number of establishments
Up to 100	35	10-100	109
101-250	15	100-1000	24
251-500	3	1000 and over	2
500 and over	5		
Total	58	Total	135

[a] In terms of number of people employed.

major multinationals; rather, they were locally owned firms which were *acquired* by (or merged with) large companies based elsewhere. In other words, external takeovers have been far more important for the employment structure of Lancaster than have patterns of branch-plant migration (except in the 1940s and 1950s with the establishment of a fertiliser factory by ICI and of an oil refinery by Shell). Lancaster has not therefore developed as a typical branch-plant economy. Nevertheless, as Smith (1979) found in the neighbouring Northern Region, it was these 'externally acquired' firms which tended to shed labour at a rate faster than 'independent firms' (see Murgatroyd and Urry, 1983, table V).

We shall now briefly consider why industrial capital did not invest in this subregion in the 1960s and 1970s. Already by the early 1960s there were a number of identifiable features relevant to this:

(a) The vulnerability of the economy because of the local dependence on a small number of important manufacturing industries, namely, fertilisers, weaving, textiles, plastics, and linoleum.

(b) The domination of the manufacturing labour market by a few large firms—this generally lowers the rate of formation of new companies (see CEPR, 1980, pages 23–24).

(c) The low unemployment rate and the small size of the labour pool, which would mean a failure both to attract regional policy incentives and to effect new plant in-migration.

(d) A pattern of increasing external ownership of the economy, so that even by 1964 the majority of workers in manufacturing were employed in plants that were externally controlled (see Fulcher et al, 1966, page 14).

(e) The development of an active policy of restructuring, especially during the later 1960s and early 1970s, which would weaken those local economies like Lancaster which were unsuccessful in attracting the new potentially mobile employment (much of which, of course, went abroad).

The last point is particularly important. It is generally calculated that the effect of regional policy was to add between 325 000 and 375 000 manufacturing jobs to the assisted regions in the period up to the mid-1970s (Moore and Rhodes, 1977). However, the main effect of this has mainly consisted in the *diversion* of investment away from certain regions and towards other areas. *The Cambridge Economic Policy Review* (CEPR, 1980) suggests that regional policy has been most beneficial for those regions which have experienced a full regional policy for all this period (namely, Wales, Northern Ireland, Scotland, and the North; see Dunford et al, 1981, figure 6, on the number of moves to Development Areas). For those other regions, like the North West, which have had only partial assistance, the effects of regional policy have been fairly limited and have not offset the effects of 'structural' and 'performance' components (CEPR, 1980, page 21, table 1.5). Keeble shows the relative weakness of moves to the North West; there were, as we have noted, no moves to the

Lancaster subregion during the period 1966–1971 (see Keeble, 1976, page 148, map 6.3a). Indeed, if we consider changes in industrial floor space between 1964 and 1972, there were only seven subregions in England which maintained about the same level, namely, Inner London, Lancaster, and the five subregions neighbouring Lancaster (see Keeble, 1976, page 97, map 5.2). What then is the explanation of this poor 'performance' in Lancaster, both in not attracting new accumulation and in failing to prevent in situ employment loss?

At this point we will introduce the distinctions made by Massey and Meegan (1982) between the different forms in which production is reorganised. We will suggest that Lancaster was one locality at whose expense the restructuring of the UK economy took place between 1965 and 1975. What then were the forms in which production was reorganised and what effects did they have?

There were three such forms: 'intensification', 'investment and technical change', and 'rationalisation'. The first is the process by which changes take place to increase the productivity of labour, but there is little, if any, loss of capacity and no investment in new forms of production. Such a reorganisation of production will generally entail less change in the distribution of employment than any of the other forms of reorganisation. In the second type, 'investment and technical change', there is heavy capital investment within new forms of production and, as a result, considerable job-loss, often highly unequally distributed. And, in the third form, 'rationalisation', there is closure of capacity without any particularly new investment or change in technique. Massey and Meegan attempt to show how in each of thirty-two separate MLHs (minimum list headings), which accounted for a job-loss of 312 100 between 1968 and 1973, one or other of these three forms are to be seen as the dominant cause of employment decline (see 1982, pages 10–11 for a summary table). In view of our present interest there are two limitations of their research: first, they focus upon a relatively brief period, 1968–1973; and second, they concentrate only on industries where there was employment decline (and incidentally where a distinctive form of the reorganisation of production can be identified). We have already noted that in Lancaster, by contrast, there were a number of industries that grew nationally in employment terms in the 1960s—the question for this study is why that growth did not occur in Lancaster. We suggest that Lancaster's manufacturing employment was concentrated in industries in which 'investment and technical change' and 'rationalisation' were to occur, rather than 'intensification'. To demonstrate this in detail is beyond the scope of this chapter: rather we will merely indicate the broad trends (for more detail, see Murgatroyd and Urry, 1983).

First, we will consider linoleum, plastic floorcoverings, leather cloth, etc industries (MLH 492 in the 1968 Standard Industrial Classification).

Table 3.6 indicates the main changes here. During the 1950s this was a relatively buoyant industrial sector with a 25% increase in the local employed labour force. However, during the 1960s there was a sharp decline in employment. The effect of this on what had been the major company since the 1860s in Lancaster has been described as follows:

> "The boom collapsed in the early 1960s, and the Mills [Williamsons] were forced into a defensive merger with a major rival: the merger led to considerable rationalisation, the disposal of surplus assets and the consolidation of both administration and production at the headquarters of the former rival [Nairns], in a government development area [Kirkcaldy]" (Martin and Fryer, 1973, page 168).

In fact, all floorcovering production was transferred to Kirkcaldy, and the Lancaster plant mainly concentrated on PVC wallcoverings instead. Overall, the rate of decline of this sector has been far faster in Lancaster than in the United Kingdom as a whole. This is because of the dramatic decline in linoleum production and the development of plastic floorcoverings and cheap carpeting based on man-made fibres. Hence there was a combination of two processes, in linoleum of rationalisation and the almost complete disappearance of manufacturing capacity, and of technical change and investment within plastic floorcoverings and carpet manufacture.

In the case of fertilisers (MLH 278) there was a similarly healthy employment pattern nationally, the numbers employed increasing from 18 000 to 22 000 between 1963 and 1970, and then declining to 19 000 (BSO, nd, page 210, table 6; 1978a, page 2, table 1). However, at the same time, there were enormous increases in net output, capital expenditure, and productivity. In table 3.7 the contrast can be seen with the floorcoverings industry.

Both output and productivity in fertiliser production increased tenfold over the period 1963–1978, whereas capital investment increased ninefold between 1968, and 1978 (all in money terms). The increases in productivity in fertilisers were greater than for any other branch of the chemicals

Table 3.6. Local and national employment (in terms of number employed) in linoleum, plastic floorcoverings, leather cloth, etc industries. The figures for 1952 and 1964 may include some employees in rubber and plastics manufacture—however, the numbers were small in this period and do not undermine the general picture of steady employment decline. There were also classification changes between 1972 and 1973. (Sources: Department of Employment, various and unpublished data; Fulcher et al, 1966.)

Region	Year				
	1952	1964	1971	1973	1977
Lancaster TTWA[a]	4019	5021	2502	1888	1483
United Kingdom	13 800	13 800	13 500	16 000	14 300

[a] Travel-to-work area.

industry between 1970 and 1975 (see COI, 1978, page 17). This capital investment was concentrated in the development of new, very large, low-cost manufacturing plant—by the late 1960s there were six major plants in the United Kingdom (ICI at Avonmouth, Billingham, and Immingham; Fisons at Avonmouth and Immingham; and Shell at Ince Marshes: see Warren, 1971, especially pages 194–200). As a consequence there was a 20% reduction in the numbers both of establishments and of enterprises between 1963 and 1978. Moreover, these enormous increases in output were achieved with little or no increase in total employment in the fertiliser industry. There was more or less constant national employment during the 1970s. Overall then the process of restructuring within the fertiliser industry was one of 'investment and technical change'. What then were the consequences for the Lancaster economy?

Local employment in this industry fell from 2285 in 1952 to 624 in 1977, for two main reasons. First, ammonia production was itself abandoned from 1977 and concentrated in the larger plants, especially in the North East. And second, the fertiliser made locally by ICI at Heysham (Nitrogel) could not compete with the new fertiliser (Nitran) which had been developed by ICI in the mid-1960s. The Heysham plant (in the Lancaster travel-to-work area) was disadvantaged in that its capacity was too small (500 tons per day, as opposed to up to 1500–2000 tons at more modern plants) and because none of its main production capacity dates from later than 1962 (interview with management, 1983). Again we see how capital accumulation in manufacturing industry did not occur in Lancaster in the past twenty years, and that this decline resulted from the development *elsewhere* of newer cheaper manufacturing capacity. Even moderate-sized plants producing for a specific regional market (for example, the ESSO plant at Warboys, Essex) were unable to compete with the major plants listed above (see Warren, 1971, pages 197–198).

Third, the production of man-made fibres had begun in Lancaster in 1928 with the establishment of Cellulose Acetate Silk Co Ltd (later

Table 3.7. Output, productivity, and capital investment in floorcoverings (Floor) and fertiliser (fert) industries, 1963-1978 (source: BSO, nd, page 210, table 6; 1978a, pages 2–3, tables 1 and 2). (Note that 'floorcoverings' refers to industries in MLH 492 of the 1968 Standard Industrial Classification; 'fertilisers' to MLH 278. Also note changes in classification in 1969, 1973, and 1979.)

Year	Net output (£m)		Net output per head (£)		Total capital investment (£m)	
	Fert	Floor	Fert	Floor	Fert	Floor
1963	36.7	33.0	2041	1644	10.1	3.5
1968	70.9	38.4	3674	2224	8.3	3.7
1970	81.6	47.4	3708	2530	16.1	4.4
1974	214.6	77.7	10875	4653	26.1	8.2
1978	366.2	117.0	19312	8963	71.2	n.a

known as Lansils), this being an era of considerable expansion in the production of cellulosic textile yarns in general. By the end of 1929 Courtaulds had thirty-three competitors nationally—yet, in the next thirty years, Courtaulds came to dominate the production of cellulose-based textile yarns (that is, rayon). By 1962, for example, Lansils was the only other producer of cellulose acetate (see Cowling, 1980, pages 81–92; Monopolies Commission, 1968, page 15). However, even in the early 1950s, the market for rayon was being eroded by the development of synthetic fibres, especially nylon and then polyesters, and of improved cotton. Over the following twenty years, Courtaulds came to dominate production in all sections of the textile industry, except that of weaving, which remained rather fragmented.

In 1978 there were 303 enterprises and 368 establishments in MLH 413 —weaving of cotton, linen, and man-made fibres (BSO, 1978c, page 2, table 1). Courtaulds partly overcame this fragmentation by establishing their own weaving plants, for example, at Skelmersdale (see Knight, 1974; also see Cowling, 1980, pages 291–293, which lists all major acquisitions, 1963–1974). Lansils was finally taken over by Courtaulds in financial year 1973–1974, having been owned by Chemstrand Ltd (a subsidiary of Monsanto) from 1962 (see Monopolies Commission, 1968, page 15 and Appendix 7).

Two conclusions are important here. First, man-made fibres constituted an industry in which investment and technical change was particularly marked, especially in the period up to 1970 (see Ewing, 1972, chapters 4 and 5, on some of the main technical changes). This can be seen from table 3.8.

Courtaulds itself was able to enlarge its monopoly position by moving into synthetics and by vertical integration (see CIS, 1974). The second point is that the effect of this in Lancaster was that the firm, Lansils, closed in September 1980 after a long period of decline. Courtaulds said that this was the result of substantial losses, but it was also partly because of the lack of updating or replacement of machinery since installation in 1952.

Table 3.8. Main developments in the UK man-made fibres industry, 1958–1978 (source: BSO, nd, pages 154–155, table 4; 1978b, pages 2–3, tables 1 and 2).

Year	Number of [a]		Output (£m)		Total employment (thousands)	Total capital expenditure (£m)
	ent	est	net	per person		
1958	10	30	49.5	1360	36.4	10.7
1963	7	26	108.8	2918	37.3	11.7
1968	5	26	163.0	4043	40.3	24.4
1970	9	26	172.8	4014	43.1	41.4
1974	27	43	293.9	6917	42.5	37.3
1978	24	36	297.3	8538	34.8	27.3

[a] Number of enterprises (ent) and establishments (est).

More generally, the reorganisation of the textile industry, the mergers, acquisitions, technical changes, and new plants in Development Areas and abroad (see CIS, 1974, pages 15 and 25–27; and Newbould, 1970, page 35, on the 1967–1978 merger boom), produced new accumulation away from the traditional Lancashire textile towns. Lancaster itself might have been protected in part from some of the worst consequences of this because of its involvement in the production of man-made fibres as opposed to cotton. However, this protection did not occur, again showing how accumulation in the 1950s has led to disaccumulation in Lancaster in the 1960s and 1970s. The total number of textile workers in the travel-to-work area declined from 5500 in 1964 to 1800 in 1977 (Department of Employment; Fulcher et al, 1966).

To summarise, in the 1950s, Lancaster benefitted from the accumulation in manufacturing and by the end of the decade had high representation in a number of growing manufacturing industries. However, these were industries that were to experience investment and technical change and rationalisation, particularly because of the increased centralisation of ownership. New plants were established elsewhere, and existing plants based on earlier technologies shed labour. Local branches of multiplant companies were run down, as these companies restructured their production away from Lancaster. Though the number of small manufacturing enterprises swelled during the later period, these did not provide sufficient employment to offset the decline in the larger establishments. It is important to note that of these industries in which there was much less job-loss in this period, two, according to Massey and Meegan (1982, chapter 3), appear as 'intensifiers' between 1968 and 1973. These are textile finishing (MLH 423), whose employment in Lancaster fell from 432 to 278 between 1971 and 1977, and footwear (MLH 450), whose employment fell from 549 to 414 (Department of Employment).

We will now consider the reorganisation of the service industries in Lancaster (for a general discussion, see chapter 2 above; also Gershuny and Miles, 1983). Between 1951 and 1977, the numbers employed in them increased by 21% (5000), compared with a 23% increase nationally. This overall expansion conceals, though, a number of divergent trends.

Figure 3.2 shows that between 1960 and 1979, employment in transport and communication declined by over one-third, while that in professional and scientific services almost trebled (rising by 180%). Other service industries maintained fairly steady levels of employment. In the relatively large size of the transport sector and the small numbers employed in financial services and government administration, Lancaster was fairly typical of the North West Region as a whole. During the 1950s, Lancaster had a lower proportion of people employed in professional and scientific services than was the national average (7.5% compared with 7.9% nationally), and in this it also resembled the average for the North West (see Marquand, 1980). However, during the 1960s and 1970s, the expansion of this sector resulted in strong local concentrations of employment in these services. 24% of the employed labour force in Lancaster were in this Industry Order (IO 25) in 1977, compared with 16% nationally.

Many of these shifts resulted not from changes in local markets or from other indigenous factors, but from decisions taken at a national level, concerning (mainly) changes in the railway, education, and health systems. As in the case of manufacturing industry, the domination of the transport and the professional and scientific services (IO 25) by organisations which extended beyond the boundaries of Lancaster resulted in reorganisation, which affected the locality to a disproportionate extent. Although the 'market' for many of these services is local, in the sense that health and education authorities cater for those living within their boundaries, there has been a concentration in Lancaster of specialised areas of health care (for example, mental health care, geriatrics) and of higher education, which serve a population far wider than that permanently living in the travel-to-work area. Employees and clients in these services are geographically mobile into the Lancaster area in order to take up the jobs or services available there (see Murgatroyd, 1981).

The tourist industry was the other major employer in the area. Here again, there is a net invisible export from Lancaster via the geographic mobility of the clientele, a large proportion of whom travel from other parts of the North West (Riley, 1974). 'Miscellaneous services' (IO 26) and 'distribution' (IO 23) are the two industries most closely connected with tourism.

In 1951, 'miscellaneous services' (which includes cinema and theatre, sport and recreation, betting and gambling, hotels, restaurants, public houses, clubs, etc) was by far the largest service industry in the area, accounting for 13.5% of all local employment—double the proportion nationally. As figure 3.2 shows, there were fluctuations in the level of employment in this industry, but by 1977 the net increase since 1951 was minimal, despite its increased *share* of employment locally.

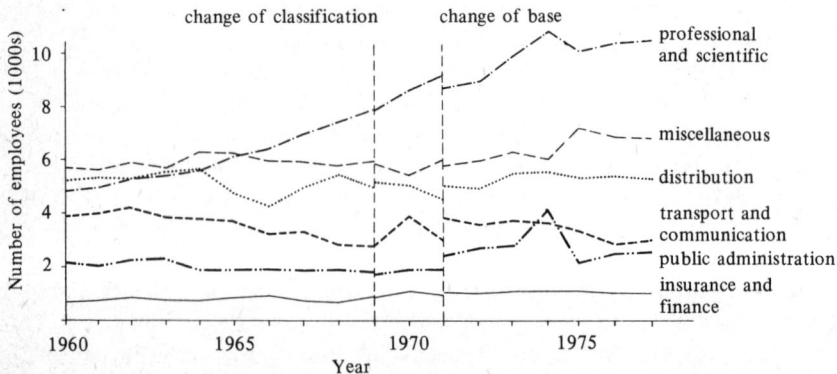

Figure 3.2. Number of employees in service industries in Lancaster, 1960–1977 (source: Department of Employment).

Similarly, distributive trades maintained a steady level of employment over the period, apart from a drop in the mid-1960s, attributable to selective employment tax. The level of employment in distribution was lower than might have been expected for a city of this size in the North West, for this region has a high level of retail employment (Marquand, 1980). The steady level of employment in distributive trades resulted from two opposing forces; nationally, retailing employment declined because of a shift towards large-scale outlets, but the population serviced by retailers in the Lancaster area increased, as a result of a high rate of in-migration of professional and retired families (Lancaster City Council, 1980). The local multiplier effects of the expanded health and education services more than made up for the slight decline in tourist-related employment over the period (Lancaster City Council, 1977).

Although little detailed information is available concerning changing ownership patterns in the local service sector, it is clear that there was a trend towards external ownership of the large enterprises in this sector as in manufacturing. There was also an increasing local dependence on public-sector employment in educational and health services. Not only has an increasing proportion of the local population come to depend directly on the state sector for employment, but also a great deal of employment in other services depends on the incomes generated by this sector. As manufacturing declined, the economy of Lancaster has become increasingly dependent on the level and direction of state expenditure (this has been further shown by the designation by British Gas of Heysham as the service centre for the Morecambe Bay Gas Field).

There are some important effects of these processes on the gender distribution of employment in this economy. First of all, although only one quarter of Lancaster's employment was in manufacturing industries in 1971, almost one half of employed males remained in manual (non-agricultural) work. This was accounted for by the small number of women in manual work. Only 21% of female employees were in manual occupations, whereas 31% were in junior nonmanual occupations; a further 15% were in personal service occupations and another 15% in intermediate nonmanual occupations. Most of the local expansion of employment in the service industries was taken up by women.

Indeed, there was a marked sexual division of labour in the local economy, which became even more pronounced over this period. There were at least twice as many men as women engaged in manufacturing employment, the numbers of both sexes declining in a steady manner over the period, with a small decline in the proportion of women. Numbers of males and females employed in the service industries both increased, but whereas in 1961 there were 127 males to every 100 females employed in this sector, the ratio had been reversed by 1977, with 116 females for every 100 males. Female employment in the service sector almost doubled during this period, while male employment, overall, increased less steadily and only slightly.

Over 80% of employed women in 1971 were in four occupational groups in service jobs; 28% were service, sports, and recreation workers, many of them cleaners, chambermaids, or engaged in serving food. 16% of women were salesworkers, 19% were clerical workers, and 18% were in the professional group. Of the latter, one half were nurses, and most of the remainder were teachers. Altogether, only 34.6% of employed males were in these occupations.

Table 3.9 shows the degree of sex-segregation among various occupational groups in Lancaster and in Great Britain as a whole. Women dominated clerical and service occupations (occupational groups 21 and 23), whereas men dominated most manual occupations, both in Lancaster and in the country as a whole. The manual occupations in which significant numbers of women were engaged in Lancaster, making clothing, textiles, or leather,

Table 3.9. Sex composition of occupational groups, Lancaster and Great Britain, 1971 (source: 1971 Census of Population Economic Activity Table; see OPCS, various).

Occupational group	Women as % of all employed	
	Lancaster	Great Britain
1 Agriculture, forestry, and fishing	17.2	14.0
2 Mining and quarrying	-	-
3 Gas, coke, and chemical makers	6.0	9.0
4 Glass and ceramic makers	-	32.0
5 Furnace, forge, and foundry workers	-	5.4
6 Electrical and electronic workers	4.9	14.0
7 Engineering and allied trades	2.5	11.0
8 Woodworkers	1.3	3.1
9 Leather workers	83.0	50.0
10 Textile workers	69.0	53.0
11 Clothing workers	90.0	80.0
12 Food, drink, and tobacco workers	17.0	30.0
13 Paper and printing workers	2.3	29.0
14 Makers of other products	10.3	35.0
15 Construction workers	-	0.3
16 Painters and decorators	-	3.0
17 Drivers of stationary engines	-	1.3
18 Labourers not classified elsewhere	13.0	11.0
19 Transport and communications	24.0	11.0
20 Warehouse keepers, packers, bottlers	22.0	37.0
21 Clerical workers	70.0	70.0
22 Salesworkers	52.0	47.0
23 Service, sports, and recreation workers	70.0	69.0
24 Administrators and managers	10.0	8.5
25 Professionals, technicians, and artists	45.0	38.0
26 Armed forces	-	4.9
27 Inadequately described occupations	54.0	57.0

were very much dominated by women. 90%, 69%, and 83% (respectively) of workers in these trades were female. These were also the only manual (nonservicing) occupational groups which were predominantly female at the national level.

Thus the expansion of women's employment did not imply a greater similarity between the positions of men and of women in the local labour market, nor indeed in the division of labour more generally. A high degree of occupational segregation persisted in Lancaster, as we have seen. Far from women entering traditional domains of male activity, it was the feminised industries that expanded. To some extent, the lack of alternative occupations for less-skilled males has meant that, if they were to avoid unemployment, they have been forced to accept work of traditionally feminine types, or else provide their own employment. However, although there is no evidence that the types of work and the conditions of employment of women noticeably improved, and there was an increasing level of female unemployment as well as male, it is clear that the local labour-market position did improve compared with that of men.

3.4 State policies and local politics
Thus there has been a substantial shift in the character of this local economy over the past thirty years. It has changed from being an economy which was dominated by a small number of private manufacturing employers, who were involved in numerous commodity and interpersonal linkages with the locality and with the surrounding textile-based region, and who mainly employed semiskilled male workers, to being an economy in which the state is the dominant employer and in which the fortunes of the small private employers depend upon the expansion or contraction of state expenditure, especially within the feminised service sector. Hardly any substantial manufacturing establishments remain (two of the three biggest have now disappeared), and there are limited linkages with other locally based firms.

We will now consider three significant political aspects of these developments. First, why was Lancaster unable to attract the mobile new employment that was generated in those manufacturing industries undergoing technical change and making new investments in the 1960s and early 1970s? Second, what were the characteristic features of the economic and social relations in Lancaster? To what extent can these relations be described as being 'paternalistic'? And third, what have been the consequences of the changes in the ownership and the structure of employment upon the local social structure?

On the first question we should note that Lancaster is part of the North West Region, and this region has performed badly in employment terms over the recent period. Stillwell (1968, page 10) maintains that the North West was among "the least attractive regions in which to locate industry" (also see Fothergill and Gudgin, 1982). This meant that other regions attracted the mobile plants which made a major difference in employment terms. Mackay and Thomson (1979, page 241) suggest that the net gain in employment from movement between 1945 and 1971 was equivalent to almost one quarter of 1960 manufacturing employment. This produced, for those less-favoured areas, cumulative disadvantage, as the age of the capital stock in those regions got progressively older and less competitive compared with the new plant being established elsewhere. Lancaster should have been partly protected from this effect, given its relative expansion in the 1940s and 1950s. However, this was not sustained, partly because the North West Region has not constituted an important force politically (in comparison with Scotland or South Wales, for example), and partly because Lancaster has had little chance of making effective representation on its own (it has maintained Intermediate Area status). The labour movement never developed a regional basis here, by contrast, for example, with South Wales or the North East of England for instance (see Cooke, 1985b, on South Wales). One crude indicator of this is given by the fact that the proportion of people voting for the Labour Party in Lancashire has generally been lower than in corresponding regions (in 1974, 50.1% in Lancashire voted Labour, compared with 59.4% in the North East).

The local state has concentrated upon two policies: first, to attract new service employment within the public sector—hence the setting-up of a university and the expansion of hospital services—and second, to develop small manufacturing firms. The latter policy was developed in the early 1960s (after the closure of the Gillow furniture workshops following the takeover by Great Universal Stores) and was consolidated in the late 1960s and 1970s; it did not change substantially, even when unemployment began to rise. Land and technical and financial assistance were made available, and a 'seedbed' experiment was set up to help very small firms to become established. Preference for these facilities was actively given to those small firms, with 'high-quality' products, in technologically based industries (Lancaster City Council, 1977). A substantial number of such firms were successfully brought to (or started in) Lancaster, using the facilities provided by the Council and the University through the local industrial initiative, *Enterprise Lancaster,* and helped by its offshoot, the *Small Firms Club,* initiated by the City Council. Large-scale manufacturing investments were less-strongly encouraged by the Local Council throughout the 1960s and early 1970s, and Lancaster's designation as an Intermediate Area during the era of regional policy after 1972 did not facilitate the attraction of large-scale capital during a period of massive industrial restructuring.

On the second and third questions above, we have already noted that the Lancaster subregion has not been an area with a strong labour movement, but, contrary to right-wing commentators, this did not result in the attraction of large flows of capital to the subregion, so that they might profit from the quiescent labour force (by contrast with the interwar period; see Chapter 11 below). It has been argued that the quiescence of the Lancaster labour force has resulted from the paternalist character of social relations both within workplaces and between the local firms and the City (see Martin and Fryer, 1973, on the firm of Williamsons; and see Urry, 1980, for some sceptical comments). Norris (1978, page 471) defines paternalism (of the sort once found in Lancaster) as existing where inequalities of economic and political power are "stabilized through the legitimating ideology of traditionalism". He suggests that there are four components to such an ideology: 'gentlemanly ethic', 'personal dependence', 'localism', and a 'gift relationship'.

Whereas traditional forms of paternalism clearly no longer existed by the 1960s and 1970s, vestiges of these practices seem to be indicated by the responses of the local labour movement to the mass redundancies and plant closures which characterised the years 1980 and 1981. These events elicited fatalistic responses from the labour force, and the only negotiations that took place were about the terms of redundancies, their necessity being accepted from the start. This can be seen by considering the closure of Couraulds's cellulose acetate Lansil works, previously a major source of local employment. Over the summer of 1980 there were a series of redundancies (120, 20, 11) before the announced closure of the works in September with a further 669 redundancies (personal communications with shop stewards, 1980). This demoralised the labour force; it was felt that decisions were being taken over which they had no control and in which their actions would have no effect. There was little sympathy for the company and, indeed, a belief that it did not 'care' for its employees. For example, it was thought that UK profits, and hence the viability of UK plants, were lower than they should have been because pulp imported from South Africa was given too high a transfer price for currency reasons (interview with shop stewards, 1980). However, this was not translated into a belief in the efficacy of industrial or political action; and in the end the workers from the Lansil works appeared grateful to accept the minimal redundancy payments paid out by Courtaulds. It is interesting to note that at the time of redundancy it was widely held that it was 'inevitable' that this plant should close, and that there was no alternative since it had lost £91 000 in the last financial year. Yet part of the reason why this was inevitable was that-there had been no major updating or replacement of much of the machinery, some of which was forty years old. And a year earlier it had been announced that Courtaulds was to build a new rayon-producing plant 'somewhere in Europe' (*The Guardian* 1979). Now although this was apparently to produce viscose yarn (rather than cellulose acetate), it demonstrated that there was nothing inevitable about corporate restructuring and associated plant closures.

The main active response to such closures was also characterised by attitudes assocated with paternalism, namely localism and personal dependence. *The Save Lancaster Campaign* was established by the Trades Council late in 1980, in the wake of several redundancy announcements, and the emphasis of the campaign was firmly on the locality rather than on class politics. This campaign did not gain much active support, even at this time, and it withered away after a few weeks. Most of those affected preferred either to depend on the provisions of the state and the efforts of of the City Council or to find individualistic solutions to unemployment. It may well be that the blossoming of small businesses during the 1970s was an accommodating local response to the decline in employment in older manufacturing firms. In addition, the existence of a large (traditional) petit bourgeoisie (the self-employed) probably undermined collectivist protests.

We have already mentioned two of the strongly localist responses to the industrial restructuring which has affected the Lancaster area, namely the *Save Lancaster Campaign* and the City Council's initiatives to encourage the establishment of new small businesses whose local interlinkages (and hence presumed local control) would be more marked than in the case of externally owned and controlled plants. Although there was considerable controversy within the labour movement about its involvement in such local initiatives, it would seem that the forms of capitalist restructuring made it difficult for employers and city officials to resist the claims of labour (particularly male labour) to some say in future developments. Indeed, to some extent, it appears that the labour movement had more involvement in trying to 'save' the City's industry than have most other groupings, certainly more than the major transnational companies who happen to have one of their plants in the locality (except Unilever). Part of the efforts of the City Council have been directed to encourage such companies to take some responsibility for the effects of their decisions. Yet, at the same time, the efforts of the local labour movement to preserve capitalist manufacturing activity in the locality clearly deflected labourist struggles away from the traditional issues of the wage-relation or the forms of capitalist control, concentrating them instead on presenting the City as a suitable site for private investment. To some extent the labour movement has also put its weight behind the 'small firms strategy'.

A number of other developments in local politics took place over this period. In particular, various 'oppositional fragments' have emerged, which have been concerned with struggles in the area of consumption as well as with production. Such issues as ecology, nuclear energy and weaponry, sexual politics, transport, leisure, and the arts have grown in importance locally as the service sector has come to dominate the area's industry, many of those active in such 'fragments' being either employed in the service sector or unemployed. The restructuring of the local economy has therefore involved not only the undermining of traditional forms of class conflict, but also the development of new struggles and a restructuring of local politics. For example, Lancaster is widely known for the strength of its local women's movement, a strength which is partly connected with the structural shifts in industry and employment noted above.

3.5 Conclusion

We have thus tried to show how the Lancaster economy has been transformed as a consequence of its location within the changing forms of the spatial division of labour. During the period of postwar reconstruction, based on the expansion of national capital, Lancaster benefitted and developed in a number of growing industries. But with the industrial restructuring of the 1960s and early 1970s, a new, in part international, spatial division of labour developed under the influence of UK regional policy. This new spatial division did not benefit Lancaster and, indeed, since its capital was of a previous vintage, the effect of the new round of accumulation was to undermine those industries established within the previous round. The main expansion was in state service employment—and partly in private service employment. There was an increasing gap between the relatively skilled employment available in the service sector (especially that of the state) and that relatively low-skilled male employment available in the private manufacturing sector. The political composition of Lancaster interestingly reflects this particular combination of forms under which the local economy has been restructured. Simple class politics mediated by 'paternalist' relations are no longer of significance; other coauthors of this book explore some of the further social and political implications of these complex patterns of industrial restructuring.

Acknowledgements. We are grateful to the Department of Employment, the Manpower Services Commission, Mr R H Kelsall of Enterprise Lancaster, and others for providing us with information, and to Mr M Lee for assistance in processing it. The work for this chapter was financed by the Human Geography Committee of the Social Science Research Council, and the Economic and Social Research Council.

Comparable localities: some problems of method

Alan Warde

The reemergence of interest in local studies raises some important methodological problems concerning comparability between localities. The problem addressed in this chapter is that of discovering how representative any chosen locality is. The demise of the UK community-study tradition in the 1960s bears witness to the seriousness of the problem of comparison. One major reason for scepticism about the value of further community studies was the noncumulative nature of the information gleaned from them; nobody knew the extent to which what might be shown about, say, Swindon could also be shown for other places, not least because authors collected different and incompatible information (see Filkin and Weir, 1972; Stacey, 1969a). This deficiency was exaggerated by the general inadequacy of sociology in handling 'space' as a concept or variable. To some extent this was the result of a lack of theory; as Giddens (1979, page 224), for example, asserts, there has been "a failure to theorise space as integral to social analysis". The community studies themselves were constricted by issues emanating from the *Gemeinschaft – Gesellschaft* dichotomy, which led to attempts at generalisation in terms of a rural–urban continuum (see, for instance, Frankenberg, 1966) and which tended to focus predominantly upon social organisation with limited regard to political and economic determinations (for example, Stacey, 1969b). Furthermore, sociologists have been reluctant to admit the existence of locality-specific practices, a reluctance instilled by a belief, inherited from modernisation theory, that space becomes more homogeneous as industrial societies advance (Warde, 1985). Yet, covertly, many sociological studies have been locality-bound: affluent workers live in Luton, deferential ones in East Anglia; dockers inhabit London, shipbuilders Tyneside. As Norris (1980, page 20) points out with reference to the study of local labour markets, it is extremely difficult to distinguish between local-specific, industry-specific, and occupation-specific characteristics. The temptation to solve this difficulty by wanton neglect of the first must be resisted. It is worth remarking that social historians, who have been making best use of local studies recently, are more aware of the problem of comparability, though their concern usually derives from an obsession with the uniqueness of historical instances rather than from any theoretical concern with the social process of spatial differentiation. The problem for the local study, of how to answer the question 'What other localities is my locality like?', is a real one. The more analysis is directed towards distinctive local economic structures (see Massey, 1983) or local social systems (see Francis, 1983, for a nostalgic invitation to revive community studies), the more important it becomes to address the problem.

No idle or maleficent disposition to make social science even more difficult inspires this question. Rather it comes from a substantive research problem, of explaining the deindustrialisation of Lancaster and the relationship of this to local political forces. Lancaster, a small city in the North West (see figure 4.1), is interesting both because it began to deindustrialise rather earlier than many localities (see chapter 3 above) and because of its particularly docile working class (see chapter 11 below). The case-study method has produced a good understanding of Lancaster, but the problem of comparability, of whether Lancaster is unique or whether its experience is a common one, remains unresolved. Upon this unresolved issue depends much of what might be said from the case study about theories of uneven regional development, deindustrialisation, labour markets, gender relations, and political militancy. It was this problem, of which other areas might have had similar or contrasting experiences to Lancaster over the past twenty years, that led to an examination of classifications—by geographers, economists, and sociologist—of areas within the United Kingdom. If classifications of local areas by socioeconomic characteristics be satisfactory, it might be expected that they should

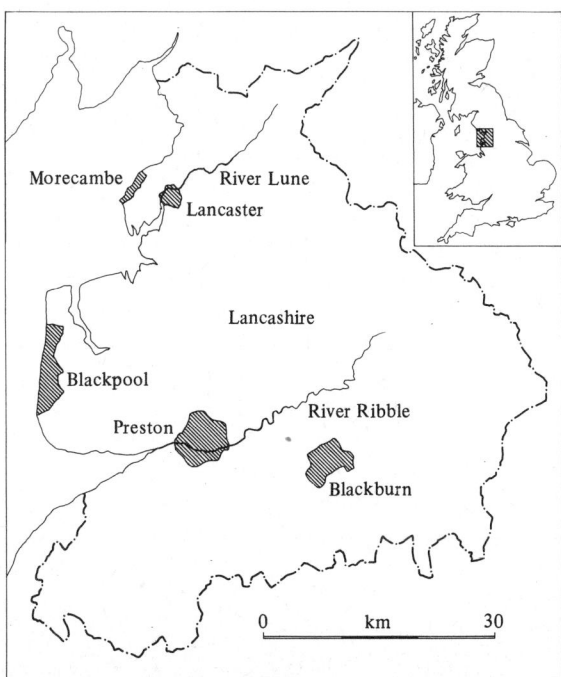

Figure 4.1. Location of Lancaster.

indicate similar and contrasting cases of local development. Armed with such information, it should be a simple matter to pursue John Stuart Mill's injunctions on scientific method.

Filkin and Weir (1972, pages 139–140), on the basis of a survey of local studies in the United Kingdom, concluded that, "given the heterogeneous nature of British locality studies, ... for the themes for which comparative research seems to be most worthwhile, there is little systematic work on which to build". Some dozen years later, despite a significant revival of interest in localities, and technical advances in the classification of data for areas, a similar conclusion might be drawn.

Recent studies have generated classifications of areas which it might be imagined would permit an answer to the question 'What other locality is my locality like?', but for many important themes the answer seems no more accessible than before. In section 4.2 of this chapter, I survey some general classifications which have a bearing on disciplined comparative studies. Each of these is of some value in its own right and, since they are not all well known, it is worthwhile to bring them to the attention of planners and social scientists. In each case, I try to evaluate the classifications.

Schemata are subject to assessment on two grounds, internal coherence and explanatory utility. Internal coherence is largely a matter of the nature of the assumptions underlying the choice of variables to be used and the technical operations undertaken in construction of the classification. Two loose tests are employed to judge explanatory utility. First, I consider how each schema deals with the area about which a lot is known on the basis of a case study, Lancaster. To the extent that classificatory schemata describe the City in inconsistent ways it is possible to judge classifications, both individually and in general. Second, I consider to what extent social practices, other than those incorporated into the bank of independent variables upon which each schema was constructed initially, can be shown to occur regularly in places identified as similar. For example, one classification is of parliamentary constituencies by the socioeconomic characteristics of the population. It seems reasonable to expect that votes will be cast in similar ways in constituencies of the same type. Generally, I examine what these classifications contribute to an explanation of local rates of deindustrialisation and to local variations in political behaviour.

Prima facie, this examination suggests that classifications are very arbitrary and of limited value. But the critique is mounted in the belief that taxonomy is essential if generalisations are ever to be substantiated on the basis of local studies. For what is sociologically significant is to what extent the course and causes of political development and deindustrialisation in Lancaster are like those of other locations. For this reason some suggestions are made in section 4.3 about how to increase the value of such classifications in social-scientific explanation, given the economic restrictions which prevent every study from compiling its own set of statistics for comparable local areas. Having considered some technical issues concerning the origins of the bewildering variety of genera to which Lancaster has been allocated, I argue that lack of theoretical concern with spatial differentiation, political process, and historical change are principal reasons for defective classification.

4.1 Area classifications

When Filkin and Weir wrote their article, published in 1972, recommending that sociologists ensure the comparability of their local studies, there were few classifications of places available for inspection. Some early 'social area' analyses of towns had been published (Green, 1971; Robson, 1969), and there was discussion of the potentiality of multivariate analysis for the classification of census material for small areas, but otherwise there was little work in the United Kingdom other than the older geographical approach to the description of an urban hierarchy and the work of Moser and Scott (1961).

4.1.1 The social classification of towns

Moser and Scott's work *British Towns: A Statistical Survey of Social and Economic Differences* (1961) probably remains the taxonomy best known to the UK sociological community, perhaps because it gains apparent sociological legitimacy through the concept of urbanism. Moser and Scott classified all 157 towns in Great Britain with a population of more than 50000 at the 1951 Census (see OPCS, various). Classification was ostensibly the goal of their endeavours, but their inspiration seemed rather to be the establishment of a particular statistical technique, principal components analysis.

Moser and Scott classified the City of Lancaster as 'a *commercial* centre with some industry' (their italics). They did not lay much importance on the actual labels given to their categories, since this was not their primary interest: they seemed fairly content, in fact, that the groups corresponded to commonsense notions of similarities between towns. Lancaster appeared with Southampton, Portsmouth, Plymouth, Bristol, Gloucester, Great Yarmouth, Norwich, Ipswich, Lincoln, Peterborough, Reading, Northampton, Worcester, York, and Cardiff. Lancaster had, in other words, some of the characteristics of a regional service centre, yet had a considerable amount of manufacturing industry as well.

Moser and Scott's work was a considerable step forward from earlier taxonomies of towns. Classifications like that of Smailes (1944), for example, attempted to produce hierarchies of towns—distinguishing between large cities, major cities, large towns, and subtowns—but the techniques available prohibited the use of anything other than ordinal numerical criteria for allocating towns to categories. Thus towns were grouped according to how many banks and cinemas they possessed, whether or not they had a Woolworths, etc, characteristics which could scarcely establish differences in social structure or quality of urban life throughout Great Britain. [3]

Moser and Scott's study was, nevertheless, a rather odd exercise in abstracted empiricism. Primarily a statistical exercise, it falls foul of many of the criticisms to which empiricism was subjected during the 1970s: the conclusion of the study, the taxonomy of towns, seemed to be an afterthought, and there was no attempt whatever to explain the origins of similarity and difference between towns.

The variables chosen by Moser and Scott were intended to distinguish social structural differences between towns. (It is, of course, the case that taxonomies can be generated on *any* dimension of difference.) There was, though, one glaring defect in their selection of variables, the absence of temporal or trend variables. As both Andrews (1971) and Armen (1972) observe, important components which accounted for variance in Moser and Scott's classification appeared to reflect change over time. Yet the temporal elements of those components were almost entirely derived from *demographic* data. It seems likely, however, that other variables, indicating economic, or perhaps political, change would be more powerful in explaining urban behaviour. For any comparative analysis of a process, like deindustrialisation, it would be infinitely preferable to include variables which explicitly express change over time. For example, changes in the proportions of people employed in manufacturing and service between 1931 and 1951, numbers of housing-starts in different years, numbers or proportions of persons employed in certain Standard Industrial Classification groups and socioeconomic groups in 1931 and 1951, these would all capture social changes. Only data of that kind, which represent trends, are likely to enhance an understanding of social *development*.

The work of Moser and Scott has nevertheless proved fruitful. It was subjected to reworking by Andrews (1971), on the basis of improved techniques, to obtain an optimal final classification. It was also used in an attempt to understand better any deviations from predominant patterns of class-voting in UK elections between 1951 and 1966 (see Piepe et al, 1969). The publication of relatively raw data in *British Towns* makes the reuse of Moser and Scott's work a continuing possibility. *British Towns* now has a successor in the work of Donnison and Soto, *The Good City: A Study of Urban Development and Policy in Britain* (1980). Though

[3]It is interesting that the geographers of the period right through to the 1960s considered the services of the tertiary sector as the key characteristic of towns and cities. In fact there appeared to have been two ways of classifying urban areas, either by function (presumably industrial, commercial, etc) or by 'importance'. Constructing an urban hierarchy has a long tradition in geography. Compare Smailes (1944) with earlier 'vertical' classifications; and note Smith (1968), who still wanted to examine 'hierarchies'. Political scientists have recently attempted to explain urban political behaviour with reference to the role of towns in the urban hierarchy. This seems to work well in some countries, but not in the United Kingdom (see Newton, 1981a).

using a different technique—cluster analysis, like that of the OPCS (Office of Population Censuses and Services) studies discussed below—the aim, to classify towns on the basis of their social structural characteristics, was similar. *The Good City*, however, is concerned both with the effects of spatial social policies and, more generally, with the quality of life in towns with different characteristics, as defined by the 1971 Census (see OPCS, various). Importantly, the authors focus on levels of economic growth and expansion, arguing that the state of local labour markets is the key to the opportunities and satisfactions which a town can offer its residents. Unfortunately, for present concerns, Lancaster was not among the towns analysed.

4.1.2 Administrative units: OPCS and CES areal classification projects

In the last decade a number of classifications have been generated for planning purposes, with the explicit intention of making the reuse of assembled data a practical possibility. Foremost among these was a joint project by the Office of Population Censuses and Surveys and the Centre for Environmental Studies (CES). This generated a number of socio-economic classifications of areas in the United Kingdom, which together constitute a potentially valuable research resource for social science and which yet has to be much utilised. Webber and his collaborators produced classifications of the 'new', post-1974-Reorganisation, local authority areas (Webber and Craig, 1978), of parliamentary constituencies (Webber, 1978), of enumeration districts (Webber, 1979), and of wards and parishes (Webber, 1977).

In each case the classification was based upon a selection of variables from the Small Area Statistics of the 1971 Census (see OPCS, various); these were manipulated by versions of cluster analysis, a multivariate technique whereby areal units are grouped by their affinity to one another on the basis of a fairly large number of social variables into a few 'families' and a rather greater number of 'clusters'. The number of possible clusters is predecided, but the number of units allocated to any given cluster can vary. The indicators are weighted, and some numerical assessment of their value in distinguishing between areal units is provided.

In one study, Webber and Craig (1978) classified the 457 local authorities, as constituted by the 1974 Reorganisation, from the Small Area Statistics. Unfortunately the changed boundaries made systematic comparison with the towns in Moser and Scott's study impossible. The new Lancaster District was assigned to family 2, 'rural and resort areas', cluster 12, 'port and retirement centres'. This cluster includes retirement centres along the south coast, the North Wales coast, and the Lancashire coast. It has a wide geographical spread and includes many small ports. Distinctively, the cluster contains "types of areas which have worse scores on measures of social deprivation than on measures of housing stress or socio-economic status" (Webber and Craig, 1978, page 43). Clearly this view of Lancaster is quite different from that of Moser and Scott. Some

of the difference is obviously because of the seaside resort of Morecambe
and adjacent rural districts both being included in the new local authority
area at the 1974 Reorganisation.

Similar techniques were employed by Webber in his classification of
parliamentary constituencies, as revised after 1971 (Webber, 1978). In
this the two local constituencies were very different, indicating major
social disparities within the subregion. Lancaster was put in the family
'stable industrial areas' and in the cluster 'poorer urban centres with some
nonmanufacturing functions'. The Morecambe and Lonsdale constituency,
on the other hand, belonged to the family 'rural areas and seaside resorts'
and to the cluster 'resorts and retirement areas'. Characteristically, such
constituencies have an aged population with residents of high socio-
economic status, and with local employment 'mostly in services'. This
cluster contained four other northern constituencies—Blackpool North,
Blackpool South, Scarborough, and Harrogate—and a number of resorts in
North Wales, the rest having south and southwest coastal locations.

The cluster containing the Lancaster constituency, 'poorer urban centres
with some nonmanufacturing functions', was said to be the least distinctive
of the thirty clusters, "though on almost all indicators it compares poorly
with the rest of the country. It also can be picked out by its somewhat
older than average and declining population and by its high proportion of
households in local authority housing" (Webber, 1978, page 31). The
constituencies are predominantly in the north of England, comprising
transport centres, administrative centres, mining areas, and some suburban
locations on Tyneside[4].

The OPCS and CES joint study appears to make distinct advances in
techniques used to classify areas. A summary and justification of its
methods is given by Webber and Craig (1978, pages 5–12), who prefer a
type of cluster analysis—a composite of stepwise progression and literative
allocation—to principal components analysis (used by Moser and Scott),
because the latter renders it "impossible to detect divergences due to
local or historical factors" (1978, page 9). The range of variables coded
from the Small Area Statistics was very large—some 300 were computed
in ratio form, though only forty were used to produce the classification,
these being selected to "represent as wide as possible a variety of
characteristics without over-representing any particular aspect" (page 6).
The aim was to provide a flexible classification oriented not to any
particular social problem or field of social policy but to a 'general'
socioeconomic taxonomy.

[4] "Ten of the 19 constituencies in this cluster are found in the Northern region.
Three of them (Carlisle, Darlington, Doncaster) are important transport centres, six of
them (Lincoln, Norwich North, Lancaster, Wakefield, Ayr, Durham) are important
administrative centres and others (Workington, Bishop Auckland, North West Durham
and Morpeth) are areas with a mining tradition. Three suburban Tyneside constituencies
also belong to this cluster" (Webber, 1978, page 31). For a full list of these
constituencies, see table 4.1 (later).

Webber's classifications are of special interest because they appear to allow some assessment of the explanatory value of socioeconomic classifications. In the case of parliamentary constituencies, for example, voting behaviour provides independent data against which to 'test' the appropriateness of the taxonomy. Whereas a perfect fit between the socioeconomic characteristics of individual constituencies and election results could not be expected, since that would entail the mistaken assumption that electoral outcomes were purely the effect of socioeconomic characteristics of the population, some correlation ought to be found. In particular, if, as has been argued by Dunleavy (1979), the way forward for psephology is to seek structural, rather than individualistic, accounts of voting behaviour, then there is reason to inquire into the degree of fit between Webber's clusters and election results.

In practice, such a 'test' is beset with difficulties. Constituency boundaries were those pertaining for the first time at the General Election of February 1974, already nearly three years after the Census data were collected and a quite sufficient time for the profile of the population to have changed. Boundary changes make it improper to compare results before 1974 or after 1979. There were but three general elections on the boundaries considered by Webber, which prevents assessment of trends within such constituencies. It must also be pointed out that Webber claimed not to be especially interested in producing a classification which was predictive of election results. Nevertheless, I have compiled the general election results of a number of constituencies, those contained in the cluster to which Lancaster was allocated and sundry other, mainly Lancashire, constituencies, the results of which are presented in tables 4.1 and 4.2.

The results of this exercise are inconclusive. It can be seen that some clusters do seem to maintain fixed patterns of voting, though others are far from consistent. Morecambe and Lonsdale, for example, votes consistently with others in its cluster. Lancaster, on the other hand, appears anomalous, insofar as there is a pattern to the 'cluster 19' constituencies, which tend overwhelmingly to vote Labour; yet, with the exception of the two Scottish constituencies, only Tynemouth has a similar record of regularly voting Conservative. For some of the other clusters, no very clear pattern at all appears, though it should be remembered that Lancashire includes some of the constituencies regularly most susceptible to change between parties.

This classification, especially, seems to be one which would have benefitted from some more focused attention to particular explanatory tasks. True, the supplementary information necessary, measures of political tradition, party organisation, etc, which are of importance in understanding voting behaviour, is most difficult to compile. It would entail an almost ethnographic knowledge of constituencies, obtainable only by the painstaking but unsystematic methods of Pelling's *Social Geography of British Elections, 1885–1910* (1967), which made a survey of newspaper reports of local political conditions in each constituency.

But certainly the absence of special emphasis on those social variables which are known to be correlated with voting behaviour—housing tenure, car ownership, religion, etc, not to mention trade-union membership and past experience of class conflict—made a close fit most unlikely. Such neglect of politically related or political variables is symptomatic of a lack of explanatory concern, which betrays many exercises of classification.

Like Moser and Scott's, Webber's works lack social variables which capture trends over time or which are sensitive to the quality of social change. Again, demographic structure would appear to be the main indicator of local social change. Thus, despite some reference to the importance of local history—as for instance when Webber and Craig observe that primarily rural local authorities in east and west England are different because of housing patterns which have their origins in the enclosure movement of the late eighteenth and nineteenth centuries— historical factors are at best casually reflected. Yet it seems probable, if comparison between constituencies is sought that the quality of social experience between, say, 1951 and 1971 will contribute to the explanation of voting at the later date.

Table 4.1. Party of Members of Parliament elected in 'poorer urban centres with some nonmanufacturing functions' (source: Webber, 1978) Key C: Conservative; L: Labour; DL: Democratic Labour; ( ): bye-election; *: no comparable constituency (boundary changes occurred between 1970 and February 1974).

Constituency	Before boundary changes					After boundary changes		
	1955	1959	1964	1966	1970	1974 (Feb)	1974 (Oct)	1979
Bishop Auckland	L	L	L	L	L	L	L	L
Durham	L	L	L	L	L	L	L	L
Durham North West	L	L	L	L	L	L	L	L
Morpeth	L	L	L	L	L	L	L	L
Wallsend	L	L	L	L	L	L	L	L
Workington	L	L	L	L	L	L	L(C)	L
Woolwich East	L	L	L	L	L	L	L	L
Norwich North	L	L	L	L	L	L	L	L
Wakefield	L	L	L	L	L	L	L	L
Newcastle East	L	C	L	L	L	L	L	L
Lincoln	L	L	L	L	L	DL(DL)	L	C
Carlisle	C	C	L	L	L	L	L	L
Darlington	C	C	L	L	L	L	L	L
Doncaster	C	C	L	L	L	L	L	L
Portsmouth North	*	*	*	*	*	L	L	C
Lancaster	C	C	C	L	C	C	C	C
Tynemouth	C	C	C	C	C	C	C	C
Ayr	C	C	C	C	C	C	C	C
Bute and N Ayrshire	C	C	C	C	C	C	C	C

Table 4.2. Party of Members of Parliament elected in various constituencies, by cluster (source: Webber, 1978).
Key C: Conservative; L: Labour; Lib: Liberal; ( ): bye-election.

Cluster	Before boundary changes					After boundary changes		
	1955	1959	1964	1966	1970	1974 (Feb)	1974 (Oct)	1979
Cluster 6[a]	C	C	C	C	C	C	C	C
Cluster 10[b]								
Clitheroe	C	C	C	C	C	C	C	C
Darwen	C	C	C	C	C	C	C	C
Chorley	L	L	L	L	C	L	L	C
Colne Valley	L	L	L	Lib	L	Lib	Lib	Lib
Barrow-in-Furness	L	L	L	L	L	L	L	L
Cluster 21[c]								
Accrington	L	L	L	L	L	L	L	L
Blackburn	L	L	L	L	L	L	L	L
Burnley	L	L	L	L	L	L	L	L
Bolton East	C	C(C)	C	L	L	L	L	L
Preston South	C	C	L	L	L	L	L	L
Stockport South	C	C	L	L	L	L	L	L
Rochdale	C(L)	L	L	L	L	Lib	Lib	Lib
Preston North	C	C	C	L	L	L	L	C
Rossendale	L	L	L	L	C	C	L	C
Bolton West	Lib	Lib	L	L	C	C	C	L

[a]Agricultural areas—Blackpool North, Blackpool South, Morecambe and Lonsdale, Skipton, Westmorland, and North Fylde—all Conservative in every election.
[b]Small industrial towns in the North West.
[c]Textile areas.

4.1.3 Labour markets

Policy concerns with the spatial distribution of both employment and unemployment, and with the separation of place of residence and the place of work, have generated a series of definitional and mapping exercises designed to plot the UK's discrete labour markets. A variety of concepts, associated with different criteria for delimiting labour market areas, have been advocated and widely discussed in the geographical literature. Thus there are maps of the United Kingdom divided into: (a) standard metropolitan labour areas (SMLAs) (Drewett et al, 1976; Hall et al, 1973); (b) travel-to-work areas (Department of Employment, 1978); (c) labour-market areas (Smart, 1974); (d) daily urban systems and functional regions (Coombes et al 1978; 1979a; 1981); and (e) local labour markets (Lever, 1979; Norris, 1980). There is a considerable debate about the merits and deficiencies of the criteria employed in each of these exercises.

The first three approaches are almost entirely mapping exercises. Their primary aim is to apply explicit and reasonable criteria to data on journeys to work in order to delimit the boundaries of local labour markets. Though such areas have been ranked by performance on certain variables —decentralisation of population and increase or decline in employment (for example, Drewett et al, 1976)—they have not yet been subjected to classification within the total number of labour markets. Critical assessments of the technical adequacy of each of these approaches already exists in the literature (see respectively, Coombes et al, 1979b; Ball,1980; Norris, 1980; Redfern, 1981; Coombes and Openshaw, 1982). The regularly repeated objections are that they comprise hybrid classifications of residence and employment locations, that their statistical cut-off points for deciding the limits of a labour market are arbitrary, and that the statistics derived for labour-market areas are incompatible with other official statistics. Moreover, they ignore class differences in commuting distances and they persistently and mistakenly attempt to include all places in the United Kingdom in their classification, thereby failing to discriminate between different types of labour markets. Nevertheless, they are not without practical value, being used both as a basis for official employment statistics in the country and for allowing some international spatial comparison. For example, the SMLA was developed and mapped to compare local economies, of differing structures and levels of prosperity, for the purposes of economic planning in the EEC.

Some of the defects of these approaches have been remedied by the fourth, and most recent, approach to daily urban systems and functional regions, developed by the Centre for Urban and Regional Development Studies (CURDS) at the University of Newcastle-upon-Tyne. Here an attempt is made to chart functional areas about which compatible information can be obtained regarding employment statistics and data from the 1971 and 1981 Censuses. The level of sophistication of the CURDS' schema is impressive. It too works on travel-to-work data, but attends more closely to the complexities of commuting patterns in densely populated areas. Whereas other classifications construct all labour markets as fundamentally of one type, CURDS distinguishes metropolitan regions from free-standing regions. The latter are relatively unproblematic: here large urban centres attract workers from the surrounding hinterland, with few residents in the urban centre leaving it to go to work. In the densely populated metropolitan regions, however, the hinterland from which a centre attracts its workers includes secondary centres which are also, to a significant degree, self-contained. The CURDS' regionalisation is therefore constructed in two tiers to represent this difference. At the upper tier are twenty metropolitan regions (for example, London, Leeds, Cardiff) and 115 free-standing functional regions (for instance, Southampton, Blackpool, Northampton). The metropolitan regions are then subdivided into one dominant functional region (DFR) and any number of subdominant functional ones (SFR). For example, the Sheffield Metropolitan Region contains the Sheffield DFR and Barnsley, and the Rotherham and Mexborough SFRs. The latter have a high degree of self-containment and represent meaningful urban centres of employment and residence, but import and export a significant number of workers each day. The free-standing functional regions, in some cases, also comprise an amalgamation of an urban region (a centre) with rural areas which themselves have a degree of self-containment (for example, the Leicester urban region and the Melton Mowbray rural area comprise a free-standing functional region). The implication is that labour-market areas are of four distinctive types, and that interlinkages between adjacent towns make metropolitan regions distinctive from other regions. The resultant map of these areas on a 'functional' basis (which is claimed to consider urban areas both as employment centres and as residential locations) is different from maps of SMLAs or travel-to-work areas. Its creators claim it to be a better representation of the urban hierarchy because it is based on a more appropriate and more complex understanding of daily travel patterns.

The CURDS' study does give an improved map, and does make a preliminary distinction between types of labour areas and urban systems. It remains however primarily descriptive and as yet is untested in analysis of social and economic processes. To the extent that it is based on travel-to-work data (it uses these as a surrogate for travel-to-services data), it remains of the same order as its precursors, despite its beginning to conceptualise what distinguishes groups of labour markets from one another. In this classification, Lancaster and Morecambe constituted a free-standing functional region (see Coombes et al, 1981).

A separate approach to this exercise, the fifth mentioned above, has been undertaken by workers at Glasgow. They developed a concept of the local labour market, whose principal distinctive characteristic was the degrees of self-containment of labour markets.

On the basis of some explicit sociological reasoning about the nature of the sale of labour power, the Glasgow group, which included Lever, McPhail, and Norris, derived a slightly different definition of labour markets by adopting the concept of the local labour market. As Norris (1980) argues, other studies ignored the internal density of labour markets in a given area. The Glasgow group, in common with other researchers, uses travel-to-work data which employ two variables for determining the boundary of the market: (1) the proportion of resident workers who work outside the boundary; and (2) the proportion of those who work inside the boundary and live outside it. But the Glasgow group observes a third variable which relates to the internal density of the market in the geographical area. This third variable records the extent to which any particular point within the area lies within the labour-market areas of all individuals and employers in the area. Internally dense markets will be those where the labour markets of a high proportion both of individuals and of employers cover the entire geographical area. However, it is very difficult to operationalise this variable in terms of available travel-to-work data; one would have to show evidence that, taking any unit within the geographical area, there was a high level of journey-to-work movement both into and out of this unit to and from almost any other area within the boundary. Certainly for the market to be dense and closed we should expect the flow of workers between any one part of the market to any other part to be greater than the flow from the first part to outside the boundary (Norris, 1980, pages 11–12).

Use of this third variable, which corresponds with Goodman's definition of a 'self-contained labour market', allows Norris to develop a typology of labour markets containing eight types (see Norris, 1980, page 12). Not every area of the United Kingdom was part of a local labour market, rather the aim was to identify areas with *locally homogeneous* labour-market conditions. Lever (1979) made the only published attempt to use the data collected on this basis for the purpose of explanation of the effects of labour-market structures. He sought to establish the effect of employer domination within local labour markets, by ascertaining in which of the 301 identified local labour markets in the United Kingdom (excluding Northern Ireland) a single employer employed more than 12.5% of the total labour force, and by showing that such domination increased fluctuations in unemployment.

The virtues claimed for the concept of local labour markets are threefold: it makes it possible to inquire whether different types of labour markets *do* operate differently; it is realistic in considering labour markets as local for a large proportion of the labour force; and it provides a way of "identifying areas which do share a common degree of labour market localisation" (Norris, 1980, page 21). Norris sums up:

"Local labour markets are areas in which both employees and firms and employers located in the same area are likely to interact with each other to a considerable extent in a situation of mutual dependence (or a relationship of exploitation). Local labour markets will vary in the extent to which such interaction occurs, the degree of self-containment can be used as an indicator of such variation. In areas which do not achieve local labour market status, however, the extent to which both jobs and workers in the market can be analysed by restricting study to that particular area must be highly questionable" (pages 21–22).

The Glasgow study has yet to prove its value in sociological explanation. It has not developed a classification of labour markets, the subclasses of which display significant variations in the beliefs, attitudes, or behaviours of workers in those labour markets. However, it would be useful to have data published which made it possible to categorise labour markets in such a way that the effect of labour-market type on social relations could be investigated. As it stands, not much can be said about Lancaster, except that in 1971 it was a local labour market, but not one dominated by any single firm or industry. Other towns in the same situation appear to be very diverse.

Norris believes that where labour markets are genuinely localised, knowledge of those markets will facilitate a better understanding of class relations, work opportunities, etc. He notes, however, that not all types of workers are subject to the constraints of self-contained labour markets: "at best we can hope to identify geographical units which represent local labour markets for almost all female workers and most manual and lower level non-manual workers" (Norris, 1980, page 13). This proviso will certainly cause problems in any empirical case study, since Norris equates labour market with job structure:

"Labour markets will ... exhibit variations in the characteristics of their job structures and it is these variations in job structure characteristics which should provide the basis for classifying labour markets of different types" (1980, page 26).

It would seem from this that if the empirical focus is the distribution of occupational places (the 'job structure'), it would be necessary to guess which of those places were subject to localisation (data not being available on recruitment and geographical mobility). Also the operation of the labour market as a local social process would be obscured, since job structure contains no reference to information networks, degrees of domination, paternalist practices, etc, which, putatively, constitute different styles of recruitment practice and social relations locally. Furthermore, the classification of labour markets on the basis of their female and 'proletarianised' occupations *alone* is unlikely to render an understanding of, for example, local class relations.

It is probably necessary to reserve judgement on the Glasgow study pending the publication of more of its results. It seems promising because it seeks to classify and to explain variations between labour markets in terms of locality and localisation. Lever and his colleagues are aware that degrees of localisation matter, considering important, for example, the role of local information networks in distributing persons to places in many occupational sectors. In this way they do appear to have thought theoretically about some of the social consequences of spatial arrangements, even though their notion of a local labour market needs further conceptual clarification[5].

4.1.4 The classification of services

Several other classifications of areal units have appeared. The interesting work of Fothergill and Gudgin (1980, pages 181–183), which tries to explain changes in the spatial distribution of employment in manufacturing and service industries, generates a classification of subregions.

[5] Probably still wider consideration of the elements which comprise labour markets are necessary before an adequate typology can be created, though if too many variables are incorporated (as seems to be the case with, for example, Storper and Walker, 1983), then comparison may become impossible.

Fothergill and Gudgin present relevant information on the distribution of UK service employment. They used a shift-share method to examine changes in total employment and in the manufacturing and service proportions of employment in sixty-two subregions for the periods 1959–1966, 1966–1971, and 1971–1975. They found that the urban–rural mix of a subregion was highly correlated with employment growth in manufacturing: the more rural an area the faster manufacturing employment grew (also see Fothergill and Gudgin, 1982). This, they suggested, invalidated centre–periphery explanations of employment change and, yet again, demonstrated the futility of regional analysis, since variations within regions were greater than those between regions.

In Fothergill and Gudgin's analysis, the Lancaster subregion is classified as an 'urban nonindustrial' area, though in fact the authors do not put great store by their taxonomy. Modifications, they claim, would not have significant effect upon their conclusions; and, to the extent that their conclusions relate primarily to the performances of subregions with different urban–rural mixes, this is perhaps correct. However, their grouping of Lancaster appears particularly unfortunate, since, although it may be like others in its group (Southwest East Anglia, that is, around Cambridge; the Sussex coast; Fylde; and the North Wales coast) on a measure of urbanisation, its employment profile is completely different (see table 4.3, which presents figures for these five subregions).

One result of considering the comparability of Lancaster with other places on the basis of these data is to be sceptical of the value of analysis at the subregional level. Comparing Lancaster's employment performance in relation to all other subregions leads to the conclusion that few generalisations can be made at this level.

Nevertheless, using the data provided, a number of points can be made about Lancaster and the process of deindustrialisation. Fothergill and

Table 4.3. Employment change in 'urban nonindustrial' subregions (source: Fothergill and Gudgin, 1980, appendix 2).

Subregion	Manufacturing employment 1959–1975			Total employment 1959–1975			Service employment 1959–1971		
	1959	1975	% change	1959	1975	% change	1959	1971	% change
Lancaster	15.0	11.7	−22.0	42.4	43.7	3.1	22.4	25.7	14.7
Southwest East Anglia	24.2	41.2	70.2	100.0	138.1	38.1	50.7	68.7	35.5
Sussex coast	43.7	64.3	47.1	251.5	292.6	16.3	164.9	182.6	10.7
Fylde	21.5	26.2	21.9	85.7	94.9	10.7	52.3	54.2	3.6
North Wales coast	3.2	5.9	84.4	31.3	37.9	21.2	23.5	23.7	0.9

Gudgin comment on the extreme features of Lancaster's employment profile. The industry mix of the subregion in 1959 was such that Lancaster might have been expected to experience the most rapid increase in manufacturing employment of any UK subregion. This projection must have been based on the presence of chemical, petroleum, and man-made fibre industries in the subregion at the time (see chapter 3 above).

Lancaster failed entirely to fulfil that expectation, manufacturing contracting by 22% between 1959 and 1975, whilst service employment, initially not expected to increase significantly (see Fothergill and Gudgin, 1980, figure 2.5, page 171), grew by 14.7% between 1959 and 1971.

Lancaster's employment profile, far from being like that of other 'urban nonindustrial' subregions, is most similar to declining industrial areas (see Fothergill and Gudgin, 1980, appendix 2). The subregions with broadly parallel profiles were the South Wales coast, Mid Lancashire, Northeast Lancashire, South Yorkshire, and Northern Ireland. Other subregions with similar experiences—these lost slightly in total employment—were West Yorkshire, the West Midlands Connurbation, and North Staffordshire. One feature of these subregions is that, with the solitary exception of the South Wales coast, all had a very much smaller ratio of service to manufacturing jobs in 1959 (see table 4.4).

Incidentally, one odd feature of this set of statistics is that the ratio of service to manufacturing jobs in 1959 seems to have no effect upon the likelihood of service employment increasing or decreasing by 1971. It might be expected that the ratio of manufacturing to service employment

Table 4.4. Employment change in subregions (source: Fothergill and Gudgin, 1980, appendix 2)

Subregion	Manufacturing employment % change 1959–1975	Total employment		Service employment % change 1959–1971	Balance[a]
		1959 (1000)	% change 1959–1975		
Lancaster	−22.0	42.4	3.1	14.7	1.49
Mid Lancashire	−20.9	131.6	0.4	26.0	0.70
Northeast Lancashire	−12.1	216.4	0.9	7.2	0.45
South Wales coast	−5.6	251.8	3.1	12.5	1.64
South Yorkshire	−12.0	329.9	0.8	16.9	0.63
Northern Ireland	−9.5	461.3	12.5	20.4	1.07
West Yorkshire	−21.0	844.3	−2.9	12.5	0.64
West Midlands Connurbation	−16.4	1151.8	−3.8	13.9	0.48
North Staffordshire	−0.9	215.8	−2.3	14.7	0.56

[a] Of employment in 1959: the ratio of total service employment to total manufacturing employment in 1959.

in 1959 would have some direct relationship with the later development of service employment. Intuitively I would expect all areas to increase their share of service employment to some degree, to account for the general increase in state-provided and other services, but that such increases would be greater in those areas with a substantial proportion of service employment at the beginning of the period. In other words, a process of centralisation within enterprises in the service sector might be anticipated. Yet there does not appear to be a correlation between the ratio in 1959, which we might describe as the *balance of the employment structure*, and the subsequent development of subregional economies. If one considers those subregions which have between one and two service jobs for every manufacturing job in 1959, there are few regularities in behaviour (see table 4.5). Again, Lancaster itself is very eccentric insofar as only London lost a greater proportion of manufacturing jobs (38%).

The absence of any pattern to changes in the balance of the employment structure may be a consequence of the inadequacies of the distinction between services and manufacturing (Walby, 1980). Or, as Fothergill and Gudgin (1980, page 173) note, rates of subregional and employment change for manufacturing may be very volatile, changing much more and much faster than service employment. In any event, it poses some interesting questions concerning the causes of differential rates of deindustrialisation across the United Kingdom.

Fothergill and Gudgin's approach apparently would not help in the discovery of places with similar profiles to Lancaster because their data suggest that Lancaster performed eccentrically. Lancaster's strange performance may simply be the effect of the subregion being very small, so that, given that manufacturing employment change is volatile, a few fortuitous movements in industrial location become exaggerated when projected onto a small population. A problem of analysis at the subregional level is that the size of the populations of those subregions varies enormously.

Forthergill and Gudgin are to be commended insofar as they attempt to consider change over time in their analysis. However, it is an oddly truncated conception of change, measured as it is by the deviation from an outcome expected for a given subregion at time t_2 on the basis of the average national performance of those industries present in the subregion (that is, the 'structural component' of the shift-share method) during the period t_1-t_2. In a sense, this is to take historical differences in industrial structures as *given* and to edit such differences out of consideration, turning time and process back into an instantaneous snapshot (for further information, see Keeble, 1976, pages 38–45).

With respect to the process of deindustrialisation, Armen (1972) also attempted to generate a classification of cities and city regions on the basis of the services which each offered. Like many of his precursors, Armen explicitly classifies towns as service centres. For geographers like

Table 4.5. All subregions with a balance of employment in 1959 between 1.0 and 2.0 (source: Fothergill and Gudgin, 1980, appendix 2).

Subregion	Balance[d]	% change (manufacturing)[a]	Total % change[b]	% change (services)[c]	Manufacturing employment[e]		
					1959	1975	change
Lancaster	1.49	-22.0	3.1	14.7	35.3	26.7	-8.6
Industrial North East	1.11	3.9	-1.0	8.6	34.6	36.2	1.6
North Cumberland–Westmorland	1.49	17.1	6.5	2.5	31.8	35.0	3.2
North Humberside	1.46	10.5	9.5	3.5	35.1	35.4	0.3
Yorkshire Coalfield	1.21	46.3	4.2	12.9	23.8	33.3	9.5
East Midlands (East Lowlands)	1.70	34.8	-3.8	13.5	26.7	31.9	5.2
Southeast East Anglia	1.60	44.5	31.3	20.7	28.7	31.6	2.9
Northeast East Anglia	1.46	38.9	27.8	25.6	30.5	33.2	2.7
London	1.67	-37.8	-11.4	2.3	34.3	24.1	-10.2
Outer Metropolitan Area	1.04	27.2	44.1	48.0	42.1	37.2	-4.9
Essex	1.70	39.4	29.6	24.0	29.0	31.2	2.2
Solent	1.83	33.6	23.3	18.6	30.0	32.5	2.5
Bedfordshire, Buckinghamshire, Berkshire, Oxfordshire	1.42	17.2	21.6	27.5	34.8	33.5	-1.3
Northern South West	1.13	0.7	14.5	20.0	39.8	35.0	-4.8
Northwest East Anglia	1.33	47.8	29.5	21.4	31.4	35.9	4.5
Merseyside	1.37	-3.0	-3.9	7.6	38.5	38.9	0.4
South Wales coast	1.63	-5.6	3.1	12.5	32.0	29.4	-2.6
Edinburgh and East-Central Scotland	1.86	14.9	7.5	10.5	26.0	27.8	1.8
Tayside	1.39	-6.9	0.4	0.4	33.7	31.3	-2.4
Borders	1.02	-2.0	-3.4	-4.0	36.1	36.6	0.5
North East Scotland	1.96	10.1	10.6	5.3	25.4	25.3	-0.1
Northern Ireland	1.06	-9.5	12.5	20.4	40.6	32.7	-7.9

a % change in manufacturing employment 1959–1975   b % change in total employment 1959–1975

c % change in service employment 1959–1971

d Of employment in 1959: the ratio of total service employment to total manufacturing employment in 1959.

e Total manufacturing employment (%) in 1959 and 1975, and % change in employment.

Smailes (1944), Carruthers (1957), and Smith (1968), what characterised towns was precisely the centralisation of services—of retailing, of recreational facilities, of financial institutions, and of various professional services. In fact, it seems to be but recently, in the context of concerns with regional policy for increasing employment opportunities, that classification of cities has been directed towards their productive rather than their distributive functions. Such classifications of services might have been expected to be useful in the study of deindustrialisation.

A perennial reservation about taxonomies is that the choice of initial data determines the conclusions, irrespective of subsequent statistical procedures. Armen extracted some 132 variables for each city and city region in England and Wales, the vast majority of which were indexes of service activities. He then grouped districts by aggregating scores for each variable, all 132 variables counting equally: "in order to overcome the shortcomings of component and factor analysis it was decided to adopt a method of classification which laid equal weight on all variables in allocating a city or city region to a classificatory group" (Armen, 1972, pages 156–157). Such a procedure had the apparently unfortunate effect of giving equal significance in the determination of clusters to number of professional workers, car ownership, annual average hours of sunshine between 1931 and 1960, and the incidence of greyhound tracks. His criteria for delineating the boundaries of city regions were more acceptable. City regions were delimited by applying "a deductive time limit of accessibility to the services provided or likely to be provided in an existing or new town" (page 152). In 1966, on empirical grounds, he decided that a forty to forty-five minute journey was the outside limit for regular use of city facilities by persons living in the hinterland. Thus city regions were determined by transport facilities, by how long it took to reach the city. Armen computed both for city regions and for cities alone—a city being defined as a settlement with a population of over 50000 in a continuously built-up area.

Armen classified Lancaster–Morecambe 'city' and Morecambe Bay 'city region' as 'holiday and retirement' areas. Although in Armen's typology areas could appear in more than one class, the Morecambe Bay region was unambiguously a vacation and retirement region, being excluded both from the 'port region' and from the 'administrative market region' subdivisions of the class 'service-biased regions'. The implication for the Lancaster Region is that as early as 1966 the characteristics of Morecambe predominated in the Region, despite the continued importance of manufacturing in the City of Lancaster itself.

One virtue of Armen's analysis was to show that varied data on service provision could be compiled: he derived systematic statistics on public services, leisure facilities, policemen, issuing of public library books, quality restaurants, and gliding bases. By comparison, Carruthers's (1957) construction of a hierarchy of service centres on the basis of bus services was perversely unidimensional. But, overall, Armen's methodology is distinctly suspect, a case where the chosen statistical procedure compounds the vagaries of the initial choice of variables. Moreover, like other classifications of service provision, it lacks any explanatory potential, despite the fact that its singular concentration on services permits one to imagine the possibility of explanations of self-sustained service growth.

4.2 Taxonomy

On the basis of this survey it would be possible to dismiss classificatory schemata as useless. It might be tempting to conclude that since any things can be classified, along any dimension, that taxonomies must be quite specific to individual explanatory tasks. Since there is no single basis upon which to classify spatial units there can be no general or multipurpose framework. The enormous variety of headings under which Lancaster has appeared in these modern surveys—from regional service centre, through poorer industrial area, to retirement and holiday resort— would give some support to such a proposition. Nevertheless, the consequences of that are unsatisfactory and probably exaggerate the difficulty of constructing useful taxonomies and underestimate their heuristic value. The classifications that I have considered do exhibit, however, several common deficiences, compensation for which might improve subsequent attempts. These deficiencies are described below.

The classifications considered in this paper are, in general, *theoretically unprincipled,* in the sense that they fail to specify the relationship between identified spatial differentiation and the social processes to which their statistical indicators refer. This is a complicated reciprocal relationship which might best be expressed as two separate critical observations: (a) these classifications are rarely explicit, and usually incoherent, about theoretical understandings of spatial differentiation; and (b) the use of a classification in explanation requires that the indicators selected correspond adequately to the social processes which determine the relevant distinctions between spatial units. This requirement itself depends upon theoretical clarity concerning the particular social processes identified as determinant.

The decision as to which spatial units should be classified is obviously important. One of the reasons why Lancaster is classified in so many different ways is that the parliamentary constituency, the local authority area, the travel-to-work-area, and the subregion cover different geographical areas with disparate population profiles. However, for Lancaster, probably rather more than for other areas, most of these areal units more or less coincide: the new local authority area, the subregion, and the travel-to-work-area are not significantly different. More important in the different descriptions of the locality have been the variables selected as a basis for classification. Sometimes these appear arbitrary; Armen (1972), for example, seemed to use all those variables that he could quantify satisfactorily, given his initial theoretical presupposition that the defining feature of spatial differentiation was the provision of services. Sometimes the variables are statistically derived. Webber (1978), for example, compiled a very large number of available indicators and processed them for their capacity to express differences between relevant areas. By this method greatest differences are identified, though there is no guarantee that the processes referred to by those indicators represent the causes, or the most salient descriptive indexes, of spatial difference. Worse, sometimes it would appear that the only criterion for selection is the existence of a data series.

It would be preferable if some adequate theory of spatial differentiation underlay the choice of variables. At one level a pious or vacuous hope, perhaps, it might be argued that such a theory is impossible to agree upon or impracticable to formulate. Rather though, it seems to me, it has not been tried. Scarce mention is to be found of theories of space. Fothergill and Gudgin (1980) alone claim to be disputing a theory, that based upon the metaphor of core and periphery. Armen, without elaboration, adopts a view of cities and city regions as constituted by the extent of their service facilities. Others simply employ administratively defined units, without apparent further reflection. None have been developed in confrontation with any of the several available general theories of spatial distribution.

That is not, of course, to say that these taxonomies are without some quasi-theoretical presuppositions about the causes of spatial differentiation. Almost all hold a weak version of economism: the primary basis of spatial variation is the uneven distribution of industries and occupations. In addition, most recognise that the quality of consumption of services (housing, educational facilities, retail trading, etc) in a locality differentiates one place from another. The interesting feature of the Glasgow concept of local labour markets was that it entailed some notion of the effectivity of social density in causing specific kinds of social practices. These, however, are very weakly elaborated hypotheses about spatial differentiation and distribution. Several more complex theories of spatial distribution exist: some based on patterns in the circulation of capital, some on the variable character of the process of production in different industrial sectors, and some on patterns of consumption. To interrogate these theories—dependency theory, the theory of the new division of labour, new urban sociology, etc—with a view to providing a theoretical rationale for the selection of indicators would be a major step forward in working towards more adequate classificatory schemes. The construction and use of a coherent model of the relationships between cycles of accumulation, patterns of employment, collective consumption, and local cultural and political processes would render classification more useful in explanation and comparison.

It does not follow from this that we should expect there to be generated one single optimal classification. Webber (1977) demonstrated, by providing alternative classifications of wards and parishes by their socioeconomic status, age profile, and housing amenities, as well as by a composite of all three, that the same data might be classified differently. It certainly seems that the explanatory tasks envisaged for areal classifications are too varied for all to be satisfied by a single taxonomy. That is not, however, to say that the possible number of classifications is unlimited. My second criticism of the 'theoretically unprincipled' nature of schemata is that greater theoretical clarity about certain social processes is necessary if selected statistical variables are to identify relevant spatial differences. Thus the theoretical considerations of the Glasgow group about the nature of the sale of labour power in the market led them, appropriately, to consider some social processes which have the effect of *determining*, rather than merely reflecting, local distinctiveness, that is, highly localised social and information networks which produce self-containment. Even though that proved difficult to operationalise, it makes more sense to decide theoretically what it is one wants an index of than to adopt accessible indicators without regard to the social processes to which they refer.

A precise understanding of social processes is reciprocally necessary for an adequate theorisation of spatial distribution. Prior to classification one must be clear how, say, a labour market works, or what an urban system is. Only then can *relevant* measures be found of that which renders individual instances distinctive. Perhaps the clearest failure to tailor explanatory purposes to a classification of spatial areas was Webber's (1978) paper on parliamentary constituencies. In this case there can be no dispute about the validity of the boundaries of the areal units classified—parliamentary constituencies are social entities which have a real and consequential existence within the UK political system. However, if their classification is to be valuable in explanation, it is absurd to neglect political indicators, since the only conceivable purpose of classifying parliamentary constituencies is to explain voting behaviour. Again, quantification of the causes of voting is difficult—the density of trade-union membership is not easily estimated by constituency, and political traditions are even less accessible—but to ignore such factors makes the exercise largely futile.

A more general point follows, incidentally, from this. Political activities are increasingly important as causes of spatial differentiation at regional, subregional, and local levels (see Lovering, 1978; Massey, 1983), yet their part in the process is nowhere specified in models either of differentiation or of classification of space. It is not simply a matter of government intervention through regional policy, important though that may be, but also of the geography of social protest and industrial militancy, the uneven incidence of which has attracted scarcely any analytical attention (though see Cooke, 1985a).

The other main reason for finding taxonomies unsatisfactory, mentioned earlier, is their failure to represent change over time within the classificatory systems. The problem is that the classifications are generally static snapshots of a fundamentally dynamic object. Spatial differentiation is the outcome of complex social processes which have to be represented if comparative analysis is to be possible. Only Fothergill and Gudgin made any attempt to make change integral to their analysis. The other taxonomies were at best restricted to making inferences about change from the demographic structure of a locality at a single point in time.

From the existing data it is impossible to say whether Lancaster and its environs changed substantially, relative to other places, in the period after World War 2, or whether, instead, the varying portrayals considered were purely the result of different criteria of compilation. Special local knowledge makes it clear that in the case of Lancaster there was marked change. However, it is not possible to answer the initial question 'What other localities is Lancaster like?' from this material unless one makes the dubious assumption that the sources of misrepresentation of other areas are systematically the same as for Lancaster. In other words, a definitive statement about the trends in Lancaster is possible only on the basis of information gained independently of the taxonomies. Yet, arguably, what is most important in sociological studies of local differentiation is precisely the character and direction of trends, trends in deindustrialisation, unemployment, the sexual division of labour, housing provision, class antagonism, etc. There is very little that can be extracted from the given data to throw light on what might be described as the *comparative trajectories of development* of towns and subregions. Recent studies of social mobility have stressed the importance of career *paths* for adequate comprehension: that male, routine, white-collar workers hold such positions but temporarily as a step on a promotion ladder, whereas their female counterparts hold them permanently, is a most significant social fact, but one which will only show up on some version of a panel study. Likewise with towns, central elements in the understanding of local social and economic systems will be systematically obscured unless development paths are consciously incorporated into classificatory schemata. Social systems develop in time, in such a way that the dimensions of historicity must be represented in any study of the social process of spatial differentiation. This requires a more creative approach to the construction of social and political indicators. The difficulties of obtaining highly reliable time-series data are considerable: comparison over time of even Census data or election results for different localities is problematic. Equivalent indicators for industrial militancy, local state provision, or patriarchal domination are bound to be less reliable. But it seems beneficial to relax criteria of reliability in the hope of improving explanation.

In conclusion, I claim that these schemata of classification, despite their limitations, are potentially useful. However, weak theoretical foundation and inadequate reference to patterns of change over time render them incapable of application to many of the explanatory tasks required by social scientists.

Explaining peripheral change

Dan Shapiro

Any spatially located study must adopt or imply a view of the significance of its location. If the focus is on purely general processes ('the development of capitalism' or 'the primary community') then all its elements must be treated as either generalisable or irrelevant. If, on the other hand, attention is to be paid to elements specific to a location—and this is increasingly the case, as witness the unfashionableness of the 'general' examples—then a set of spatial problems arises. What defines a socially significant spatial unit? How are general social processes or elements to be 'mapped onto' localities and how is their operation affected by their coexistence with other elements and processes in concrete spaces? If surface empirical phenomena occur in particular places, how can we determine whether this reflects a sociospatial logic or whether it is arbitrary?

In this chapter, I attempt to relate recent developments in the sociological treatment of space and time to research on social change in the North of Scotland. In the case of my own research the focus was on social change as a consequence of North Sea oil-related development. Here—as presumably with most extractive processes—the usual concerns of a development study, to account for the presence or absence of certain kinds of activity, are reversed, since the presence of much of the activity surrounding North Sea oil can be explained on clear technical and economic grounds. This differs, then, from the tendency towards the economic 'homogenisation of space' observable for much of production. The concern is to account for the precise form of developments and for the changes they imply for local societies. This requires the identification of appropriate social spaces, of social forces operating upon and within them, and of the temporal (historical) dimension already in train.

Established theories of development, whether Marxist or modernisation, generate relatively clear, simple, and well-known contents for these categories. Throughout the 1970s these were under attack by proponents of 'dependency' theories in an attempt to explain three main problems: decline, in either absolute or relative terms, of per-capita income; unemployment and underemployment; and the failure, or extreme slowness, of development of forces of production. Despite some obvious difficulties with these measures, they seem to be conceivable in spatial terms, and the results *appear* unfavourable to whole populations of areas regardless of class. It is this that fuels 'externalist' accounts of their underdevelopment. Dependency-type theories propose that the development of some areas is necessarily at the expense of the underdevelopment of others; that participation in trade under capitalist relations of exchange can lead to the imposition of detrimental structures of production; and that under these circumstances control is externalised and the capacity for 'autonomous' decisions on production is lost.

It can be observed that the expansion of commodity exchange throughout the world has not brought about economic development [contrary to Marx's famous 'Chinese walls' passage in the *Manifesto* (see Marx and Engels, 1952, page 47)]. 'Neo-Marxist' theorists (especially Frank and Wallerstein) seek to explain this by proposing that capitalist exchange gives rise to a world capitalist system in which the development of the core depends on and creates underdevelopment in the periphery: surplus is expropriated from the periphery and appropriated in the core. This world system is 'capitalist' because it involves production for profit in the market: hence its origin lies with the discoveries and establishment of trading routes in the sixteenth century. According to Wallerstein, for example, this profit incentive determines increased production, innovation, specialisation (according to a 'natural' fit between areas and products), *and* the application of the 'appropriate' system of control of labour. Thus slavery, feudalism, free wage labour are *all* forms of *capitalist* reward to labour and are determined by trade—free labour is the form used for skilled work in the core, coerced labour for less-skilled work in the periphery. Each maximises output within its own setting. Because capitalism rewards capital rather than labour, the outcome of this specialised world system is a transfer of surplus from labour-intensive periphery to capital-intensive core, food production necessitating less capital and skill. The development of this world system, then, is determined by: (a) expansion, (b) specialisation, (c) surplus transfer.

Given the generality and apparent explanatory power of this model, it is hardly surprising that it was taken up by researchers concerned with issues of uneven regional development, particularly in 'semiperipheral' or 'peripheral–metropolitan' regions such as the European fringe. If the account is accepted, it has strong implications for regional uneven development. If the operation of the capitalist world market can 'call forth' a world division of labour and the appropriate systems of labour control, incorporating such vast disparities, then it is surely capable of determining finer gradations of disparity. We need look no further than to the 'fittedness' of regions for particular specialised production, and to the degree of skill and capitalisation 'entailed' by that production. The degree of regional disadvantage in the form of expropriation of surplus can then be read off. The continuing centrality of such theories—even if only as a central focus of criticism—can be seen in the contributions to the 1983 British Sociological Association Annual Conference on the theme of the periphery of industrial society (see Littlewood et al, 1984).

It is perhaps worth noting that although Massey (1978a), in one of the founding contributions to current work on regionalism, does dismiss "approaches 'borrowed' from underdevelopment theory" (pages 109-114), her reasons for doing so seem to me inappropriate. For the most part she does not proceed by querying the basis of these theories themselves—though she does state that they are subject to debate and criticisms at international level—but by querying the validity of translating them from inter' to intranational levels. She raises three main objections: first, that there are empirical differences between nation-states and their constituent regions, for example, monetary unification, customs policies; and that the state as a focus for class relations is usually less strong at the regional than at the national level. Though this is certainly true, it hardly seems adequate to dismiss the possibility of useful parallels, and one could equally point to empirical similarities that render national boundaries relatively arbitrary from the point of view of production or exchange relations. Similarly, one can identify radical disjunctions of class relations within nation-states. In the 1840s and 1850s, peasants throughout Europe were starving to death through successive waves of potato blight, while urban proletariats subsisted on imported food, by virtue of the nature of class relations connecting peasant and landlord, wage labourer and capitalist, in certain *regions* of *all* of these countries. This objection, then, can at best be a note of caution—to differentiate 'regional' and 'national' uneven development is *more* arbitrary than conflating them. Second, she objects that such a translation implies a general problematic of 'the spatial', writ large or small, forgetting that we are dealing with *social* divisions of territory and socially different types of territorial division. I agree with this, but I do not think it makes Massey's point. It is applicable to *any* consideration of spatial differentiation, whether 'regional' or 'national', and could condemn or condone either without demonstrating any necessary incommensurability between the two. Third, Massey considers the most important objection to be that these theories tend to take nation-states as objects given to analysis, whereas she wishes to argue that regions are *not* necessarily pregiven. Here, I think Massey is simply mistaken in her reading of the literature, which—though it sometimes works with 'national' examples—does not constitute areas as significant units for study on the basis of 'nation'. Indeed the more usual criticism is that such theories are far too vague with respect to particular social formations, rather than that they predefine them.

If dependency theories were adequate at an international level, then I do not believe these objections would suffice to dismiss them from consideration as accounts of regional uneven development too. The *locus classicus* of critiques of dependency-type theories is provided by Brenner (1977), who argues that the processes of expansion, specialisation, and surplus transfer cannot determine economic development. The expansion of trade, even for profit in the market, does not itself constitute capitalism—such trade has occurred repeatedly in precapitalist history.

Where this occurs under feudal social relations there will indeed be an attempt to increase production for exchange, but this takes the form of increasing absolute surplus labour (intensified coercion). Because feudal production is essentially static, this is very limited and indeed often damaging. Far from being *chosen* to maximise surplus, the retention of these production relations *curtails* the production of commodities for exchange and tends to increase the world market price. This cannot be conceived as in the interests of the 'centre' or the 'world capitalist system', and so must be interpreted as the *outcome* of class struggle in the periphery—the relative strength of the feudal ruling class *both* against the local bourgeoisie *and* against international capital. For this feudal class the maximisation of surplus is not the same as maximisation of output, the freedom to interfere with social relations is limited, and direct access to the means of subsistence robs 'market pressures' of their compulsion.

Similarly, Brenner points out that specialisation is not new, nor does it itself constitute capitalism, which develops through continuing innovation and the adoption of new methods of production so as to increase relative surplus labour and the productivity of labour. Specialisation, by contrast, is a 'one-off' recombination. But capacity for innovation depends on the freedom of labour and capital to combine at the highest level of technical development and the necessity for it to do so: that is, 'free' wage labour separated from the means of subsistence and production. This again can only occur as the outcome of class struggles, not as a mechanical response to the extension of trade.

As for transferred surplus (wealth) this is not in itself 'capital', nor (argues Brenner) was it necessary for the development of capitalism in the core. And it is nonsense to suggest that specialisation entails a given level of skill and capitalisation, and hence transfer of surplus (positive or negative): compare US agriculture with manufacturing in the Third World.

Another—and as it happens roughly contemporary—possibility for delineating significant social spaces arose from the structuralist emphasis on social formations as structures in dominance embodying articulations of different modes of production. The specificity of an area, then, could be understood in terms of the combination of modes present and their relative weight. Hence, perhaps, the centrality of the peasantry in many accounts of the peripheries of metropolitan areas—a weight that they have difficulty in bearing. But the permutations allowed by this approach are limited, and they do not appear to be capable of accounting for major empirical differences in formally indistinguishable areas.

One of the most promising avenues is the recent development of realist theories of space and time, and the combination of these with the work of the 'new' regionalism with its emphasis on the constitution of social and economic spaces through successive superimposed rounds of the restructuring of capitalist production. I shall discuss one such formulation

(Urry, 1985) and consider its implications for existing studies of peripheral change and for the development of an adequate programme for such study.

This theorisation of social relations in space and time may be summarised as involving the following propositions about significant entities and their causal relations:

(1) Some entities persist through the realisation of certain powers, not through the properties of space and time themselves: space and time are not 'particulars'.

(2) There are two 'orders of the social world': relatively enduring social entities with (variably realisable) causal properties; and specific events to which the former contingently give rise. This involves the rejection both of positivism and of 'naive realism': the derivation of events from a *single* structure or essence (frequently the capitalist mode of production).

(3) The conditions of *realisation* of entities' causal properties often include the (partial) realisation of the causal properties of *other* entities. It is in this sense (rather than just 'empirically') that things are *concrete*: events, and their spatial patterning, are to be explained in terms of complex, overlapping, and spatiotemporally structured relations between entities, with the realisation or part realisation or blocking of their causal powers.

(4) *Space* is currently the more salient aspect of the space–time couple. This is because:

(a) two objects can occupy the same point in time, but not in space—if an entity is to exert effects on more than one object it must act, therefore, at more than one point in space;

(b) space is limited (constant sum), so competition for the control of space is fundamentally political, involving power.

(5) It follows that spatiotemporal transformations are more difficult to effect than simply temporal ones: the latter, therefore, happen first. An example of this is the three stages of capital accumulation:

(a) absolute surplus-value production;

(b) relative surplus-value production with spatial transformations within the sphere of circulation;

(c) relative surplus-value production with spatial transformations within the sphere of production.

(6) The current hypermobility of capital can be contrasted with civil society which presupposes the constitution of individual subjects (crucial interpellations of the subject being spatiotemporal location and gender). Subjects are necessarily spatially distributed (especially into households) and constrained. Wage labour is produced and reproduced in civil society; hence there is a contrast between the production of capital, which is spatially indifferent, and of wage labour, for which 'place' is of particular significance.

(7) Processes of capital restructuring tend to a 'dual economy': in the case of the United Kingdom, London vs the rest. Urban areas are reduced to labour pools, sites for the production and reproduction of wage labour, and their important linkages are hence those of civil society rather than of the economy. This heightens the significance of *locality*, and its possibilities for collective organisation, while lessening that of region and nation. Localities are structured more by civil society than by relations of production.

(8) Relations between capitalist production and civil society take on a complex combination of necessity and contingency through the interdependencies of their respective causal powers.

(9) The spatial organisation of the division of labour can be contrasted with that of civil society. Six main forms of the spatial division of labour can be identified:

(a) regional specialisation;

(b) regional dispersal;

(c) functional separation—central management and research and development (R and D), skilled labour in old manufacturing centres, and peripheral unskilled labour;

(d) functional separation—central management and R and D, peripheral semi- and unskilled labour;

(e) functional separation—management, R and D, and skilled labour in a central economy, and unskilled labour in a peripheral economy;

(f) areas with investment, technical change, and new products, and static areas with decreasingly competitive production and job-loss.

Particular areas result from the complex superimposition of such patterns (past and present) in different production sectors. And seven dimensions of civil society can be identified, namely the degree to which:

(a) the built environment can be transformed;

(b) there is *integration* of the social relations of civil society into the capitalist economy;

(c) the social relations of civil society are based on *community* or *commodity*;

(d) there is *heterogeneity* of class experiences;

(e) there is spatial *concentration* of different social classes and social forces;

(f) civil societies are organised *vertically* (class-specific) or *horizontally* (non-class-specific groups or practices);

(g) civil societies are long-established, *sedimented*.

Three general difficulties, plus a number of more detailed ones, occur to me with this schema. First, the contention that spatial changes occur only when the possibilities for spatiotemporal change have been relatively exhausted is striking and interesting, but the derivation of this from the general properties of space and time is less convincing. The difference between discussion of the properties of single points in space and time

and the complexities of real spatiotemporal events is such that I doubt
the significance of the observation that two objects can occupy the same
point in time but not in space. Nor is it clear that controlling one
'moment' necessarily guarantees the next 'moment', so that controlling
the disposition of time may be as infinite a problem as controlling space.

Further, I wonder how true it is that space is 'constant sum' whereas
time is not. Even taken as absolutes ('particulars'), this is doubtful;
taken as social appropriations of space and time it is more uncertain. For
most of human history, agricultural 'space' was unlimited; that is, the use
of land for improvement (forest, scrub, moor) was limited only by the
availability of labour, a constraint more of time than of space. With the
development of capitalist agriculture, the amount of land available to it
again becomes, relatively, unlimited. And how much sense does it make,
currently, to speak of industrial space as limited? On the contrary, the
problem is its superabundance—what has been redolently termed the
'lumpen-geography' of capital.

This in turn casts doubts on the distinctiveness of space as *uniquely*
political, involving power and control, since it seems obvious that the
disposition of time is also political, sometimes intensely so.

A second and rather basic problem is: 'what is an entity?' Even
within one particular paper, all of the following terms could qualify:
entity; enduring entity; structural mechanism; social object; something
which possesses a realised or unrealised or partially realised causal power;
discourse; and interpellation. How do these terms relate? What are the
criteria for entities? How many entities are there? Very few? If so,
standard realism hardly seems all that naive. Rather more? In which
case, how 'hard' is the distinction between entity and mere event? What
scale (space) of causal effect and what degree (time) of longevity or
persistence are to count as constituting an entity? Are these arbitrary
decisions? And if so, is this 'really' a realist position?

The third problem is what seems to me to be an overidentification of
civil society with households. There is (obviously) a large difference
between the formal properties of capitalist relations of production
pertaining to the economy and the actual condition of struggle ('industrial
relations') obtaining in production units. The production of wage labour
(together with forms of resistance) thus occurs to an important degree in
the production unit, in ways which may be quite distinct from, or in
conflict with, its production in the household. To speak of households as
the 'cell form' of civil society is therefore useful as an analogy for the
'friction of distance' between them, but misleading in suggesting that all
forms of civil society are built up from combinations of these units.

Some subsidiary points flow from this. First, the extent to which the
important linkages within the city pass through the household may be
exaggerated. The hypermobility of capital may make it 'spatially
indifferent'—but this does not mean indifferent to the space in which

particular capitals are located. *Having located*, capital faces costs in premature relocation, which will be resisted through local political engagement. Mobile capital certainly engages in struggle with local labour, and often in local politics, and this will contribute to the 'constitution' of urban areas, both as a power in its own right and through its part in the production of labour and its collective experience. It follows from this that the distinction between local and nonlocal capital may not be so clearcut—that both contribute in some sense to the reproduction of local wage labour. Second, it is not clear that the potential influence of labour and intermediate classes is strengthened at the local level. It may well be weakened regionally and nationally, but it does not follow that it is strengthened locally. Spatial indifference is an *additional* asset for capital which, as above, still engages in local struggle too. Similarly, why should the erosion of local or regional particularities created by capital (the demise of regional production specialisms or functions) *heighten* the distinctiveness of each locality through the distinctiveness of each one's civil society. Even if the latter *were* the only distinctiveness to remain, it does not follow that this is *greater* than before. Last, it seems to me that plenty of scope remains for production relations to transform or to determine the condition of a locality through transforming or determining (part of) the condition of its civil society. Suppose a locality (for example, a new town deserted by its principal industry—there are now many such cases) has a large unemployed (and relatively unorganised) population and a correspondingly large number of (fragmented) households. Then suppose an employer moves in to take advantage of the possibility of employing female, perhaps part-time, labour. In this case relations of production would profoundly affect (structure) the condition of local civil society, with a particular effect on gender relations.

The import of this discussion is not, however, to undermine the project in general. If the current importance of space cannot so confidently be derived from the general properties of space and time, then this would certainly reduce the elegance of the model, but would not necessarily interfere with the project of seeking out the temporal and spatial operations and interrelationships of entities. The question of what is an entity might be ameliorated by developing a closer definition 'in use', and it may be necessary to reconcile ourselves to some softening of the dividing line between entity and event, while retaining the objective of indentifying the extent (space) and persistence (time) of the effects of putative causal objects and their interrelationships, and of attempting to identify a rank order. And finally, the distinction between civil society and the production sphere of the economy will be blurred by the intrusion of subjectivities constructed in civil society into the labour process and by the realisation of labour power, and by the contribution of interpellations from the world of production to the constitution of subjects in civil society.

The question next arises of what light this model casts on existing studies of semiperipheral development, their adequacy, and the possibilities for their reformulation. In considering this I shall concentrate on the area with which I have the closest empirical research connection—development, and especially oil-related development, in the North of Scotland. Much of my own work on migrant labour could be said, in retrospect and in common with other contemporary work, to have adopted a class-determinist framework in seeking to reduce all issues to relations between economic classes. In particular:

(1) the features of, and differences between, groups were identified and explained primarily in terms of class position (peasantry, wage labour, semipeasantry, etc);

(2) relations between groups (for example, migrant and local labour) were similarly related to their class positions;

(3) class relations, and changes of class position, were the principal explanations sought for social change;

(4) class was itself one-dimensionally treated in terms of economic relations.

The distinctiveness of the local situation, then, was conceived mainly in terms of an unusual clash of class positions. The effect is to reduce the account to a set-piece class confrontation, the possible outcomes and explanations of which are largely pregiven. This was, at least in part, in reaction to popular accounts of developments in terms of a crude notion of culture and unique 'ways of life'.

An exception to this was the consideration of dependency, discussed above, and in particular an attempt to explore the possibilities of a 'dependent industrial relations' (Shapiro, 1981). This involved identifying those aspects of the industrial relations of oil which could not be accounted for in terms of the properties of formally free wage labour and which seemed to require an account in terms of nonwage constraint. The conclusion, however, was that these forms of ascriptive constraint were by no means unique to peripheral locations, but could equally be found at the centre. The effect of this is, first, again to reduce the significance of 'the local'; and second to leave a range of phenomena theoretically unaccounted for under the label (after Corrigan, 1977) of 'ascriptive constraint'.

What, then, of the adequacy of other work? Though there was little current sociology of interest, there were, through the 1970s, some impressive contributions to the social history of the North of Scotland, mainly by Malcolm Gray, Ian Carter, Jim Hunter, Ian Prebble, and Peter Mewett. The kinds of issues these writers were concerned with included:

(a) the development of crofting as a distinctive form of peasant agriculture;

(b) the development of capitalist agriculture, both in the form of mixed farming in the fertile eastern counties and of sheep 'ranches' in the west;

(c) the relationship of crofting agriculture to these forms;
(d) the means of survival, especially forms of occupational pluralism, of the remaining semipeasantry; and
(e) the consequences of all these in terms of class formation and organisation, political mobilisation, migration, and family structure.

There is a tendency to think of crofting as a 'traditional' system which has existed from time immemorial. The work of Hunter and Carter underlines how recent it is, being a product of the clearances in the eighteenth century. It arose out of the preceding 'runrig' system through the assumption by clan chiefs of legal property rights in clan lands. This could, after the eviction of the population, be very profitably let for the breeding and fattening of sheep. Crofting—the subsistence of families on small coastal plots of land—arose in its initial form through two further factors: the growth and prosperity of the kelp industry (involving the gathering and processing of seaweed) between the 1760s and 1820s, which meant the clan chiefs and landlords wished not simply to be rid of the cleared population, but to retain them on the coast to work on kelp. Clan families were granted small coastal plots, but at exorbitant rents which could not possibly be paid from their agricultural production, thus forcing family members to work in the landlord's kelp industry. The second factor was the introduction of the potato, which, as in Ireland, made it possible for enough food for subsistence to be produced from tiny parcels of land. The kelp industry collapsed after the end of the Napoleonic Wars, from which date crofters became the 'Highlands problem' of an excess redundant population. The potato blights, the worst of which occurred in the period 1845–1850, were accompanied and succeeded by waves of emigration. Carter, in his earlier work (for example, 1974), explicitly relates the development of crofting to theories of the development of underdevelopment, and, citing Frank, argues that far from being the backward consequence of the absence of 'modern' (capitalist) development, the crofting system is itself a *product* of the penetration of capitalist (market) relations to the Highlands.

History's apparently clear verdict on crofting was arrested, however, by massive agitation and political mobilisation by crofters during the period 1881–1886, culminating in the Crofters Act. This was largely in the wake of Irish agitation, and on the same issues: rent control, security of tenure, and compensation for improvements. This special legal 'protection' achieved by crofters has meant their survival to this day, though in a manner increasingly dependent on occupational pluralism. This aspect has been pursued by Mewett (1977), who documented the varieties of strategies employed in the Western Isles for maintaining household income, from fishing to seafaring to long spells of labouring and factory work in urban centres; and also the transformations in crofting activities towards those requiring less labour input, despite consequent reductions in production in subsistence terms, as wage earning increased in salience.

Carter (1979) takes up the question of why agitation by crofters was successful in the West Highlands but not in the North-East. Up to the 1880s there was no rational criterion for separating much of the (now) Grampian Region from the West Highlands, and the Gladstone government was forced into bizarre contortions to justify the exclusion of the (now) Grampian Region from the Crofters Act of 1886. Capitalist agriculture arrived late in Aberdeenshire, but by 1840 it was supreme in agricultural production in Scotland, having overtaken that of the Lothians. Nevertheless, right into the twentieth century the great majority of agricultural holdings were crofts. Peasant agitation erupted in the North-East in 1880, a year *earlier* than in the west—but while the peasant class in the West Highlands formed an effective political organisation and achieved all of its main aims, peasants in the North-East did not and were defeated. Carter accounts for this in terms of the intimate articulation between the dominant capitalist mode of agricultural production in the lowland areas and the subordinate peasant mode in the uplands. Peasant farmers raised cattle to be fattened on capitalist farms to the East, while their children provided nearly all of the wage labour on capitalist farms under the 'bothy' system. Peasant farmers also brought waste land into cultivation, through backbreaking and 'unprofitable' labour, on a system of nineteen year 'improving' leases (at nominal rents), after which time the improved land was resumed by landlords. In the West, by contrast, there was no possible articulation between crofting and sheep, just a stark visible, and hostile conflict of interests. In terms of political consequences, by the end of World War 1, bereft of protective legislation, the North-East peasantry was dead. In the West, by contrast, crofters came back from the War and intensified the land grabs.

Hunter's (1976) work combines elements of a class analysis with an engaged account of the crofting community forging itself (the title of his book, *The Making of the Crofting Community*, deliberately alludes to E P Thompson). The other accounts are couched explicitly in terms of class.

These accounts make fascinating reading and are an immeasurable improvement on the prior barrenness of 'Scottish history', but might nonetheless be amenable to a broader perspective. For example, the success of crofters in the west is attributed to the stark opposition of their interests to those of capitalist agriculture and, by implication, to the continuing strength of peasant production. It would be wrong, however, to characterise peasant economic production as 'strong' at this time—it was already weak and steadily weakening, as in the rest of Europe. Its strength lay, rather, in its relations of reproduction and production of peasant labour, apparently resulting in a particularly fierce determination to cling to an (economically) miserable existence. The subsequent commitment to ingenious and very varied forms of occupational pluralism—including extensive periods in wage labour in different corners of the globe—seems to call for a similar account in terms of the strength of the 'civil society'. Equally, the political strength found by crofters in the 1880s was not the consequence of any established political structures— previously entirely nonexistent—but again of the strength of 'civil society' in the form of households and cooperation between households; and with an important contribution from religion, not in relation to content or belief but as an organisational practice.

As for East coast developments, these could be seen as, at least in part, an accommodation of capitalist agriculture to a strong form of peasant 'civil society', forcing it to make special arrangements for the subsistence and day-to-day reproduction of its labour. This in turn produced a particular form of social organisation involving a sharp separation of age-cohorts and the development of a distinctive 'youth culture', with consequences as diverse as the bothy ballads, satanistic secret societies which acted in some respects like trade unions, and the contemporarily much-lamented soaring illegitimacy rates in the counties of the North-East.

One might attempt, then, to draw up a formula to treat a spatially located study in accordance with the theoretical scheme discussed above. Thus one could:

(a) Identify the principal entities 'in play'. Consider their respective causal powers, especially in terms of their extent (spatial range) and duration.

(b) Consider the ways in which these causal powers interrelate, transform, and modify each other, and the pattern produced by the 'overlapping' of their spatial and temporal ranges.

(c) Consider especially the forms of spatial organisation peculiar to principal entities, and the consequences of these for the constitution of different kinds of 'locality'—spaces related to each other ('isomorphic') in terms of the logic of the entity concerned. For this purpose, historical entities and their legacies in terms of constituted localities should be considered.

(d) At a minimum, principal entities should include forms of division of labour, civil society, and the state.

Pursuing these prescriptions for the North of Scotland could produce some instances, as described below.

Division of labour—historical development

The spread of capitalist social relations in agriculture involves fairly clear causal powers: in the West, first the displacement of a subsistence population to the coast to work in a geographically dispersed industry, and, subsequently, its ejection from all areas of capitalist agriculture; and, in the East, transformation of the peasantry into capitalist farmers and landless labourers, with a progressive ejection of agricultural wage labour accompanying increased capitalisation. These causal powers might be seen as having been *facilitated* by the translation to an alien social and economic context of legal rights in property developed in the capitalist south; that is, a reinforcing effect of the causal powers and spatial extent of the UK state. On the other hand, these powers were in turn *resisted* through the strength of existing 'civil society', resulting in the freezing of the process at one particular stage in the west (a process which, some argue, is now continuing to its postponed conclusion as a result of recent legislation allowing crofters to buy, and subsequently resell, their crofts); and in its delay and partial modification in the east. The Highland edge between east and west therefore occupies an ambiguous position in between these two processes. Perhaps this may be related to the fact that the 'kilts and cabers' aspect of 'Caledonian idiocy', an insulting and apparently 'free-floating' appropriation of Highland culture, has its base in this area.

Division of labour—oil developments

Large-scale oil developments off Scotland constitute rather a special form of the division of labour. Rather than any of the six forms identified above (page 82), with oil quite high management, skilled labour, and unskilled labour are all located in the periphery. The 'spatial indifference' characteristic of modern capital does not apply to it in anything like the same way (true also, presumably, for most extractive industry). In terms of a balance of contingencies and necessities, oil relations of production are necessarily capitalist, necessarily located in limited areas of the North of Scotland, but only contingently utilise any category of local labour. The scale of activity, by comparison with what existed before, means that oil-related activities cannot avoid actively reconstituting these spaces and entering very rapidly into 'local' relations. The potential impact both on local civil society and on the local state is very large. In terms of its own causal powers, its pressure is to gain unrestricted, unsupervised, and untaxed access to local land, transport, communications, and unskilled labour. These may all be subject to resistance and constraint from the national and local state, local labour, local capital, and local popular struggles.

Local capital

There is scope for disagreement about the significance of local capital and the extent to which it may be expected to act differently from nonlocal capital. I would argue that the more relevant distinction is between large and small capital, and that capitals are local as a by-product of being small rather than vice versa. This might be modified through the possibility of local capital accommodating production to particular features of local civil society—in this context, perhaps patterns of shift and seasonal production which take account of occupational pluralism, croftworking, etc. A further conflict of interests is obviously that between capital located in a peripheral area to take advantage of low rates of pay and more advanced sectors of capital. This is not necessarily a local/nonlocal distinction, however. Some capital (large and small) may be tied to the locality by its raw material (for example, food processing); others by raw material *and* the need for cheap labour (for instance, wool processing and manufacture); others just by cheap labour (for example, engineering). A further distinctiveness of local capital may be its relation to the local state, where it may be thoroughly entrenched (in such cases organised labour can represent the interests of large-scale capital temporarily).

Local state

An increasing *proximity* between state and civil society has been remarked (Urry, 1985), referring primarily to the national state. The local state has always been more proximate to local civil society, with fewer layers of mediation between them. As such there is scope, within limits, for the local state to be 'captured', either in the interests of local capital or by local popular struggles.

However, the power of the local state, once captured, to act against large-scale capital is affected by (amongst other things) the precise legal restriction of its spatial extent. There is an interesting contrast to be drawn between North Sea developments and the Morecambe Bay gas field in the Lancaster area. Though the latter is smaller by many orders of magnitude, it is in a much stronger position against the local state than North Sea operators are against the Shetlands Council or the Grampian Region. This is simply because the North Sea operators have no economic alternative to a landfall somewhere within the territory controlled by these authorities, whereas British Gas has a choice. This is enough to make British Gas, in effect, hypermobile.

Gender relations in the division of labour and in reproduction

A number of 'routine' aspects of gender relations in the division of labour are observable in oil, for example, the confinement of female labour to relatively poorly paid (often part-time) 'caring' and domestic occupations such as catering and cleaning. In locations where there are workcamps. many such jobs may be created.

This involves the translocation of 'urban' expectations of women and women's work, but these expectations may intrude considerably in local production and reproduction relations. For example, it may be women who work crofts while men are in paid employment, so that the employment of local women has a large impact on croftworking in an area.

A quite different aspect is gender relations between men at work. Oil-related work shows a particularly strong version of 'masculinism', often encouraged by employers, with a probable effect of defusing and diverting conflict and discontent. This accentuated discourse of masculinity, almost cultivation of brutality, is presumably related to the total immersion in this constrained single-sex environment, and the patterns of frustration and desire which this involves. This ought to be related to a broader treatment of the 'sexuality of the workplace'.

A connected issue is the intervention of new patterns of working in civil society through the household. Continuous periods of work followed by continuous periods of leave involve quite new patterns of 'presence and absence' in the household, which may throw into relief or make problematic existing gender relations and relations of reproduction.

Civil society and agencies of reproduction

A further intervention in civil society arises through novel involvements in producing and reproducing labour. An obvious implication of the above paragraph is that, for workers in workcamps and on rigs and platforms, the employer has taken over a substantial amount of the immediate day-to-day production and reproduction of labour power. This goes far in explaining the vulnerability of labour in these circumstances—without the employers' good offices the worker cannot even reproduce himself or herself from day to day.

Relatedly, the state has taken on a pronounced role, vis-à-vis civil society, in determining the availability of households for labour. Thus some local authorities decreed that no 'family' accommodation would be made available to oil-related workers, so restricting them to the kind of regime described above. Elsewhere (for example, East Ross) the local authority built housing estates and encouraged migrant workers to relocate with their households as part of a programme of 'development'.

These issues are referred to in chapter 6 below.

Civil society, household, and locality

Two aspects of civil society that have been emphasised are (1), spatiotemporal location, as one of the strongest and most constitutive interpellations of subjects, so that 'locality' becomes a key principle of organisation, identification, and struggle, sedimented over time; and (2), the 'household', as the key unit ('cell form') of civil society and the site of reproduction. In the remainder of this chapter, I wish to explore some aspects of these. First, one may note at least a superficial proximity between these themes and central concerns of social anthropology: the particularity of local small-scale societies and systems of kinship. This connection holds out both a promise—that recent anthropological studies of semiperipheral societies might be assimilable to such a framework—and also a warning of some of the pitfalls that could attend a rediscovery of community and tradition.

It would be salutary, perhaps, to start with the warnings. I will relate these to the tendency—temptation—to use 'community' and 'tradition' as shorthand terms: 'community' for local social relations in general; 'tradition' for the longevity of such relations ('sedimentation'), implying their unchanging continuity, rootedness, and entrenchment. This general problem has a pronounced application in treatments of the 'Celtic periphery', with well over a century of 'Celtic twilight' in literature and social commentary, depicting a golden tradition of authentic community, usually on the very point of disappearing, though still barely discernible to the assiduous gaze. There is also an anthropological *locus classicus* of this position, and of its criticism, dealing with a Celtic peripheral peasantry. Though this is based on western Ireland rather than on northern Scotland, many of the issues are the same. The 'origin' is the well-known Arensberg and Kimball (1968) study *Family and Community in Ireland*, carried out in the 1930s and republished in 1968. The relevant 'interlocutors' are Brody (1973), in his book *Inishkillane*—often held up as the very model of a sensitive, informed, modern local study—and Gibbon (1973), in his extended review of Brody.

Rural society in County Clare is depicted by Arensberg and Kimball as a strong and successful peasant community, based on patriarchy (in its extended sense, domination of women and sons by the male head of household); inheritance, by *one* son (usually the eldest) on his father's retirement (which might well not be till this 'lad' was himself in his fifties); and junior status (including the impossibility of marrying) for such a son. According to Arensberg and Kimball this peasant production is relatively independent of the market and other external forces, it is an enclosed system; it is governed by 'tradition', ties of mutual aid and obligation, and family exchange of labour—'cooring'; there is no significant differentiation within the community by class or status (by which they obviously mean *interhousehold* differentiation). This traditional community is characterised by them as healthy and, indeed, strengthening.

When Brody came to study this same area in the early 1970s, he found the rural peasant community in a state of advanced degeneration. He graphically illustrates this through showing:
(a) a withdrawal from the positive evaluation of this community, a sense of its subordination and 'inferiority', and hence a collective depression;
(b) individual manifestations of this anomic condition in terms of the high incidence of depressive mental breakdown;
(c) the ridiculing and devaluation of fathers (patriarchs) by their sons, in their presence and with their apparent acquiescence;
(d) the progressive penetration of rapacious entrepreneurs, taking advantage of community demoralisation to gather the economic reins of the local society into their grasp—the 'cash nexus' replacing or displacing non-commodity relations.

The explanation Brody offers of this apparent paradox (a society 'strong and strengthening' in the 1930s now in collapse) is in terms of *external* interventions: first 'modernisation', through the media, resulting in the importation' of 'urban values'—the consequences are demoralisation and emigration; and second, the undermining of the local subsistence economy by the flow of 'remittances'—money sent 'back home' by emigrants, which becomes a prime source of income and results in a withdrawal from peasant farming. This in turn undermines the communal culture, allowing it to be penetrated and subordinated by entrepreneurs.

Brody thus superimposes a certain historical process on top of Arensberg and Kimball's enthnography; first, by criticising the 'timelessness' of their view of the traditional community, and showing that this patriarchal form arose from the famines of the potato blight (mentioned above); and second, by demonstrating that the idyll of the 1930s was actually on the point of destruction through modernisation. He also criticises the 'functionalism' of their account, but despite this retains their characterisation of the 'community' and its roots in 'tradition'—it is a usage which falls apart in his hands as he finds himself forced to refer to an 'older tradition', a 'newer tradition', and 'the incorporation of elements of an older tradition into a newer tradition'. The very concept of 'tradition', one might say, implies the reification of time and space, their treatment as 'particulars'.

Gibbon in his review sets out to demonstrate the falsity of the entire 'problem', as posed by Brody, through the falsity of Arensberg and Kimball's original depiction. The 'eclipse of community' is not new; indeed, as we saw, its demise has been mourned for well over a century (compare Carter, 1976). Gibbon shows from the agricultural statistics that, for the period of Arensberg and Kimball's study, there was a steady trend towards the amalgamation of holdings, involving the demise of smaller holdings. What is more, Gibbon argues that the supposed mechanism of stability, cooring—the exchange of family labour, and of machine time for family labour—was actually a mechanism of *differentiation*, undermining the smaller peasantry. He then goes on to show that the incidence of mental breakdown leading to institutionalisation has always been high since the famines, and was actually declining at the time of Brody's research. The fragility of patriarchy and its legitimated 'respect' is attested for the period since the famines, in literature (most celebratedly in Synge) and in trials for parricide; and the activities of the Gombeen men (local entrepreneurs) and their dominance over communities through debt-bondage is equally well attested.

Because Brody accepts Arensberg and Kimball's 'myth of origins', their false functionalist depiction of community (while superficially rejecting the functionalism), he is inevitably drawn into a false 'functionalist' explanation—external intrusion into a stable system. The *real* explanation is the steady development of capitalist agriculture, producing larger units, specialisation in beef production, the progressive marginalisation of peasant subsistence farming, and the ejection of agricultural labour.

"The vicissitudes of the majority (of the middle peasantry) and the upward social mobility of its minority have for the entire century underlain the most striking features of this society, namely the undermining of the status, security and ideology of this group. It is not necessary to go outside Ireland to understand this process or its basis, since it is no more than the local form of the development of capitalism in agriculture" (Gibbon, 1973, page 496).

One could say, then, that, although Brody recaptures the process for history (albeit an erroneous history), Gibbon recaptures it for theory. He roots out the untheorised usage and false problem, but at the expense of asserting a thoroughgoing reductionism privileging economic-class and class-production relations[6]. In withdrawing from this reductionism it is necessary to avoid returning to a functionalist or ahistorical or merely romantic alternative. I would hazard the contention that the terms 'tradition' and 'community', or their various synonyms (and these could sometimes include 'sedimented' or 'spatiotemporal location'), nearly always signal one or other of these problems.

With respect to anthropological promise, a recent collection entitled *Belonging* (Cohen, 1982) sets out precisely to explore identity and social organisation in UK rural cultures, and includes contributions on the Scottish Isles. From our particular perspective, however, these are disappointing. One example is provided by Mewett, whose very interesting, though also reductionist work, on the changing balance of occupational pluralism on Lewis was referred to above. His paper, on the same settlement (Mewett, 1982), identifies three significant associational categories, which are, he claims, the basis of local social organisation. These are kinship, neighbouring, and church; class, he says, is not salient, at least *within* the community. There is no spatial congruence between these three categories.

Taken separately, each of these categories potentially generates conflict; for example, between neighbours through sheer proximity and the possibilities of transgression (wandering stock, mending fences, etc); and from the Calvinist Church, through the polarity 'communicant–drunkard', each pole involving negative imputations of the other. But these conflicts are contained through the intersection and crosscutting of the associational categories, so that those potentially divided on one dimension are likely to be brought together again on another. What is more, this containment 'function' is taken by Mewett (1982, page 111) as the explanation for the category; thus:
"this means that people divided by the schisms of the other associational categories are brought together by the obligations of neighbouring. This suggests, moreover, a reason for the social boundary surrounding the neighbourhood set. Without it ... the schisms of family and church would not be controlled ...".
And elsewhere (page 116) a particular technique for 'keeping the peace'— carefully placing messages about a grievance with a third party who can be relied upon to relay it—is said to work *because* otherwise disruptions would undermine the system of generalised reciprocity; hence they *have to be* diverted through the 'placing' of complaints. The functional necessity involved in all this is the material one of cooperation in croft production.

[6] Bearing in mind, of course, that this is Gibbon circa 1973.

And to cap it all, Mewett describes the incipient dissolution o̶ɪ̶ ̶ṵ̶.̶.̶
through the 'intrusion' of increasing noncroft income and state welfare
provision. This, then, represents exactly the regression from economism
to functionalism to be avoided, despite the richness of the ethnographic
observation.

To conclude, I wish to give some preliminary consideration to the
relationship between entities as structures of intersecting, blocking, or
facilitating causal powers, and individual subjects constituted primarily in
civil society. If the concept of the interpellation or hailing of subjects
and the resulting constitution of subjectivities is to be taken seriously (and
I believe it should be), then the implications of translating this concept
from a 'naive' or monostructural environment to one of a plurality of
related entities must be considered. In its earlier formulations (as in the
works of Althusser and Lacan), subjects stand in a clear relationship to
the Subject (capital S) of their hailing (whether as the Subject of bourgeois
ideology or of the entry into language).

If the all-powerful constituting structure is replaced with a range of
entities in complex interrelationships, then we must consider that each
entity can, perhaps must, stand in a Subject relationship to subjects which
it partially constitutes. The interpellation of subjects, then, would be at
least as complex and multifaceted as the network of entities. 'At least',
because interpellations constitute and reproduce subjects discursively,
through the production of meaning. Entities are thus apparent to subjects
discursively, if at all—that is, as systems of meaning which are contested
interdiscursively in conditions of ideological struggle, and which stand
alongside the structures of possibility and constraint embodied in entities
themselves. Amongst such complex interpellations will be differing and
often contradictory spatial identifications.

Policy, planning, and peripheral development

Dan Shapiro

This chapter continues to take oil-related development in the North of Scotland as its empirical focus, concentrating this time on issues of formal development planning and development policy. Sociological treatments of development generally pay scant attention to planning. If considered at all, the formal planning framework is usually taken simply as an adjunct of the state, requiring little independent analysis. Though theories of the state of course differ, the interpretation of planning simply reflects these differences.

Some social theories do generate a more particular place for aspects of planning, however. Habermas's discussions (1970; 1974) of the conditions under which an 'ideal speech' situation may be attained, and of those under which 'systematically distorted communication' actually arise, lend themselves well to the analysis of planning inquiries as paradigm examples both in terms of the privileging of professional expertise and technocracy, and in terms of the framing of appropriate and permissible discourses. Indeed an analysis of the public inquiry system in these terms, which happens to take as its example proposals for a North-Sea-oil-related petrochemical complex in Scotland, is available (Rodger, 1980). Though I return to this briefly later in the chapter, it is not its main focus.

Aside from its centrality or peripherality for social theory, however, the speed, novelty, and particular location of oil-related developments in the North of Scotland have made planning issues and development policies very prominent, and offer some varied examples of planning struggles and outcomes. These events relate to planning in several ways: the overall exploitation of offshore oil and gas is subject to planning attempts by central government; particular developments are 'planned' by their protagonists (oil companies and their agents); developments and development proposals connect with existing planning policies and environments in the areas they affect; and development proposals nearly all pass through a hierarchy of statutory planning agencies (local, regional, and sometimes national)[7]. Plans and proposals are themselves a focal point for struggles between individual and collective agents—local and central state and state fractions, local and nonlocal particular and collective capitals, classes and class fractions, and nonclass social groupings. The planning nexus is not, of course, neutral as between these agents, but serves to construct them in particular ways and to modify their powers and efficacy, enhancing some and diminishing others.

[7]Some statutory authorities are not required to obtain planning permission from local authorities, though they may be subject to planning inquiries.

It is not easy to separate out 'planning' as an object of study and to identify the points at which 'it' begins and ends. The very notion of a planned event is itself problematic. Policies and plans may be identified, and so may sets of events, however contentiously; but the relation between them is irretrievably messy. Events may occur—or equally fail to occur—in response to plans, despite plans, or quite independently. Neither the congruity of plans and events nor their temporal sequence can reliably fix this relation. Plans and events both exist in a complex environment of causal influences which may intersect with each other in such a way as to be mutually facilitating or mutually blocking. It follows that planning and development must be considered together, and, not surprisingly, theories of each are generally held in connected pairs— functionalist planning theories with functionalist theories of development, etc.

In this chapter, I attempt to consider this aspect of oil-related activity more systematically. I have been greatly aided in this by Cooke's (1983) recent work *Theories of Planning and Spatial Development*, partly because of its very comprehensive coverage, but more importantly because his approach to the topic meshes well with the work and interests of members of the Lancaster Regionalism Group[8]. Cooke argues for and adopts a realist epistemology and a neo-Gramscian theoretical position, emphasising struggles occurring in the spheres of civil society. The book falls into two parts, in the first of which Cooke reviews the deficiencies of atomistic planning theories, deriving from classical economics, and of functionalist unitary and consensual theories. He also reviews the existing critiques of planning theory and their posited alternatives, each of which is faulted in terms of one or more of the flaws of rationalism, essentialism, idealism, functionalism, abstractionism, and resultant chaotic conceptions.

In the second part of the book, Cooke builds up a more adequate planning theory by reviewing and seeking to integrate theories of development, theories of the central and local state, theories of labour-market differentiation including spatial differentiation, and the relation of these to local, regional, and central planning. On the way to this he continues to use the above list of cardinal sins, at times in rather an absolutist way as hatchets with which to excise whole realms of literature. Behind this, though, lies a more sympathetic treatment in which the advantages of theories are accreted as successive approximations to a satisfactory theory.

Cooke rejects all established theories of regional development—regional equilibrium, regional disequilibrium, and Keynesian models—primarily for their rationalism and abstractionism, and varieties of core–periphery theory are rejected for similar reasons. Turning to urban development theories, he dismisses Castells for his emphasis on the structural determination of the urban, with which his theory of change derived from

[8]Indeed, Cooke draws heavily on Urry's published work in developing his own position.

consumption movements sits uneasily in a manner similar to Althusser's difficulties in accommodating class struggle. The most valuable urban development theory is that of Scott (1980) for his emphasis on the role of the state in reproducing the basis for capitalist civil society by seeking to unscramble the knots arising from changes in the location of production and ensuing changes in the location of reproduction. Scott sees planning as bridging the interface between the public and the private, state and civil society. For Cooke, the deficiencies of this position lie in its state essentialism and its functionalism in deriving agencies and their actions— the state, planning, the family—from the needs of capital.

Another useful area of development theory identified by Cooke is Massey's treatment (1978a; 1981) in terms of successive rounds of accumulation, with firms relocating in whole or in part so as to seek out the best circumstances for continued accumulation. This produces the overlaying of historically specific spatial divisions of labour, sector by sector. The deficiences of this approach lie in the tendency to prioritise the logic of accumulation which appears to drag all else behind it.

Theorisation of the state is crucial if theories of development are to be connected to planning. In considering the central state Cooke rejects class theories, such as those of Miliband and Poulantzas, and crisis theories such as those of Habermas, Offe, and O'Connor, the latter for their idealist emphasis on normative legitimation and their concentration on distribution rather than on production relations. Reviewing the work of Jessop (1982), Urry (1981a), and others, Cooke proceeds to argue for the separation of state, civil society, and economy, with civil society standing between state and economy. The economy is divided between spheres of production and circulation, with the state barely able to enter the sphere of production relations. Civil society is the site of class struggles, reproduction struggles, and popular struggles; and an important consequence of these various separations is the ability to specify the distinctiveness of the local as opposed to the central state, and the possibility of contradictions between these levels. The individuated relationships which emerge from exchange relations in the sphere of circulation are fundamental constituents of civil society, and subjects may mobilise around a variety of collective interests besides class: gender, region, ethnicity, nationality, status, etc. The distribution of these overlapping dimensions in space will obviously not be even, hence the heterogeneity of local civil society, local labour markets, and local struggles, the nature of which differentiate and specify the local state.

Cooke derives planning itself as located in Gramsci's 'civilising process' of the state, the process whereby the state engages the societal chaos and anarchy which is itself the product of increasing rationality of capitalist production within the firm. The distinction between central and local planning can be mapped onto the three spheres of civil society in circulation, reproduction, and popular struggle. Within the sphere of circulation, central state planning involves general or selective regional assistance;

regional planning involves discretionary assistance through development agencies, etc; and local planning, operating through the medium of law rather than money, intervenes in circulation through zoning, compulsory purchase, redevelopment, etc, in ways which favour large capital at the expense of small. Within the sphere of reproduction, at a central level the relative success of labour in circulation struggles produces locational shifts in production, exposing previously industrialised regions and diverting their struggles towards reproduction issues directed at the state; and at the local level, local class and other relations affect the outcome of reproductive planning, as in the balance between public and private provision in housing, transport, employment, education, etc. And within the sphere of popular struggle, oppositions between the state and nonclass groupings often crystallise around planning issues (roads, amenities, etc).

A vital step is still missing, however, in connecting development, civil society, the state, and planning to processes of spatial relocation: namely to specify the nature of the accumulation advantages embodied in different spaces, which requires a consideration of labour-market differentiation. After reviewing the deficiencies of dual labour-market, internal labour-market, and segmented labour-market theories, Cooke goes on to employ Kreckel's (1980) discussion of five mechanisms of labour-market differentiation (demarcation, exclusion, solidarism, inclusion, and exposure), and to combine this with theories of spatially uneven development (Cooke, 1981, 1982; Massey, 1983; Urry, 1981b) which emphasise the permanent dynamic process of recomposition and reconstitution of classes and labour markets in the tension between accumulation and resistance. On this basis Cooke tentatively proposes a twelvefold classification of spatially discontinuous labour markets.

However, it would clearly be sinful (in Cooke's terms) to 'read off' class organisation and struggle from spatialised labour-market features, hence a further consideration of class theories is required. Cooke discusses theories of the economic and political determination of class, adopting Hall's (1977) solution of the absence of any necessary correspondence between them, and emphasising the spatial variance of classes and local class structures. In asking what mechanisms activate local classes to threaten the accumulation process, we turn again to the relation between places in production and production relations, and civil society, the realm in which individuals engage in struggle, hence recognise collective interests, hence become classes. Within the sphere of production, struggles may arise around the labour process, around mechanisation, and between craft and general unions. Within the sphere of circulation, conflicts may arise around fluctuations in real wages, intersectoral differentials, and primarily intrasectoral differentials. Within the sphere of reproduction, struggles concern the reproduction of capital, of capitalist social relations, and of labour power.

As the culmination of this scheme, Cooke seeks to connect the state's development planning to the sociospatial recomposition of classes in labour markets. The planning nexus is the location of the necessary meeting of land, labour, and capital. Cooke argues that it is labour's success in circulation and then reproduction that has *obliged* the state to assist capital accumulation through the planning system. The state is obliged to enable capital to take advantage of inherited patterns of uneven development, which it meets via five key strategies: concentration, decentralisation, containment, semiperipheralisation, and recycling (for example, inner-city redevelopment) (see pages 103–104 below).

Cooke's is, so far as I know, the only work which attempts to theorise planning so comprehensively and on such a 'congenial' theoretical basis, hence its importance. A detailed critique would be out of place, but in the remainder of this chapter, I attempt to identify what seem to me to be some difficulties in Cooke's analysis, and subsequently to consider some planning examples drawn from North Sea oil-related development.

One problem is a degree of uncertainty and inconsistency in Cooke's use of terms, particularly in the way he applies distinctions between the spheres of production, circulation, reproduction, and popular struggle. Occasionally this has significant consequences, as in his discussion of shifts in dominance between struggles in production, circulation, and reproduction. In places (for example, pages 179 and 239) he espouses a position, drawn from Blanke et al (1978) and discussed by Urry (1981a, page 111), in which the period of dominance of the sphere of circulation is accompanied by struggles to generalise legal rights in citizenship and representation such as to establish fully legal subjects with property rights in their own labour power. After the attainment of this, struggles over levels of wages, conditions, etc occur under the dominance of the sphere of reproduction. Yet in many other places Cooke refers to struggles over wages, conditions, etc as occurring under the sphere of circulation, and the renewed centrality of such struggles as signalling a return to dominance of the sphere of circulation.

Cooke then uses this to develop an argument in which continuing successes for labour in its struggles with capital in the spheres of production, circulation, and reproduction have produced a shift in the relations of power between labour and capital in favour of the former, and has also meant that labour has succeeded in capturing resources for reproduction via the state (pages 199–200, 220, 231, 236–237, and 274). This has engendered a crisis of accumulation for capital, producing a return to dominance of circulation struggles, and a shift in the primary concern of the state from the reproduction of labour to the reproduction of capital. This is uncomfortably close to a Thatcherite analysis of the UK condition, and is by no means the only possible account.

A second difficulty concerns the derivation of spatially discontinuous labour markets (pages 222–228), and within this the treatment of gender

in particular. For Cooke, "The division of labour is precisely the major
outcome of the asymmetrical relations between capital and labour, on the
one hand, and within labour, on the other" (page 214). Though this
formula certainly leaves a place for gender relations (and others, such as
race), it is a somewhat subordinate place, and Cooke's gender-related
categories are rather 'tacked-on' to a class-dominated model. This
produces a quite different result from, for example, Murgatroyd's
demonstration in this book (chapter 7) that positions in the division of
labour are not simply occupied by different categories of labour, but that
gender relations significantly structure the characteristics of the places.

Cooke is led from this into relatively weak accounts of gender relations
in the division of labour. For example, he cites (without criticism) Offe
and Hinrichs's (1977) account of 'unresistant' groups of workers (which
include women, especially wives) as being able to gain subsistence outside
the labour market, and as not conforming to the image of the normal
worker held by trade-union functionaries (pages 214–215). This is rather
different from emphasising the enforced dependence of married women
on husbands through the denial to them of categories of unemployment,
and the active organisation of male against female workers [see the
contributions by Walby to this book (chapters 8 and 9 below)].
Elsewhere, Cooke cites Friedman (1977a) (again without pertinent
criticism), who identifies 'peripheral' workers, including women and ethnic
minorities, as groups "demonstrating the lowest levels of solidarism"
(page 220). This locates disadvantage negatively, as a failure to demonstrate
solidarism, rather than positively, as the object of active organisation by
male workers.

A third problem concerns Cooke's analysis of the state. He is careful
to locate the state in the relation between capital and labour, but even so a
tension persists between explanations of state activity, and state expansion,
as a consequence of pressure from labour, and explanations in terms of
ensuring conditions for continued accumulation for capital. Thus Cooke
argues that "as struggles in the sphere of reproduction have been
progressively more successful, with the result that the scope of the state
has grown *vis-à-vis* the lives of its citizens, greater numbers of people of
all classes have a stake in retaining the services which the state provides"
(page 204); and that "[Gramsci] insisted that pressure could be, and as
we have seen, has frequently been put upon the state to bring about a
diminution of the power asymmetry between capital and labour. We have
argued that planning meausres are one expression of this pressure, so are
certain legal and welfare measures" (page 254). Yet Cooke also argues
that:

"what the state, through its planning system, is obliged to undertake
under the conditions of late capitalism is to enable capital to take
advantage of inherited patterns of uneven development. These patterns
themselves become deeply inscribed into the territorial settlement
pattern where labour successfully defends its reproduction space.

This process entails the planning system in laying the foundations for long-term, and occasionally rapid social and spatial recomposition, the reproduction of capitalist social relations, the restructuring of local labour markets, and the maintenance of capitalism as the dominant mode of production in the national territory" (page 240).

And again,

"The clearest tendency is for the state to be assisting capital, in whichever ways it can, to escape from the recent reduction in the power asymmetry between capital and labour" (page 274).

Elsewhere Cooke ascribes to state planning what appears to be an 'ideology-like' function:

"Hence, it is in mediating through the form of bourgeois law that the capitalist state (and planning system) supplies temporary solutions to conflicts emanating from the social relations of production" (page 263).

These are, of course, not straightforwardly incompatible, and such situations may indeed arise; it is rather that, to avoid a state essentialism, the conditions for this must be specified. Cooke, drawing on Urry, does discuss this issue of *transmutation*, the process whereby:

"changes produced by popular pressure are transmuted into something less acceptable to those popular forces. This has the following paradoxical consequence. Many of the changes produced in this manner within capitalist societies satisfy none of the major classes in such societies. The end result has been unintended by any major social element" (Urry, quoted in Cooke, 1983 pages 241 and 254).

There are, however, problems with this discussion. The most fundamental is that the conditions for what are really more transformations than transmutations of outcome are not specified; the *possibility* of such a process is not a sufficient account. The second is that Cooke confines his discussion of transmutation to *statism*, that is the oppressiveness of the *form* of state action, whereas the major matter to be explained is a *change* in state action. The third is that statism is considered in terms of an *appearance* of oppression, whereas the changes involved concern rather more than appearances (page 254).

Cooke is perfectly in command of these relationships at the level of theory. He says, for example, that:

"The implication here is not that the state or, more pertinently, the state planning apparatus is 'functional' for capital by 'guaranteeing' its property relations 'automatically', but that the planning system is itself fraught with the contradictory lines of force found in civil and political society. This means that planning does not simply serve capital, it helps to provide conditions for accumulation or valorization to continue. This is carried out in a context set by resistance to those activities from labour and a variety of ethnic, regional, local, gender, religious and other interest groups. The outcomes of this process are uncertain" (page 264).

The difficulty is rather that in his discussion of planning and location issues, he shows these as always resulting in outcomes favourable to continued accumulation and/or valorisation. For this always to emerge from a nominal condition of struggle is as essentialist as for it to emerge from a theory of state function.

The most important instance of this is Cooke's elaboration of:

"five 'strategies' by means of which development planning meets a fundamental obligation of the state *vis-à-vis* capital, which is to supply it with appropriately composed wage-labour under conditions in which it is not possible for this to occur automatically" (page 240).

"There are at least five distinct development 'strategies' available to the planning system, each of which combines the state's temporary responses to the conflicting pressures of capital and labour by bringing labour and land together in ways which assist capital accumulation" (page 273).

"Such a 'strategy'-complex involves the state, at various levels, providing conditions for profitable production by bringing together land, subsidies and labour" (page 274).

Cooke is careful, through the use of quotation marks and in a footnote (footnote 7, page 240), to distance himself from the intentionality implied in the term 'strategy'. Despite this, however, his account of these state actions shows a strong tendency towards a 'purposive' explanation in terms of continued accumulation and valorisation. Thus, for example:

"The [semi-peripheralisation] policy 'undercurrent' has clearly become a more blatant 'strategy' in that both the Industry Department and local states in relatively prosperous regions have, increasingly, responded to the demands of small to medium capitals for new locations" (page 246).

"As 'strategic' planning emphasis has slipped away from being dominated by the sphere of reproduction and back towards domination by struggle in the sphere of circulation, so the central state, in particular, has developed policies which are *aimed at recycling* the subemployed and underemployed *in ways which* assist the recapitalization of capitalism" (pages 247–248; my emphasis).

It is not that this is purely a theoretical problem. Rather the tendency (a) to emphasise purposiveness with respect to continued accumulation and valorisation, and (b) to emphasise wherever possible a spatial relocation logic to such purposes, produces an account of state action which I believe is often distracting. *Decentralisation*, through such measures as regional aid, clearly has a spatial relocation purpose; but it is hard to see its distinctive 'recomposition' aspects—the intrafirm decomposition of production taking advantage of unskilled and supposedly unorganised peripheral labour—as in any way anticipated or intended by the state. In relation to *containment*, through zoning measures etc, it seems far less relevant to consider this as an aspect of relocation policy (for example, pages 198–199) than as the outcome of (largely middle-) class and popular struggles to defend residential amenity. And it is doubtful whether permitting firms to relocate to the *semiperiphery* has either the intent or the result of providing compliant labour, since appropriate labour will often either move or travel (see Flowerdew and Salt, 1979, on the successive migration of firms and workers). Finally, although *recycling* is clearly purposive with respect to location and reproduction, to consider it as part of an elaborate strategy to resubordinate organised resistant urban labour—or to decontrol capital—is ultimately misleading.

A fourth area of difficulty concerns the definition of 'planning', its scope, and its extent. It will already be clear that 'planning' includes not only formal planning institutions, but also any aspect of the activities of the central, regional, or local state with development or location effects. We have already seen that this includes the provision of appropriate categories of labour, including, in general, the provision of individuated legally separate subject-bearers of labour power. This in itself implies the involvement of the coercive and repressive apparatuses of the state, a point Cooke explicitly acknowledges:

"if as seems possible from currently visible tendencies in the restructuring of production relations, labour power in advanced economies enters a prolonged period of over-supply, at least as far as larger internationally competitive capital is concerned, the implications for development planning cannot be clearly deduced, although some extension of the social control function may be implied" (pages 250–251).

Planning, then, appears to involve the whole of the state, and it is difficult to see how 'planning' and 'the state' are to be conceived as in any way distinct.

It does not stop here, however, since Cooke also includes inputs to development and location from outside the state. So, for example:

"we have argued that there is no space for state intervention directly in the sphere of production, hence there is no involvement of state planning in this sphere. However, this does not mean that there is no planning performed in production, the opposite is in fact the case except that the planning which is done, and which is highly rational, carefully controlled and monitored, is private. That is, it is conceived and executed by the representatives of the interests of capital largely against the interests of labour" (page 192).

The obverse of this also applies, namely the development by labour and popular classes of 'counterplanning' for socially useful production (discussed on pages 256–261). Ultimately, then, it is unclear whether 'planning' excludes any significant aspect of the social formation. Of course, I do not wish to advocate that real linkages be ignored simply for the sake of a more manageable object of study, but if 'planning' is to retain any specificity in relation to spatial development then I believe it should be more precisely focused. I offer some suggestions for this later.

A fifth area of difficulty concerns the overall form of Cooke's argument. He criticises the linearity of other recent planning theories:

"by focusing upon a fundamentally linear idea of capital accumulation to which the remainder of the complex determinations of capitalist society, state, classes, culture, ideology, are conceptually subordinated, a large slice of material reality which, for part of the time at least, exists in opposition to accumulation imperatives, and modifies their spatial manifestations, remains untheorized" (page 166).

Yet Cooke's own argument does tend—and I certainly do not wish to put it any higher than that—to resolve itself into a linearity of its own. This results from the very creative connection between the various arguments and areas of work which Cooke proposes, which takes something like the following form. 'Class' production relations (somewhat ritualistically commencing the sequence, since their effects are not really set out) produce both state reproductive activity and accumulation crises for capital, which produce capital spatial restructuring imperatives, producing state action to secure capital restructuring, producing planning strategies, producing a changing spatial division of labour. This is a most illuminating and suggestive model—though with some problems, as I have tried to indicate—provided sufficient scope is allowed for ambiguity and indeterminacy both in the derivation of the elements and in their effects. As before, appropriate theoretical caveats are entered [for example, "We would conclude, therefore, that it is of key importance that urban and regional development planning under capitalism is conceptualized as a somewhat limited and indeterminate part of an equally indeterminate framework of uneven social relations" (page 264)]. It is, rather, that the model does not fully express these caveats.

To return briefly to the issue of delineating a more specific location for planning, I would suggest, first, that planning should be conceived not as *any* nexus of forces with development or location effects, but specifically as those which are mediated by and pass through the state. The rational elaboration of aims and interests by different groups in the economy and in civil society is not 'planning', but a far more universal phenomenon, largely inseparable from practices within those spheres. The submission and negotiation of those through the state, with the distinctive possibilities for 'legitimate' coercion this entails, has its own specificity which inheres in the institutions. Hence where progressive professional planners turn their energies to assisting workers to develop socially useful methods of production, as Cooke advocates (page 260), they no longer do so from within the state.

Second, within the state, it would seem useful clearly to distinguish those measures which involve a spatial locational *logic*—such as regional aid or inner-city redevelopment—from those which have spatial *effects*. Within the latter one might distinguish between macrospatial effects—such as the concentration and rationalisation of nationalised industries or the

use by the military of peripheral areas (see Spaven, 1983); mesospatial
effects —such as the concentration of health service facilities into regional
centres or the development of semiperipheral industrial and residential
estates; and microspatial effects, such as zoning. Again, the purpose is
not to ignore links and causal relationships, but to allow these to be more
plausibly and variably derived, and to conceive planning relationships
more satisfactorily through distinguishing internal and external connections,
retaining the specificity of the state.

The purpose of this excursion into planning theory was to ground a
consideration of planning struggles from the North of Scotland. These
must appear rather small in scale in the wake of this general discussion,
but my aim has been to select three out of many possible instances to
illustrate the strength of, respectively, the local planning framework,
'popular' struggles in civil society, and the local state.

First, though, some peculiarities of the situation must be noted. The
major oil companies and the central state both shared a strong interest in
the rapid exploitation of North Sea oil and gas. This was not only to gain
exchequer revenue and balance of payments advantages, but because of
the insecurity of the whole financial basis of North Sea oil in the middle
and late 1970s. Throughout this period the escalating 'resource cost' of
North Sea oil extraction greatly exceeded that of the principal land-based
sites such as those in the Middle East. The vast expenditure was only
viable, therefore, given the continuing success of the OPEC cartel in
holding the market price well above these costs. Historically such cartels
have been fragile; hence the rationality of extracting and selling as much
as possible while these conditions obtained. It follows from this that
action by the central state in support of large-scale capital cannot be used
as evidence of any general relationship of this kind; but it also enhances
the significance of any local or popular forces capable of resisting or
modifying the actions of such a powerful combination.

A second peculiarity concerns the 'underdeveloped' character of the
North of Scotland. Without wishing to go into the underdevelopment –
dependency debate regarding the area (see Carter, 1974; Moore, 1980;
Shapiro, 1981), it remains the case that it was regarded by central and
local planners as 'backward' and in need of positive intervention to
prevent continued emigration, unemployment, and underemployment, and
economic contraction (see Carter, 1972). It was, therefore, a precursor of
the trend towards the discretionary direct-initiative forms of development
planning discussed above. This took shape most clearly in the establishment
of the Highlands and Islands Development Board (HIDB) in 1965, a body
with then unprecedentedly sweeping financial and legal development powers.

The first example, that of the Cromarty Firth (see figure 6.1), illustrates
this well. One of the first tasks of the HIDB, in conjunction with the local
authority, was to designate the whole Moray and Cromarty Firth area as
a centre for industrial growth and development. The physical basis of this

is the presence of reasonable infrastructural provision in the shape of railways, airport, and an existing small city (Inverness), and the identification of the Moray and Cromarty Firths as one of the best undeveloped deep-water harbour sites in Europe. It would be difficult to claim that the establishment of the HIDB was a result of local political

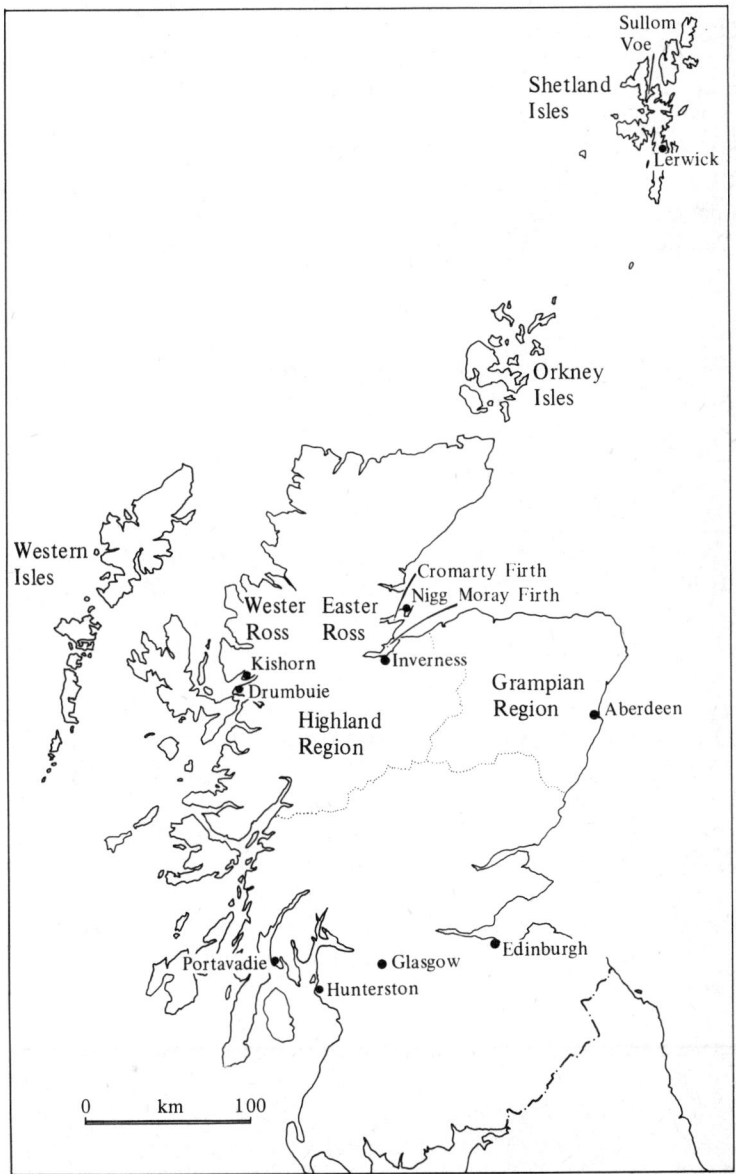

Figure 6.1. Scotland, showing selected oil-related sites.

mobilisation or effective labour demand for the state to underwrite
regional conditions of reproduction. The planning history of the 'Highland
problem' is itself a topic of some interest. The response to the ejection
of a redundant population after the collapse of the kelp industry and the
failure of potato crops, discussed in chapter 5 above, produced a response,
partly in terms of famine relief, but more concertedly for the provision of
assisted passages for emigration to the New World(s) (Hunter, 1976).
Later, in the 1880s, with effective political organisation around the
interests of the peasant crofting sector, the special protective legislation
embodied in the Crofters Acts of 1886 and subsequently were indeed
achieved through political mobilisation in conjunction with the very
particular circumstances of the Gladstone Government and its need to
secure a parliamentary majority for Irish legislation. Crofter activism was
pronounced until at least the interwar period, but there has been little
evidence of it since. One is tempted to identify the establishment of the
HIDB with the Wilsonian white-heat-of-technology trend to major planning
intervention in development, applied to the Highlands through a concern
to preserve a perceived cultural heritage and 'way of life'.

The promotion of the Moray Firth produced, after much fruitless
activity, a single success in the Alcan aluminium smelter established
at Invergordon in 1967. This highly capital-intensive venture, which
incidentally has recently been abandoned because of the prolonged decline
in the demand for aluminium, turns out largely to have been based on the
negotiation of extremely cheap electricity from the North of Scotland
Hydro Board, electricity being the major input to the smelting process.
This produced something of a scandal through the continuing multimillion-
pound losses of the Board in consequence under its contractual obligations.
In the euphoria produced by, at this stage, just the prospect of this
development, HIDB commissioned in 1967 a planning report on a plan for
growth for the Moray Firth, published in 1968 (JHPG, 1968). This is a
very good example of the kind of simple comprehensive unitary plan,
produced by a consultant team, castigated by Cooke (1983, page 38).
Starting from highly simplistic assumptions about impending industrial
development, it proceeds to elaborate in copious detail the best and most
'rational' plan for an expansion of the area's population to as many as
300,000 people. This involves multiple major housing developments,
radical infrastructural provision proposals, detailed studies of the most
favourable housing types, and the intricacies of their location and
interrelation in terms of water tables, ground frost patterns, pollution
smoke-plume footprints, average carriageway speeds, and an entire
technical utopian paraphernalia, all based on the speculative house of
cards of massive industrial development.

The advent of proposals from Highlands Fabricators in 1972 to
construct a steel-production-platform fabrication yard on the shores of the
Cromarty Firth at Nigg was received, therefore, with great relief as a

blessed saviour and as confirmation of at least a part of these grandiose development plans. The impetus from the beginning was to regard this as a spur to, and consistent with, permanent industrial development in the region; and the developers, taking their cue, emphasised the longevity, employment, and spin-off effects of their proposals. As it happens, the Nigg development has turned out to be one of the more lasting and successful of the oil-related projects, but in my view this was not at all predictable at the outset and, indeed, there was a period in the mid-1970s when the outlook for steel-platform fabrication seemed poor. It is entirely possible that the whole venture could have closed within three to four years. Lobbying on behalf of the development was only aimed at the very few people resident in the immediate vicinity of the site, who proved only too happy to accept the financial inducements offered by the developers.

As part of its planning application Highlands Fabricators gave strong undertakings to train and to employ local labour, and they honoured this obligation by setting up a training school and by giving welding and metalworking skills to locally recruited labour, which formed a substantial proportion of their total work force. This is in contrast with oil-related employers elsewhere who have been content to rely on immigrant skilled labour, usually temporarily accommodated in work camps. One may speculate as to whether this undertaking and its fulfilment resulted from local pressure to provide employment opportunities, or as a dispersal strategy on the part of the Company to take the opportunity to use 'green' labour and to avoid highly organised craft labour in metalworking trades. Another aspect of interest concerns reproduction, and specifically the provision of housing by the local state as a consequence of its perception of these activities as part of a process of permanent development. The local authority was quick to provide 'family' accommodation for migrant labour working in oil-related activities. Indeed, as part of this it held out against the Company providing a work camp for temporary migrant labour and delayed the granting of planning permission for this for two years. Family accommodation has been taken up by many whose 'home' on some longer view is elsewhere in Scotland or the United Kingdom, and this implies a change in the gender and domestic relations that have previously applied to many construction engineering workers. Whether this is a permanent change is doubtful (see the treatment of housing in East Ross by Grigor, 1980). It may also have meant a move out of paid employment for wives of male oil workers through their moving their household to an area with very limited paid-employment opportunities for women. This may be made as part of a more general point that large-scale employment developments in peripheral locations will increase the dependency of labour's conditions of reproduction. This may mean either increased dependency on the state for the total provision of housing and facilities for subsistence, or on the employer through the provision of work camps and company housing (Shapiro, 1981).

Part of the interpretation of these developments is best postponed for a comparative treatment with the next example, that of platform fabrication in Wester Ross. We may note, however, the confluence of two forces in moulding the form of development. The actions of the 'regional' state, HIDB (acting rather as a delegated regional arm of the central state than as a 'local' state), helped to establish a planning environment strongly conducive to development. Although the Board certainly consulted widely and was subject to varieties of local pressure, this arose primarily through the combination of central state policy and the relatively autonomous perceptions and prescriptions of professional planners.

From a different social source, the properly local state was generating similar possibilities and imperatives. Grigor (1980) documents the manner in which the Ross and Cromarty County Council also evolved plans for major industrial development in this area, and of its experimentation with discretionary nonpublic modes of inducing development activity. Ultimately, the local state has no power to compel industry to locate within it; but it does have power over its own activities, such as infrastructural and housing provision, and it is perhaps not surprising that the Council appended to its theory of the developmental potential of the Moray–Cromarty area the theory that the provision of such infrastructure would generate the development. "Put crudely, one could say that for Ross and Cromarty County Council, houses means jobs" (Grigor, 1980, page 72)—not, of course, that this kind of reaction was unique to this area.

An immediate effect of this was estimates of additional housing need, including oil-related requirements, of up to 8600 houses, a massive increase in the area's housing stock. Though nothing like this number was ever built, the result was nonetheless a substantial excess of provision. Oil-related activities were also affected by these policies, however. It was necessary for them to comply as far as possible with the 'permanent development' model, claiming, preposterously, that work would be provided for forty or fifty years, and complying with the County's (equally absurd and arbitrary) definition of all married employees as permanent residents requiring family accommodation. The substantial effort put into the training of local people for 'skilled' craft jobs is a further aspect of this requirement.

This issue relates to another local nexus of competing interests, between organised craft labour and 'local' (in practice almost Highland-wide) popular desires for good jobs. Construction of steel production platforms involves a high proportion of craft-apprenticed labour in welding, plating, and construction engineering skills. The unions concerned acquiesced quite readily to the training of locals for these jobs in a manner virtually unprecedented in peacetime, though considerable resentment and disapproval of the 'six-week wonders' was to surface later.

The value of turning attention next to platform-fabrication developments in Wester Ross is precisely the contrast that they offer to materially similar production activities in Cromarty. In 1973 the combine of Mowlem–Taylor–Woodrow applied for planning permission to construct a concrete-production-platform fabrication yard at Drumbuie on the south shore of Loch Carron. This site offered flat coastal land with immediate access to deep water, and also a rail supply line. It was claimed at the time that this site was unique, though this has frequently been disputed. The preference of companies for northwestern locations in preference to ones in striking distance of the Clyde is generally attributed to their desire to avoid organised Glasgow labour. The proposal immediately sparked off organised local opposition on the grounds, first of the unique cultural character of the Drumbuie community, and second, of the beauty of the area. It would make sense to identify this opposition with the vocal, often professional, holiday-home and retirement-home group in the area— known locally as 'white settlers'—though in fact evidence for this is mixed. The point, however, is that this local opposition group succeeded in making the Drumbuie development into a national conservation-versus-development issue, at roughly the height of popular interest in ecological and environmental concerns. The Drumbuie public inquiry was major national daily newspaper and television news, and the outcome was a clear rejection of the proposal by the public inquiry Recorder.

Immediately in the wake of the Drumbuie rejection, the Howard–Doris combine lodged an application for planning permission for a similar concrete-production-platform fabrication yard across the bay of Loch Carron in Loch Kishorn. Despite the public inquiry Recorder's view that a development at Kishorn would also be undesirable, the opposition to Drumbuie totally failed to materialise against the Kishorn proposal. Despite this the developer was careful to frame the proposal in terms of minimising impact: there would be a limit of 400 site-workers, a work camp and all facilities for migrant workers would be contained within the site, there would be no Sunday working, and all materials for the site would be transported by sea or by rail and ferry, not by road. A remarkable aspect of this from the planning perspective is the way in which fundamentally similar developments—steel- and concrete-production-platform fabrication—were given diametrically opposing interpretations by one and the same planning authority: Ross and Cromarty County Council, subsequently the Highland Region. The Nigg development, as we have seen, was interpreted as an integral part of permanent industrial development in the subregion, whereas the Kishorn development was interpreted as an essentially temporary activity to be contained and its impact limited. The point is that this was not done as the result of a decision based on cultural or aesthetic criteria—which would in any case be difficult to justify—to *render* one development temporary while encouraging the other, but rather that a schizophrenic evaluation of the activity was presented as a rational basis for the differing plans. This clearly rationalises in technical terms a differing political reality; to what extent this was consciously the case is difficult to determine.

At Kishorn as at Nigg, then, accommodation to local state and popular pressure modified the form the development would take and imposed various constraints on its operation. Once established, however, the Company was able to set about systematically stretching and diluting the planning conditions and undertakings. The work force steadily increased from the permitted 400 to over 2000; Sunday working commenced on the site; the undertaking to supply it solely as an island site was ignored, resulting in much damage and obstruction to the local single-track roads; further applications were lodged to enlarge the work camp substantially. The local authority appointed a planning enforcement officer to operate full-time on the site; he resigned after it became apparent that his work was completely ineffectual.

The imposition of a 'constrained' employment regime as a planning condition made it necessary for the Company to use a limited work force intensively—though this may well have been their preference in any case. Once some of the contradictions around this had been resolved, at local expense, the way was open to further work-intensification. A twelve-hour working shift became a thirteen- to fourteen-hour working shift (including time spent travelling by boat) once the production platform moved out to its floating 'wet site'. The effects of this on all sections of the work force were extreme (though it was the regime preferred by the migrant labour housed in the work camp), but particularly so for the local and semilocal components whose private and household relations were distorted to a degree that most of them soon found intolerable (these and other aspects of the 'industrial relations' situation at Kishorn are explored in more detail elsewhere—see Shapiro, 1981). This, together with an attempt by the Company to cut labour costs through cutting the bonus, resulted in a short but bitter strike in which the work force was completely defeated. A consequence of this was a substantial 'remanning' of the project, based largely on recruitment from the Isle of Skye. Two aspects of this may be particularly noted. One is the contribution of the 'regional' state, in the shape of the Manpower Services Commission, to whom recruitment had been delegated, to defeating labour through supplying a replacement work force. The second is that, though opportunities for Skye labour were obviously enhanced, this labour market was much too small to supply the Company's needs. The consequence, predictably, was that many unemployed construction workers got themselves to Skye and applied for work as locals. The result was, first, a breach of undertakings for facilities for the work force to be self-contained on site; and second, an off-loading of much of the burden of immediate reproduction from the Company back onto labour.

We may attempt to draw conclusions from these sets of events about the initial and subsequent efficacy of struggles around planning in determining outcomes. It has often been noted (for example, in Rodger, 1980) that there is a disjunction between the real operation of planning procedures and inquiries and the way these are imagined to operate by objectors. Although objectors expect to be able to debate the general necessity or desirability of projects, and preferable alternatives in a national or even global context, the procedures themselves tend to be confined to examining minute technicalities concerning siting, operational procedures, safety, mitigation of nuisance, etc. Objectors find this intensely frustrating and come to regard the procedures as loaded against them—which is generally true, though as a result of the structure of the planning procedures rather than of 'bias' in their conduct. The Drumbuie planning inquiry was a striking exception to this. In introducing his summary, the Recorder wrote:

"Unfortunately a development of this magnitude in a rural area whose landscape is of great scenic beauty will have profound effects on amenity and on the social, cultural and economic life of the community. It is therefore necessary to look closely to see if there are (a) compelling reasons in the national interest why the applications should be granted, and (b) compelling reasons in the national and local interest why they should not. The one side must then be balanced against the other" (RE, 1974, page 172).

Though possibly relevant considerations for a planning inquiry commission, these are most unusual elements of a planning inquiry. Here, the intensity of the popular struggle was such that it actually succeeded in 'capturing' the planning inquiry for the 'popular' definition of its role and purpose.

This leads directly into the second area of conclusions, namely that a particular planning outcome is rarely the end of the issue, and its prescriptions may bear little relation to eventual outcomes. The planning 'moment'—through constituting certain legal relations between groups and interests in struggle—can modify significantly the causal powers of such groups and interests. But when the planning moment has passed, a reversion to unmodified relations of power is likely to ensue. This can be seen both on a general and on a local scale. Generally, if the issue is important enough there may even be a change in the planning framework itself; the initiation of the planning inquiry commission is a 'liberal' example. In the Drumbuie case, the central state was seriously alarmed at the outcome and at its implications both for the speed of North Sea oil extraction and for UK participation. It therefore commissioned a coastal survey of Scottish waters to identify the most suitable sites, and took steps to remove platform fabrication from the normal planning framework by directly acquiring two sites—Hunterston and Portavadie—and by constructing the fabrication docks and facilities itself; despite advice that there might be no demand for them. In the event this advice proved correct, and these 'white-elephant' yards were never used. An example from Shetland will be introduced below.

On the local scale, we can see that in the Drumbuie case the rejection resulted simply in a new proposal which, though modified and though coming from a different consortium, was broadly equivalent. The opposition was exhausted (and more counterforces mobilised) and this one got through. At the level of detail we can see that virtually every one of the conditions and undertakings attached to the consent was breached, and both the local state and local popular forces were quite powerless to prevent this. The 'planned' settlement between these parties was retroactively dismantled.

Also at Nigg, in East Ross, Highlands Fabricators was able to recoup ground. The training school, so central to local employment opportunities, was quite soon shut down on the grounds that its job was done. The Company's response to refusal of permission for a work camp was to bring in two moored Greek cruise-liners as temporary accommodation for migrant labour. Although at one level simply a 'logical' response to a problem, the notoriety and scandal that quickly grew up around the 'Highland Star' and 'Highland Queen' rubbed the Council's nose in the contradictions of its policies and helped to force a change. And when faced with industrial conflict the Company was not slow to threaten to close the yard down, assurances of permanent development notwithstanding. It is not only that, once in place, developers can cynically employ 'wedge tactics' to improve their position; it is also that circumstances change, forcing interests to engage in further struggles. Both at Kishorn and at Nigg, management engaged their work forces in conflicts aimed at worsening the terms for labour, presumably in response to the escalation of labour costs beyond estimates or the intensification of competition. These struggles, apart from their consequences for labour, had profound 'planning' consequences too. A schematic summary of events and relations at Drumbuie and Kishorn is attempted in figure 6.2.

In Shetland we find the most celebrated instance of local resistance and autonomy in the planned control of North Sea oil developments. The main features of the Shetland achievement are:
(1) an early determination to seize initiative and control when it became clear that Shetland would be the site of major oil-pipeline landfalls and transshipment facilities;
(2) the successful promotion of special legislation (Zetland County Council Act, 1974) to enable this to be done;
(3) the use of this legislation to act as a commercial profit taking partner in various aspects of the developments, and in effect, to extract a Shetland 'barrelage tax' on all oil passing through.
The principal questions that arise in relation to these achievements are: what aspects of Shetland social organisation enabled so uniquely 'competent' a set of objectives to be formulated; how was the passage of

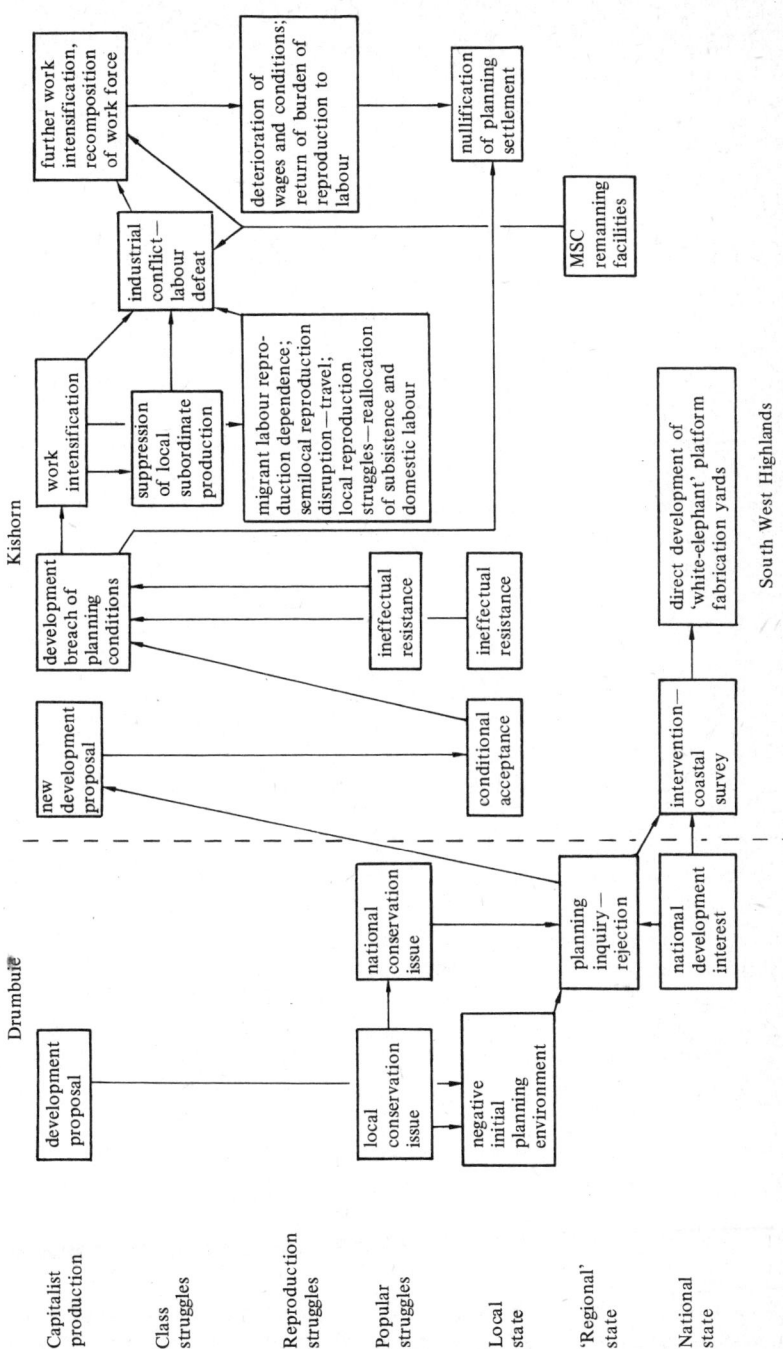

Figure 6.2. A schematic summary of events and relations at Drumbuie and Kishorn (MSC stands for Manpower Services Comission).

legislation achieved; and why was the Shetland Islands Council allowed to persist in its 'aggressive' use of this legislation in the face of the interests of oil companies and central state?

Two main popular accounts of the first of these questions prevail. On the one hand, it is asserted that the history of Shetland is a history of the guile, wit, and energy of its inhabitants pitted against a constant procession of privations, vicissitudes, and attempts at external exploitation. Oil is merely the latest of these, and, once again, Shetlanders have proved equal to the task. In explaining this 'difference', reference is often made to the distinctive Norse origins and qualities of the Shetland people.

On the other hand, credit for its achievement is often accorded to the professionalism and ingenuity of the Council's management team, and particularly of its Chief Executive, Ian Clark, in a 'David and Goliath' confrontation. Oil companies dutifully upheld this image, with one representative claiming that only Colonel Gadafy has been as awkward to deal with (Davies, 1978, page 44). These accounts can be seen as alternatives; as complementary; and also as antagonistic, through-connecting to lines of division within Shetland. Thus there is a partial coincidence of class divisions (Lerwick bourgeoisie versus the rest), 'centre-periphery' divisions (Lerwick and county), and native-outsider divisions (incomer local government professionals). In these terms, the Shetland Bill could be interpreted as an imposition by outside interests and outside consultants against the interests of many Shetlanders, and was opposed as such by a 'Shetland Democratic Group'.

Even a cursory review of the economic history of Shetland reveals its close integration with the Scottish, English, and European economy since at least the seventeenth century. It also reveals that the Norse 'myth of origins' is much exaggerated, the Shetland dialect being far closer to that of Lowland Scots in derivation, and several of the most famed Norse ceremonies being Victorian revivals (Smith, 1977). It would be very difficult to sustain a view of Shetland economic history as distinctively harsh or the response to it as especially resourceful. The point, however, is that such representations may be much more easily sustained in a locality with such clear boundaries. It may be more pertinent to emphasise the continuous recent experiences of groups in Shetland of negotiating finance from the state through the White Fish Authority, the Ministry of Agriculture, and the Crofters Commission since the 1950s, and the Highlands and Islands Development Board since 1965. A rehearsal for legislation existed in the successful lobbying in the early 1970s for Shetland to have its own all-purpose authority rather than being subsumed under the Highland Region.

Regarding the attainment of legislation and its use, it is generally acknowledged that there were always limits to the extent to which the Council could attempt to constrain development without provoking central government resistance. Extracting maximum concessions was thus a matter of finely judging these limits. Peculiarities of Shetland's geographical location and legal jurisdiction are also highly significant. For oil developers to avoid a Shetland pipeline landfall would have been impossibly expensive, and so too would delays in granting planning permission (see Grieco, 1980). At the same time, the rise of the Scottish Nationalist Party and its claim to 'Scottish oil' was a significant potential threat to the UK treasury—but Shetland was *opposed* to separation from the United Kingdom and more inclined to separation from Scotland. In the event of any such separations occurring, many 'Scottish' oilfields would 'belong' to Shetland, hence the political desirability of humouring Shetland political demands. Shetland's autonomy, then, may have emerged in the space opened by a contest between the national state and regional popular struggles in Scotland. This shows interesting parallels with the political contingencies that resulted in the Crofters Acts under Gladstone, discussed in chapter 5 above, with major local effects.

For this to have been successfully pursued required clarity of purpose and the determination to act swiftly to avoid the *faits accomplis* experienced in other areas. Underlying this is a local willingness to regard the impending developments as clearly negative and hence to be resisted, or at least contained and manipulated to maximum advantage. It is possible to make out a general case for this on the basis of the strength of the Shetland economy in the early and mid-1970s. The principal Shetland economic activities of agriculture, fishing, fish processing, and wool textiles were all in a phase of prosperity and expansion at this period. This is summed up in the popular contemporary saw that 'oil needs Shetland more than Shetland needs oil'. This situation was to be short-lived; but the health of these activities was in any case dependent on very low rates of pay and it is obviously superficial to represent the persistence of these conditions as to the advantage of all Shetlanders.

There was in fact a clear conflict of interest between Shetland labour, for whom oil-related activities brought the prospect of more work and much higher pay, and Shetland employers who stood to lose labour and to be forced to compete with oil wages. Hence the domination of the Shetland Islands Council by local small and medium capital—who had for years succeeded in blocking planning applications for Shetland branches of national retail chains—goes far in explaining the decisiveness of the Council's response. There was a determined attempt by the Council, in the name of the long-term interest of the Islands' economy, to insulate oil activities and to impede the employment of Shetlanders in them. This was partially overturned by united action by Shetland and migrant labour (see Shapiro, 1980). A schematic summary of these relations is attempted in figure 6.3.

In general terms, then, 'planning' is grounded in relations of struggle—which include, but are not restricted to, the capital relation—over spatial development. It is the formal 'space' constituted by and in the state

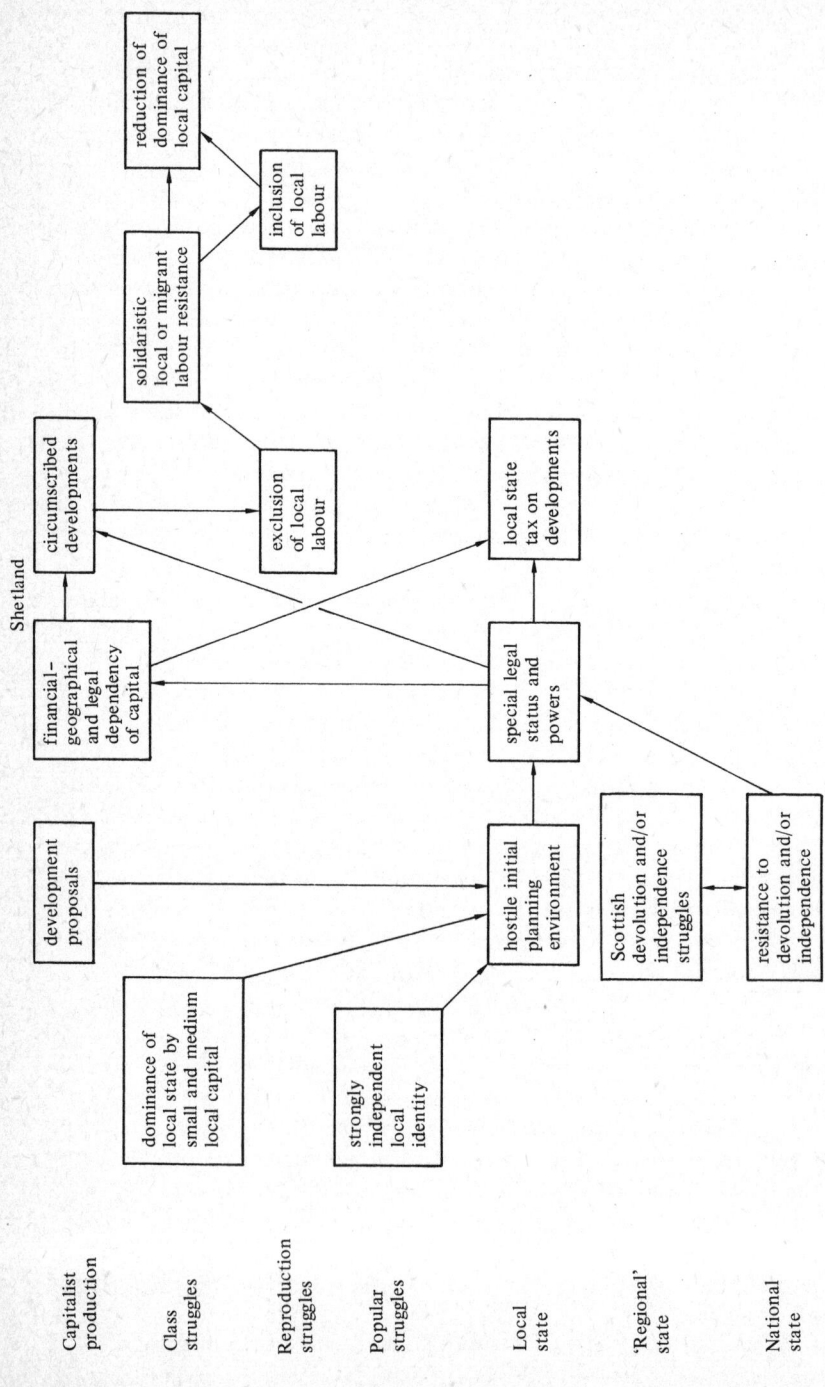

Figure 6.3. A schematic summary of events and relation in Shetland.

where such struggles occur. Various contradictions are embodied here.
Formally, such struggles occur independently of particular events or
proposals and are abstractly contained in general planning settlements (for
example, structure plans, development area statuses, new towns, protected
areas, enterprise zones, etc) against which particular proposals are
measured.

In practice, particular events or proposals may engage or mobilise forces
exceeding those engaged in the abstract planning struggles. Some parties
are necessarily engaged: the proponents of physical developments (in this
case large-scale capitals), the local state, the regional state, and (always in
reserve) the national state. Others, such as organised labour or rival
capitals, are contingently engaged, but institutionally grounded. Others,
such as various alliances of popular forces, are contingently engaged and
normally without institutional grounding—popular struggles are necessary
for these even to achieve a state of organisation, although, once organised,
they are recognised within the formal procedures.

The relative powers of these parties are not pregiven and 'directly'
engaged, but are modified by the 'terms of engagement' embodied in the
planning framework of the state—the formal space, which, as theorised
above, is itself the outcome of relations of struggle. The engagement of
these forces in this context is the 'planning nexus', and its outcome is the
'planned settlement' for a particular set of developments. This, however,
is not coterminous with the developmental outcomes; these are the results
of struggles which continue after the planning 'moment', which occur (in
varying degrees) outside the planning nexus, and in which the forces
engaged may be much less subject to the modifications of the planning
framework. The struggles at all of these levels may ultimately produce
changes in the planning framework itself, thus altering the context for
future struggles.

Turning to the cases I have briefly described, various examples of this
process can be identified. The different treatment of production-platform
fabrication in Easter and Wester Ross can be attributed to the strength of
the planning framework applied in those areas. This appears as the strength
of the local state, but is better conceived as the strength of local forces
whose struggles produced these planning environments. This had substantial
effects in the planning nexus on the form of development proposals and
on the conditions under which capital and labour were constrained. But
we can also see that in both areas the developmental outcomes diverged
from the planned settlement as the result of continuing 'postplanning'
struggles. In the case of the Drumbuie inquiry, we can see that the
strength of local and national popular forces in the planning nexus
actually succeeded in modifying the operation of the planning framework—
but that the institutional fragility of such forces made them incapable of
sustaining a block on development.

In the case of Shetland, local struggles were engaged directly against the planning framework, first in establishing the Shetland Isles as an all-purpose local authority, and subsequently in attaining special planning and development powers for that authority, with major effects on the planned settlement. However, here again continuing struggles modified the developmental outcome and altered the relative strength of class forces in Shetland. Finally, we can see that, after the Drumbuie inquiry, the planned settlement itself engendered changes in the planning framework, through the action of the national state in bypassing planning controls to develop directly the 'white elephant' yards in southwest Scotland.

The planning process in relation to physical developments in space, then, can be conceived as a cycle of struggles in a continuing state of flux. This is schematised in figure 6.4.

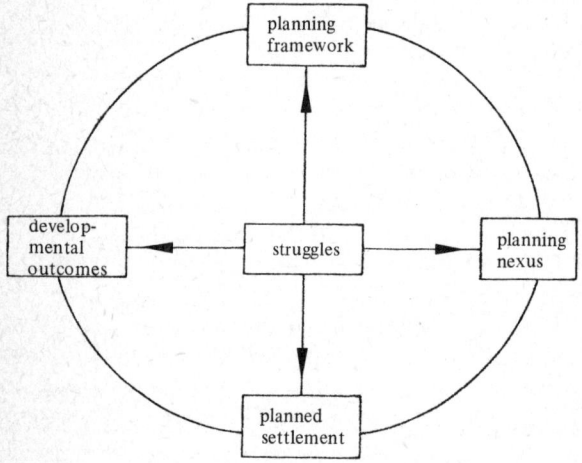

Figure 6.4. The planning process.

Occupational stratification and gender[†]

Linda Murgatroyd

7.1 Introduction

In a modern United Kingdom, as in most known societies, gender is a
central feature of the social division of labour—some tasks are socially
defined as 'men's work' and others are considered to be 'women's work'.
Although the sex-typing of tasks is less rigid in advanced capitalist
societies than in some others (some men do 'feminine' jobs and a few
women do 'masculine' work), and despite the fast-changing labour process
and occupational structure, sexual divisions remain a central feature of the
social division of labour.

In this chapter, I contend that gender is of crucial importance, not only
in assigning people to 'places' in the division of labour, but also in the
very definition of occupations, and thereby in shaping the division of
labour as a whole. The social relations of gender are central to the labour
process. As such, gender must be included as a central feature of any
analysis of social stratification, whether it is concerned with the social
characteristics of people in particular occupations or whether it seeks to
analyse the social relations in which they engage. The present discussion
will be confined to the realm of paid work, although, as I have argued
elsewhere (see Murgatroyd, 1979; 1982a; 1983), the scope of studies on
the organisation of work and on the labour process must eventually be
broadened to include unpaid work also, before the sexual division of
labour and the social relations of gender can be given due importance.

Within the sphere of formal paid employment, there remains a high
degree of segregation by sex, and most jobs are considered to be better
suited to one or other sex. These 'men's jobs' and 'women's jobs' have
become so defined through a variety of specific historical processes. The
sexual division of labour has altered, along with the social division of
labour as a whole; similarly, social definitions as to the suitability of men
or women for performing different tasks have changed, and more general
cultural conceptions of masculinity and femininity have been modified.
Although the degree to which different occupations are associated with
one or other gender varies, most 'places' in the occupational structure
carry such an association to some degree.

[†]This is a substantially revised version of an article which was first published in the
Sociological Review, in November 1982 (Murgatroyd, 1982b). Early drafts of this
paper were presented to the Oxford University Seminar on Women in the Labour
Market (March 1981) and to the British Sociological Association Sexual Divisions
Study Group (May 1981).

Most UK stratification studies, even in recent years, have concentrated exclusively upon stratification among men. Though these are useful and valid sociological enquiries, they should not be mistaken as being studies of stratification in the society as a whole. Yet this elision has often been made, and this has resulted in several inconsistencies and inadequacies regarding the treatment of women (for example, see Acker, 1973; Delphy, 1981; Garnsey, 1978). Furthermore, analyses of stratification and social mobility which exclude women are not even able fully to explain mobility patterns and changing occupational distributions among men, since the changing pattern of women's employment affects these at the same time (see Goldthorpe and Llewellyn, 1980).

The relationships between different occupational classes and the changes of personal mobility between them are profoundly affected by the sexual composition of occupational groups as well as by the gender of the individuals considered (see Heath, 1981a, chapter 4). The sex of different groups of workers has a major impact on workplace conflicts and on negotiations over the definition of jobs, the assignation of skill labels, and pay levels (see Hartmann, 1979b; Phillips and Taylor, 1980). Indeed, struggles centred around the sexual division of labour have been crucially important in determining *which jobs* are created, and what skill level, status, and pay are allocated to them. As a result, they also shape the social relations between capital and labour more generally. If women are omitted from studies of the labour force, not only is one-third of the employed population ignored, but due consideration cannot be given to the question as to why the particular occupations in the two remaining thirds are male, and how the existence of women in the labour force, or as a reserve labour force, affects the position and action of these males. Despite all this, attempts continue to be made to explain male mobility patterns, even in highly feminised occupations, without reference to women and the changing sexual division of labour. For example, Stewart et al (1980) make a number of conclusions about the stratification position of clerical workers in general, from their study of the careers of male clerical workers. The latter are a minority of the clerical work force, and the authors nowhere argue that they are representative of the whole group of clerks—evidence suggests the contrary.

These result in conclusions which may be highly misleading, and much of the discussion in this chapter is aimed at producing a clearer understanding of the processes which produce particular occupational structures and divisions of labour by sex. In particular, I am concerned that, given the limited information which is generally available to planners in such fields as employment, this information should not in future omit the crucially important dimension of gender, as it so often has in the past. The incorporation of gender along these lines has far-reaching implications for social stratification theories, which cannot be fully investigated here, but which have importance in a number of policy and planning fields.

Most obviously, they have implications for policies relating to employment and training policies, to sex equality policies, and to policy areas (such as transport, taxation, social security) which impinge directly on these. But, in addition, the gendered nature of paid employment has a wider impact on income distribution (between households, cohorts, etc) and also on the nature, amount, and distribution of labour within households and on the wider informal economy, whose importance is expected to increase in the near future (for example, see Gershuny, 1978; Gershuny and Miles, 1983; chapter 2 above).

In the next section, I discuss the high degree of sex-segregation in the labour force. Then I turn to the labour market and labour process for an explanation of how such segregation has been produced and maintained. Some of the jobs done principally by women are then discussed in a little more detail, as is the centrality of gender relations to the labour process in many of these jobs. I then further pursue two sets of implications which are of central importance in understanding, first the evolution of the structure of the labour force, and second how this may be appropriately documented.

The argument presented here calls into question the simple distinction between fixed places in an occupational structure and the persons who fill them. Though at any given particular time, there exists de facto a given set of jobs, the occupational structure is in a constant state of change, and, although some 'places' disappear, others are created. These occupations take on some of the characteristics of their incumbents, and indeed are partially shaped by the characteristics of recruits. One aspect of this is that they become defined as 'masculine' or 'feminine'; they are not 'empty places', independent of the people who fill them. This calls for the development of more dynamic stratification theories, investigating the historical development of occupational structures in the context of contemporary social changes and struggles, including the social relations of gender.

Further, the discussion of gender relations and of the nature of many 'feminine' jobs has implications for the classification of occupations. If the gender of the incumbents is an important characteristic of an occupation, then this must be considered in drawing up occupational classifications. Some suggestions are made as to how these might be modified in order more explicitly to account for gender, and better to distinguish among the occupations into which women are concentrated, in particular, service sector occupations. These modifications are of particular interest in the light of the current economic restructuring, and the debates about the shape of 'postindustrial' societies, and their occupational structures, with the associated growth of feminised service occupations (for example, see Bell, 1974; Bruegel, 1979; Gershuny, 1978; Gershuny and Miles, 1983; OPCS, 1980; Thevenot, 1977; Touraine, 1974).

7.2 Gender and the occupational structure

Women now make up around 40% of the employed labour force, a proportion that has risen since World War 2. Until then it had remained at about 30% for some decades. Within the labour force, women have been concentrated into a small number of occupational groups. The high degree of sexual segregation within the labour force, whether divided by occupation or industry, has been demonstrated by a number of studies (Chiplin and Sloane, 1976; Hakim, 1979; 1981; Milkman, 1976).

Hakim (1979) has discussed a number of measures of occupational segregation, distinguishing between horizontal and vertical segregation, which she defines thus:

> "*Horizontal* occupational segregation exists when men and women are most commonly working in different *types* of occupation. *Vertical* occupational segregation exists when men are most commonly working in *higher grade* occupations and women are most commonly working in lower grade occupations, or vice versa. The two are logically separate" (page 19).

Her analysis is based on Census data, and the occupational classifications she uses are those of the Registrar General, used in the Census (see OPCS, 1971a). Her distinction between horizontal and vertical segregation is implicit in the ways in which this occupational classification has been made. These indications of segregation have a number of limitations. Hakim argues that these types of occupational segregation are logically separate, but in practice they are inextricably combined, since the classification of occupations on which they are based is itself differentiated both in horizontal and in vertical senses. The Office of the Registrar General has provided a vertical grouping of occupations into five or six ranked social classes. This intuitive scale groups together occupations whose incumbents are thought to have 'broadly similar standing'. Whether this is a ranking of life-styles (or possibly, of prestige), as opposed to one of economic class positions (as associated with market capacities) to which Hakim's 'vertical' dimension is more closely related, women rank low both in social class and in occupational hierarchies. The interpretation of these hierarchies, however, presents some thorny problems. Gender is not mentioned in the Registrar General's discussion of the construction of occupational or social class categories, so we must assume either that the classification was of 'places', and the gender of their incumbents was deemed irrelevant, or that it was assumed that incumbents were male[9].

Occupational scales have been constructed on both bases. For example, the first course is that taken by Duncan (1961), whereas Hope and Goldthorpe (1974) constructed their scale on the basis that male incumbents of each occupation were compared.

---

[9] Oakley (1972) discusses the distinction between 'sex', a natural attribute, and 'gender', which is a cultural product that, though based on sex, may take different historical forms. As such it is the product of social relations (see Rubin, 1975).

The importance of specifying gender in such exercises has been clearly demonstrated by Haavio-Manilla (1969). Table 7.1 shows the results when she asked respondents to assign scores to men, women, and the nonworking wives of men in different occupations. In any single occupation, males are ranked more highly than females (who are ranked above the wives of men). But the ranking of occupations is not consistent across different sex-groups. These findings raise further questions for the interpretation of occupational scales; the inclusion of personal characteristics implies that it is no longer occupations as 'empty places' that are being ranked. If the rankings measure an ordering of positions in the labour market, or workplace hierarchy, then the lower grading of females is consistent with the concentration of women into lower reaches of occupational hierarchies. However, if life-style is being measured, one might expect the opposite effect, given that most working women who are married have husbands in higher status and higher paying occupations than themselves, and are therefore likely to have higher status life-styles and to be better off than their male colleagues of equal rank. Whether occupied women are excluded in the intuitive construction of the social class scale, or whether gender is deemed irrelevant, then social class is a poor indicator of women's position in the occupational hierarchy, and a discussion of whether it measures their 'prestige' or their 'life-styles' seems irrelevant in the face of other questions of the relation between women's occupations and their social position in general. Nonetheless, social class is the only basis on which occupied men and women have been grouped into a vertically ranked ordering. Table 7.2 shows that, in 1971, 65% of males and 44% of females were in manual jobs. Whereas the manual–nonmanual distinction has been a simple and meaningful way to make a

Table 7.1. Mean ranks of male and female representatives of occupational groups, and of nonworking wives of men in these groups (source: Haavio-Manilla, 1969, page 130, table 6).

Occupation	Male	Female	Wife
Physician	1.6	2.5	9.1
Architect	2.4	3.7	8.9
Psychologist	2.8	4.2	9.3
Bank director	3.4	4.7	10.1
Foreman	6.3	7.8	13.1
Advertisement agency secretary	6.6	7.2	12.8
Head porter	7.8	9.4	13.2
Student	8.9	9.4	13.5
Chimney sweep	10.4	12.2	15.5
Furniture salesperson	10.6	11.6	15.1
Milkwagon driver	12.1	13.5	16.5
Office messenger	13.1	13.9	16.3

broad vertical differentiation among males, it poses a number of problems when applied to the labour force as a whole, or when used to distinguish among women workers.

First, within each of the 'manual' and 'nonmanual' categories, it is clear that women are concentrated at the lower end of the hierarchy within each group. Whereas 56.5% of women were in nonmanual work, 39% of the total were in social class III (routine nonmanual work), and only 1% were in social class I (professional and managerial occupations). 5.2% of men were in this highest social class. Table 7.3 indicates that 23% of men, but only 17.6% of women, classified by their own occupation were in social class II or above. In fact, it is these two classes which include the 'upper' and middle classes: proprietors, employers, manager, administrators, and people with technical or professional jobs. Within the manual sector, men were concentrated in skilled work (social class III) and women in 'semiskilled' work (social class IV); though about the same proportion of men and women were in unskilled manual work, women are in the lower grade occupations.

Table 7.2. Social class composition of economically active persons, by sex, in Great Britain in 1971 [percentage of men and women in each social class (own occupation)] (source: 1971 Census of Population; see OPCS, various).

Social class	Men	Women
Nonmanual (N)		
I	5.2	1.0
II	17.8	16.6
III N	11.9	38.9
Total	34.9	56.5
Manual (M)		
III M	39.0	10.0
IV	17.8	26.1
V	8.3	7.5
Total	65.1	43.6
Total classified (100%)	15368000	7918000

Table 7.3. Social class composition of economically active persons, by sex, in Great Britain in 1971 (cumulative percentage of men and women by own social class) (source: 1971 Census of Population: see OPCS, various).

Social class	Men	Women
I	5.2	1.0
II and above	23.0	17.6
III and above	73.9	66.5
IV and above	91.7	92.6
V and above	100.0	100.1

Second, there is a considerable overlap between these two groups in the 'social standing' of their members, whether this is measured in terms of earned income, social origins, or ascribed status. Table 7.4 indicates the spread of earnings among full-time manual and nonmanual workers, and shows the extent of this overlap, even among workers of the same sex. The overlap was greater still if men and women were taken together (also see Routh, 1980).

Heath (1981a; 1981b) found that the social origins of women personal service workers differed hardly at all from those of female manual workers, but were much 'lower' than those of clerical workers. In the exercise carried out by Hope and Goldthorpe (1974) to obtain a social ranking of occupations (men only), there was a significant overlap in the prestige accorded to 'blue-collar' and 'white-collar' men. The proletarian-isation of many areas of white-collar work has brought them closer to manual jobs in terms both of financial rewards and of job content, as demonstrated by Braverman (1974).

A third problem with the manual or nonmanual distinction is the primary division within the labour force, in that it may be less significant than gender itself. Table 7.4 shows clearly the much greater difference between the earnings of men and women than between manual or nonmanual workers of the same sex. In terms of grading and ranking occupations, gender is again a major criterion for differentiation. Haavio Manilla's findings (mentioned above) have clearly demonstrated that gender is in some way important when occupations are being ranked, and there is evidence that in formal (as well as informal) job demarcations, the maintenance of sexual divisions has been a central consideration. Phillips and Taylor's (1980) investigation into the definition of work tasks and their gradings in terms of skill support this hypothesis. They concluded that: "Skill definitions are saturated with sexual bias. The work of women is often deemed inferior simply because it is women who do it" (page 53).

Table 7.4. Gross weekly earnings (£ per week) of full-time workers, manual and nonmanual, by sex, Great Britain, April 1979 (source: Department of Employment, 1979).

Type of worker	Earnings category				
	lowest decile	lowest quartile	median	upper quartile	upper decile
Males—nonmanual	59.5	68.1	101.0	129.6	166.0
Males—manual	54.3	68.1	85.4	105.4	128.6
Females—nonmanual	39.7	48.1	59.6	75.7	96.9
Females—manual	36.3	43.0	52.4	63.0	74.4

   The difficult problems of introducing women into occupation-based
social classes, and other occupational rankings, suggests that unidimensional
hierarchy of the kind represented by existing scales is not appropriate for
this purpose. Nonetheless, all the available socioeconomic indicators
suggest that women are unambiguously concentrated into lower grade
occupations. This arises from a combination of 'vertical' and 'horizontal'
types of segregation within occupational groups containing both men and
women; men dominate the upper reaches whereas women are in the
lower grades. Simultaneously, women are concentrated in a range of jobs
which themselves rank low among occupations on most counts, in
comparison with occupations dominated by men (although there is
considerable overlap among these groups). Furthermore, as Llewellyn
(1981) points out, those men who are in female-dominated areas of the
occupational structure are frequently mobile out of them, whereas women
remain in the same position.
   In addition to 'vertical' segregation between men and women in the
broad groupings mentioned above, there is a high degree of vertical
segregation within occupational groups, and what Hakim calls 'horizontal'
segregation among occupations. Her analysis has shown that in 1971 over
half of all male workers were working in occupations in which women
made up less than 10% of workers. Half of the women workers were in
occupations where less than 30% of the workers were male. Among men,
87% were to be found in occupations where most workers were of their
own sex, and among women the corresponding figure was 77%. This
represents a high degree of occupational segregation, although the level
had declined since the turn of the century. At the time 11% of female
workers and 47% of male workers were in occupations which were the
exclusive preserve of their own sex; but by 1971 there were virtually no
exclusively female occupations (a negligible proportion of women worked
in them) and only 14% of males were in exclusively male occupations (see
table 7.5). Men made greater inroads into typically female occupations
during this period than did women into male-dominated ones. Measures
of horizontal segregation which took account of the changing proportion
of women in the total labour force confirm the pattern, that women's

Table 7.5. Changing sex-segregation of UK occupations, 1901 and 1971 (source:
adapted from Hakim, 1979).

Year	Percentage of men working in occupations which had the following percentage of male workers						Percentage of women working in occupations which had the following percentage of female workers					
	100	90+	80+	70+	60+	50+	100	90+	80+	70+	60+	50+
1901	47	74	83	89	92	95	11	52	54	71	74	82
1971	14	53	69	77	84	87	0	25	44	51	75	77

underrepresentation in typically male jobs was more marked than their overrepresentation in typically female jobs. There was a slight reversal of this trend towards decreased horizontal segregation more recently; between 1961 and 1971, most measures indicated a slight increase in segregation.

Table 7.6 shows the sex-composition of the main occupational groups in 1979. Two-thirds of occupied women were in three occupational groups: clerical and related (31.1%), personal service occupations (22%), and professional and related occupations in welfare and health (12.1%), while the greatest concentrations of males were in processing, making, and repairing metal and electrical goods (21%), managerial occupations (10.8%), and transport and related occupations (10.6%).

Women overwhelmingly dominated the catering, cleaning, hairdressing, and other personal service occupational group (82% of these workers were women). They were also very much overrepresented among clerical and related workers, professional and related workers in health and education, and in selling occupations. In the manual occupations, women were slightly overrepresented in repetitive assembly, finishing, and packaging occupations, whereas men dominated the other groups, especially the more skilled of the metal- and electrical-processing occupations. All professional and managerial occupations other than in health and education were dominated by males, as were security and protective services.

Within each occupational group, women were overrepresented in the less skilled, lower status, or lower paid jobs, whereas men were overrepresented in the highly skilled and managerial jobs. Where women had some measure of relative economic and social advantage it tended to be in spheres where a majority of their collaborators were also women. Hence, in the professions, women were concentrated into occupations which were low in the professional hierarchy and which were dominated by women. For example, in 1971, 91% of nurses were women, but only 9% of medical consultants were; 64% of schoolteachers were women, but only 2% of university professors were. In management, women were concentrated either in personnel management or in industries where the majority of workers are women; for example, in services, textiles, or clothing industries. Thus it would appear that, as occupational groups and industries are disaggregated, the level of sexual segregation increases. The national data analysed here mask further segregation at regional, local, and establishment levels (for further details see EOC, 1981 pages 16–19).

In this section, a number of features of the occupational structure regarding gender have been noted. First, most occupations are dominated by one or other sex; there is a high degree of occupational segregation and most occupations are sex-typed. This is a central feature of the occupational structure, and as such must be incorporated in the core of stratification theory.

Table 7.6. Sex-composition of main occupational groups in Great Britain, 1979 (source: OPCS, 1979b).

Occupational group	Workers, % women	Women, under- and over- represented[a]	Occupational distribution	
			male	female
Professional and related supporting management in public sector	20.6	0.53	5.3	2.2
Professional and related in welfare and health	63.5	1.63	4.4	12.1
Literary, artistic, and sports	32.5	0.84	0.9	0.7
Professional and related in science, engineering	8.9	0.23	5.6	0.9
Managerial	20.5	0.53	10.8	4.3
Clerical and related	72.5	1.86	7.5	31.1
Selling	59.9	1.54	3.9	9.2
Security and protective services	9.8	0.25	2.4	0.4
Catering, cleaning, hairdressing, and other personal services	82.0	2.10	3.1	22.2
Farming, fishing, and related	1.3	0.30	2.1	0.5
Materials processing (excluding metal and electrical)	33.8	0.87	8.3	6.6
Processing, making, repairing, etc (metal and electrical)	5.0	0.13	21.0	1.7
Painting, repetitive assembly, product inspection, packaging, etc	45.8	1.17	4.3	5.6
Construction, mining, etc not elsewhere specified	0.4	0.01	5.6	0.0
Transport operators— material-moving and storing related	5.4	0.14	10.6	0.9
Miscellaneous labourers, etc	7.7	0.20	3.3	0.4
Inadequately described and understated	42.9	1.10	1.1	1.0
All groups	39.0		99.2	99.6

[a]Index is greater than 1 if a larger proportion of those in the occupation are women than in the employed labour force as a whole (that is, 39%), and less than 1 if a smaller proportion of these in the occupation are women than in the employed labour force as a whole.

Second, feminised occupations tend to rank lower than male-dominated ones on most criteria. Women are also generally concentrated in the lower positions within occupational hierarchies. A number of critics have commented upon the historical association of 'deskilling' with the feminisation of certain occupations. Not only are the women in such occupations as clerical work or personal service poorly paid and ascribed low social status, but so are the males, when compared with other males, with the exception of a minority of males whose position in a feminised occupation is transitional or who are in elevated positions within the hierarchies of such occupations. The female-dominated personal service or lower grade white-collar occupations have been characterised as 'pink-collar occupations' (see Kapp Howe, 1978). They deserve far more notice than has hitherto been accorded them by stratification theories, and they will be discussed further below.

Third, gender itself carries with it implications for social status which are at least as great as whether one's occupation is 'white-collar' or 'blue-collar', and is also important in determining earnings levels. This suggests that the distinction between 'people' and 'places' in stratification theory is unsatisfactory, in so far as social characteristics of workers (of which gender is one) affect their social standing at least as much as job content. Furthermore, I would suggest that a dynamic analysis of stratification, which systematically includes women as well as men, would reveal gender to be of central importance in the very shaping and defining of the occupational structure. Thus, for example, a 'dynamic' analysis which considers the structuring of individual careers would show different rates of career advancement for men and women. Similarly, the collective recruitment of particular groups of people to newly developing occupational classes has been shaped by preexisting sexual divisions, as has been shown by particular case studies (for example, Mackintosh, 1979). A historical macrosociological study of the type developed by Bertaux (1977), but with the inclusion of women and gender, would be a particularly interesting direction for future research.

In the next sections, I discuss some of the processes which have produced the patterns of sex-segregation discussed above. The occupational structure at any point in time is the result of past social struggles, as well as of technical and physical factors. One dimension of these social relations is organised around gender, and this affects not only the sexual division of labour but also the relationships within the labour process. Patterns of income and status inequality, at any particular time, have resulted from such processes.

7.3 The production and reproduction of sex-typed occupations
In this section, I argue that sex-segregation has not arisen purely by accident, or through the workings of impersonal markets, but has been a systematic and enduring feature of the social division of paid labour.

It is the result of a combination of forces, some of them aimed specifically at maintaining sex-segregation. I discuss some of the processes whereby occupational segregation and sex-typing are produced and maintained, and I advance some crude hypotheses. This is not the place for a detailed historical analysis of the emergence and sex-typing of particular occupations, nor for a full discussion of all the particular cultural, historical, and institutional influences at play in this process. My more limited aim has been to show that sex-segregation is the result of social relations in which gender per se has a crucial part to play (in addition to, and independent of, its influences via marriage), and briefly to outline the main features of these. This reinforces my more general claim that gender must be centrally incorporated into stratification analyses, and provides the beginnings of a basis for doing this.

Occupations are formed at times when technical and social changes (such as new inventions, or changes in the supply of labour) effect changes in the social division of labour. The restructuring of the production process, or parts of it, takes particular forms which are the result of conflicts and struggles. At the same time that particular sets of work tasks are (re)grouped into occupations, and that these are redefined in terms of skill, wage rates, etc, these occupations, I suggest, are assigned (explicitly or implicitly) to workers of one or other sex. Once an occupation has been 'sex-typed', normative and other forces operate which maintain segregation. These vary in different segments of the labour market and over time. Only when labour-market or technical conditions change substantially is there likely to be any change in the sex-typing of an occupation, and this is only likely in the context of a more general renegotiation of that part of the division of labour. Cockburn (1981) has illustrated such a renegotiation, in the context of the introduction of new microtechnology to the printing industry.

The persistence of low-paid sectors in affluent, advanced, capitalist societies has been attributed to the emergence of noncompetitive, or structured, labour markets. Indeed, without some degree of structuring of the labour market, the effect of a reserve of unemployed or underemployed labour would serve only to lower the wage rate as a whole (in general here, see Kerr, 1954; Reich et al, 1980; Rubery, 1978). Persistent sex-segregation is one aspect of the social division of labour which is maintained by structured labour markets. Although an explanation of which particular jobs are done by men and which by women cannot be found simply by investigating the *general* working of these labour markets, the structuring of the labour market permits such segregation, and provides some mechanisms whereby it is reproduced in different sectors. The degree of support for segregation of male workers, and the attitudes of employers and of women themselves, have varied in different times and places.

The existence of division among the working class and within particular work forces often benefits employers by facilitating their control over employees. Different groups of workers and potential employees may be played off against one another, and lack of communality of interest and solidarity permit lower wages to be paid, strikes broken, and so forth. But in other cases, such divisions within a work force may actually hinder the pursuit of profit or other managerial goals. In the particular case of sex-segregation and associated pay inequalities it is not clear that employers profit directly from segregation, even without taking the costs of maintaining segregation into account. Bergmann (1980b) has shown that, assuming hiring practices are entirely in the hands of employers, and that the only goal of the latter is profit maximisation, segregation and the implied possibility of maintaining a low-wage sector do not necessarily produce maximum gains to employers, although they may do so.

In practice, employers have shown considerable variability in their attitudes to sex-segregation, both individually, as Hunt (1975) has shown, and as a group, as illustrated by the stance of the Confederation of British Industries (see Coote and Hewitt, 1980). These varied and changeable attitudes reflect not only different perceptions of the value, rationale, and/or justice of sex-segregation, but also different interests in (benefits from) segregation, according to the specific situation in question.

Employers, however, do not have autonomy in their hiring practices; worker organisation has been of great importance in constructing and maintaining a segmented labour market. Since the early days of the craft unions, employees have combined together effectively to create structured labour markets in which access to particular jobs and skills have been controlled by unions each having a monopoly of particular sectors of employment. By these means, jobs have been kept secure and wages high in some structured sheltered labour markets, despite the deskilling of other sectors and the extension of unionisation. These controls have been variously based on occupation, firm, or industry, and the unions' power in defining 'skills'—who should have access to them, how they should be rewarded—have often carried over through technical changes which have rendered this expertise obsolete, to maintain privileged positions for the 'skilled' workers in the new organisation of work. Indeed it has been argued that "from the viewpoint of Trade Union development, at least, workers are thus skilled and unskilled according to whether or not their organisation is deliberately restricted" (Turner, 1962, page 114). Parkin (1974; 1979) has shown that the operation of various mechanisms of 'closure' (such as control over apprenticeships, guilds, and entry to professions and the maintenance of standards within them) has structured the formation of occupational classes in particular ways. One of the ways (not mentioned by Parkin) is the structuring of occupations into 'men's work' and 'women's work'. The processes of labour-force segmentation, actively and explicitly constructed by workers, and often upheld by employers, provide valuable insights into sexual segregation.

   From the earliest days of industrialisation, we can find evidence of
employers who were eager to recruit women workers to new or expanding
occupations. Women have accepted lower pay than men, and have been
less likely to become unionised, and are more tolerant of boring repetitive
work. The 1971 General Household Survey (OPCS, 1971b) found that
60.7% of female workers were 'very satisfied' with their work, as
compared with 47.2% of males. Furthermore, the successful recruitment
of women undermined the bargaining position of male workers within
those particular segments of the labour market. The entry of women into
these fields of employment enabled employers to pay lower wages than
would have been accepted by males, and thus enabled the occupations
and/or industries in question to become low-waged work. For just as long,
working-class men have organised themselves, first to fight against women's
entry into factory employment as competitors with themselves, and then
to limit the participation of women in the labour force, their pay levels,
and their chances of gaining a strong foothold in particular sectors.
Hartmann (1979b) has demonstrated how groups of male workers have at
times successfully organised themselves to exclude women from particular
jobs. A variety of other factors have also been of importance in excluding
women from specific types of employment, at different times, and the
maintenenace of a male monopoly has not always been the main
consideration (for further discussion, see Coyle, 1980; Humphries, 1981;
chapters 8 and 9 below). But one of the effects of protecting the
employment conditions in some sectors of the labour market was that it
was at the expense of employment opportunities for women, among
others. Though the aristocracy of labour excluded many men, all women
were kept out on the very ground that they were women. Although there
have been exceptions, for example, in the case of the wives or widows of
male members of the labour aristocracy (see Lewenhak, 1977), these
generally pertained to women by virtue of their specific relations to
particular men, rather than in their own right.
   The monopoly power of trade unions was explicitly used to exclude
women from apprenticeships as late as the 1960s (although the 1977 Sex
Discrimination Act has outlawed this practice) and to prevent women
from gaining equal employment opportunities. There is some evidence to
suggest that skilled unions have been those most hostile to the employment
of women on equal terms with men and have used their power to try to
prevent this, although systematic evidence is not available [for example,
see Victor Feather's evidence to the House of Lords (1972) Select
Committee on the Anti-Discrimination Bill, concerning an employer who
wanted to offer equal opportunities to men and women]. Of the three
unions involved, that with the least-skilled membership had no objections,
equal pay having been a long-standing demand. The second union would
permit the employment of women only when unemployment in the
industry was low, stipulating that they should be the first to go in a

redundancy situation. The third, the most-skilled union, would accept no women under any condition. This supports the hypothesis that the exclusion of women has been part of a wider process of occupational closure. Where women have entered occupations in large numbers, these have indeed become areas of comparatively low pay, and regarded as low-skilled. The exclusion of women from protected sections of the labour market crowded them into the remaining occupations.

Although some occupations remain the preserve of males, others have become defined as 'women's work'. The particular jobs which became so defined have depended on historical circumstances. I would hypothesise that the state of local and national labour markets at the time of a new industry developing or a new technology being introduced was crucially important in determining whether new or expanding occupations should be worked by men or by women. The piecemeal evidence which is available suggests that those occupations which became defined as female were expanding at a time when the skills needed to do them were commonly held or easily learned, and when there was either a particularly high demand for labour or an especially large pool of women seeking work (for example, see Lazonick, 1979). These are circumstances in which it was particularly hard for groups of workers to obtain or keep monopoly powers. So, although some areas were protected, for men, others were permitted to become feminised.

In the case of clerical work, for example, in 1911, 21% of clerical workers were women; in 1971 the figure was 73%. The feminisation of clerical work occurred at a time when the skills of literacy were in any case becoming widespread through mass education. Male clerks had tended not to be unionised and had often been promoted to partnerships in the firm. Such upward mobility could not have been possible for the whole of an expanding junior white-collar work force, and promotion in more recent years has been largely confined to men (see Barker and Downing, 1980).

The nursing profession was established at a time when there were few 'respectable' courses for impoverished women of bourgeois and petit bourgeois origins to take. These women constituted a potential labour force who were already schooled in the necessary qualities for nursing, since it was character and familiarity with servicing tasks and roles that mattered. At that time, the main qualification thought necessary "to be a good nurse [was that] one must be a good woman" (Florence Nightingale, quoted in Gamarnikow, 1978). This, by definition, is a widely held qualification.

In general, then, particular occupations have become defined as 'men's work' or 'women's work', as a result of conflicts between employers seeking to employ women as low-wage labour, and groups of male workers attempting to exclude women from particular sectors of employment in order to protect their own wage levels. Once occupations have been culturally defined as appropriate to one sex, entry to them by individual members of the other sex is controlled through a number of mechanisms. They range from explicit barriers to entry, or other formal measures, to norms which make it inconceivable that a woman should do job X or a man job Y. Though the specific forms of ideology rendering jobs gender-appropriate for women or men vary over time and among different groups within a single society[10], they are often very strongly held. Where the normative boundaries are transgressed, verbal and physical harassment and insults may be resorted to; these range from joking, teasing, and innuendo to physical assault. By these means, women are generally deterred or prevented from pursuing traditionally male occupations, even where they are legally entitled to do so.

Where women have entered traditionally 'male' preserves despite these pressures, their performance and promotions may be impaired by sexual harassment and discrimination from colleagues, clients, or superiors. Thus, women bus drivers in London (where bus driving has long been a 'man's job') have been harassed by passengers, motorists, and male colleagues and disapproved of by their instructors (*The Guardian* 1971). Similarly, as shown by Smith (1976), women journalists have been deprived of access to information, skills, and experience crucial to their success and eventual promotion. In general, such practices have prevented women from doing their jobs as easily and as well as might otherwise be expected, and have hindered their promotion both directly and indirectly. Mackinnon (1979) documents and discusses these practices more fully.

The sexuality and gender-identity of males entering nursing or other female-dominated occupations may also be questioned by specifically sexual teasing and mocking. However, there are fewer occupations which are exclusively female than are entirely male—even taking account of the differenct proportion of men and women who are in employment. There is also an asymmetry here insofar as many of the men first entering 'feminine' occupations do so in the (realistic) expectation of rapid promotion to higher reaches of the occupational hierarchy, in which men are once again in the majority. These social arrangements are, then, the means whereby sex-segregation, and hence a sexual division of labour, have been maintained through periods of rapid social and economic change. Ideologies of gender have served to legitimate a sexual division of labour which, albeit changing, has been crystallised and built into occupations at particular times as a result of specific historical struggles.

[10]Milkman (1981) has demonstrated the changeability of gender ideologies as related to specific occupations, and how power relations affected them in two manufacturing industries, during the employment changes associated with World War 2 (also see Summerfield, 1977). Chombart de Lauwe et al (1963) have illustrated the range of gender ideologies that coexist within one advanced industrial society, at a single moment in time.

It has not been my purpose here to discuss the power relations underlying these struggles (for a more general discussion of the ideology of gender and the power relations underlying it, see Guillaumin, 1981). Neither can their implications be discussed here, though they are wide indeed. I have merely argued that sex-segregation in employment in industrial capitalist societies has been wrought as a result of social relations around gender. As such, segregation is a central feature of the occupational structure, and the sex-typing of occupations is a reflection of these social relations. To ignore this dimension of occupational stratification is to omit from the analysis an element which has been crucial to the historical structuring of occupations, as well as being of importance in determining patterns of personal mobility among occupations, and social relations within them.

7.4 Occupational classifications

In the last two sections, I have noted the concentration of women into a small number of occupational groups, and have discussed the social processes which have produced this segregation. I now suggest that the importance of gender in structuring the division of labour in general, and the occupational scheme in particular, must be taken into account when classifying and grouping together occupations. Further empirical work both into the social relations embodied in some kinds of work and into particular segments of the labour market would be needed to test the value of the present suggestions before they might be incorporated into future occupational classifications. But gender, 'female' occupations, and women workers have for so long been given a secondary place in studies of work and stratification that such a reworking is timely.

Occupational classifications are constructed for a variety of purposes, and I do not propose to discuss these here. Similarly, studies of social stratification may be made in pursuit of different theoretical concerns. However, they all make use of one or other classification of occupations. For most purposes it is desirable that such classifications distinguish sufficiently among occupations as to be able to regroup them according to a number of different criteria. These include position in the labour market, the nature of the job (including technical, social, and environmental features), and even the characteristics of the incumbents (life-style, social standing, etc). If gender is to be recognised in occupational classification, and women included in stratification studies, changes must be made to classification schemes, the relative importance of criteria for differentiating among jobs must be reassessed, and the relation between occupation and 'social standing' must be investigated further.

Two themes are taken up in this section. The importance of segregation and sex-typing for occupational classifications is discussed. The lack of distinctions within many women's occupations is then related to the dearth of theoretical work on the social relations of servicing employment, and I suggest that servicing relations are closely associated with the wider social relations of gender. In combination with further work on patterns of job mobility and on career histories, these would be useful ways of approaching some gender-related problems in the classification of occupations.

7.4.1 Segregation

The importance of gender-related occupational characteristics suggests that the proportions of men and women in an occupation is itself a feature worthy of inclusion in the classification of occupations. If the hypothesis is correct, that occupations are sex-tuped at the same time as they crystallise as occupations, and that the sex-typing is unlikely to change unless the jobs themselves change substantially in other respects (either the labour market changes dramatically, so that the market situation of incumbents also changes, or the tasks are restructured, or both), then whether a job is mainly a 'man's job' or a 'woman's job' is an inherent characteristic of the occupation. As we have seen, both the degree of segregation within an occupation and the sex-group which dominates it are important indicators of the market position of, and social relations engaged in by, men and women in that occupation. This would seem, then, to be a theoretically meaningful distinction to make, as well as being one relatively easy to operationalise. The empirical relation between segregation per se, social relations, market position, and other characteristics of occupations needs to be investigated. But the very fact that an occupation is exclusively female, or male, or that it has a particular mix of men and women, is in itself an important feature of that segment of the labour market. In addition, the sex-composition of occupational groups may, in combination with other characteristics, indicate something about the type of social relations dominant in that sector.

Stewart et al (1980) have also argued that the distinction between 'people' and 'places' in the stratification scheme is not very fruitful, and that is should be abandoned in favour of an approach which better reflects the social processes which produce a stratified society, and the processes of the labour market. The present suggestions are in line with such an approach, and indeed support and develop it. Further research on job histories and on particular segments of the labour market are necessary, however. In combination with the results of such research, segregation can very usefully be used to differentiate among occupations and to group them together.

Table 7.7 indicates the main occupations which were dominated by women in the early 1970s. Very few of these occupations were manufacturing jobs; only 'sewers and embroiderers' and (possibly) 'packers, labellers, and related workers' were engaged in making goods; the others were in service occupations of some kind.

The social relations engaged in by people employed in these 'servicing' occupations urgently require further study. Service occupations and industries have been expanding rapidly in recent decades, both in absolute terms and as a share of total employment, and the importance of servicing work may be expected to grow. Though the sociology of a

'service class' of managers, administrators, and technicians has been
developed, there has been relatively little sociological interest taken in the
majority of lower level servicing occupations. They have been largely
confined to the periphery of occupational sociology and of the sociology
of class and stratification, although there have been recent exceptions.

In servicing jobs generally, work tasks are defined in terms of meeting
the needs or requirements of particular people, as opposed to producing a
certain quantity of goods, or working at a specific rate. A servicing
relationship is characteristic of most of the jobs mentioned in table 7.7.
Thus secretaries are the secretaries of one or more particular people, and
have to perform secretrial duties for these people, as the latter require.
The work tasks of maids, nurses, hairdressers, waiters, and watresses are
all defined in relation to particular people, such as their clients, patients,
or employers. It is these people whose needs or requirements define the
work (the typing, the waiting, the tending); the service worker must be
available to perform tasks as, when, and how the boss, client, or patient
requires. The products of their labour are directly appropriated or used
by the latter, and it is in general hard, and often impossible, to accumulate
the products of service work.

Table 7.7. Female employees in selected occupational groups, Great Britain, 1971
(source: 1971 Census of Population Economic Activity Tables; see OPCS, various).

Occupational group	Number of women workers (thousands)	Percentage of workers who are women
Typists, secretaries, shorthand writers	759	98.6
Maids, valets, etc	428	96.6
Hand and machine sewers and embroiderers	230	96.6
Canteen assistants	293	96.4
Nurses	394	91.2
Charwomen, cleaners, and sweepers	456	87.3
Office machine operators	153	86.4
Telephone operators	89	83.2
Kitchen hands	100	82.0
Shop salesmen and assistants (SIC)	789	81.1
Hairdressers, manicurists, and beauticians	124	78.0
Packers, labellers, and related workers	217	72.9
Waiters and waitresses	82	72.6
Bartenders	73	70.9
Cooks	121	66.1
Primary and secondary schoolteachers	318	64.1
Clerks and cashiers	1546	62.5

Servicing work does not fall neatly into the 'blue-collar'–'white-collar' distinction between manual and nonmanual work, but straddles the two, being characteristic of neither archetype. It may involve widely varying degree of autonomy, responsibility, and skill, and be performed in a number of different locations, and dealing in a variety of ways with people, data, and things. The occupational classification used in the US Census, and again in the Australian National University Study of Social Mobility, makes some interesting empirical classifications of occupations according to the way 'data, people, and things' are handled (see Broom et al, 1977; Miller, 1966). However, social relations of what Stacey (1981) has called 'people-work' require further study before such distinctions can be interpreted sociologically. Clearly, such distinctions, traditional to occupational classification, must be maintained, but where the latter group puts together large numbers of service workers into undifferentiated categories, such as 'typists, secretaries, shorthand writers', or 'shop salesmen and assistants' (sic), further distinctions are needed. Fruitful progress might be made, I suggest, by investigating *for whom* the services are being done, asking the questions 'To whom?' and 'At whose behest?' We might then be able to distinguish between the shop assistant at a supermarket and one in a high-class specialist boutique, between the secretary of the managing director of a multinational corporation, the typist in a typing pool, and the secretary of a suburban self-employed travel agent.

A corollary of this might be to argue that, for many servicing jobs, status accrues to some extent by ascription and that chances of occupational advance are related to those of the boss (the boss gets promotion and takes his secretary with him). A parallel may be drawn here with the way in which married women (and other household members) are ascribed status according to their husband's ('head' of household's) occupation. However, a further component is necessary to the analysis, namely an account of the different relationships between the people concerned. The contract between marriage partners is different from those between a secretary and her boss, or between nurses and the medical profession. Access to, and control over, resources, and status acquired through these attachments, vary according to the formal contract between the parties, as well as being subject to a large amount of informal negotiation within the bounds of this contract. Bell and Newby (1976) have characterised relations between husbands and wives in terms of a 'deferential dialectic'. I would suggest that we need to study the relations of service employment in these terms as well. The wage contract may specify the rewards to these jobs (though not tips, etc), but it does not specify exactly the work that has to be done or how it should be done.

A hidden job content is an important part of women's work in servicing jobs performed for men. The deference and negotiation which is a component of most, if not all, servicing relationships takes on particular characteristics when the service workers are women and the people they

are servicing are men. This is a particular and frequently occurring case
of the social relations of gender discussed in more general terms above.
Many women in jobs whose official content, as stated in their contract of
employment, is confined to quite different tasks are expected also to
render various personal services to their bosses and/or clients. A number
of writers have documented how female secretaries and typists, for
example, are expected to nurture and care for their male superior in ways
which extend far beyond the bounds of doing the typing and office work.
Feeding them, mending their clothes, buying presents for their wives,
looking after their pets, and arranging social events quite unconnected
with work, are all things which it is quite commonplace for these 'clerical'
workers to be asked to do (see AMB, 1976; Barker and Downing, 1980;
McNally, 1979). These duties may sometimes be extended into more
explicitly sexual servicing. These are not reciprocal arrangements, and
they are not explicitly recognised in the employment contract, but they
are expected services nonetheless. Chodorow (1978) has argued that
'femininity' is culturally defined in terms of mothering, with all the caring,
nurturing, servicing work that that implies (albeit taking different cultural
forms), and masculinity is defined in opposition to this. This suggests
that an explanation of the 'servicing' nature of so many 'women's
occupations' must take gender into account per se. A servicing component
to work tasks reinforces the definition of the occupation as 'women's
work', and the hierarchical relations implicit in servicing reinforce the
gender hierarchy present elsewhere in societies[11]. In these tasks, the
general ideology of gender, which associates femininity with nurturing,
and hence with servicing, may be translated directly into specific
occupational terms. This implies that the tasks in clerical and servicing
'pink-collar' work might need to be restructured, in order to become
defeminised, in such a way as to separate out the informal personal
service components of these jobs from other parts.
    There are some strong similarities, then, between the traditional
servicing relations of domestic work within marriage and relations of
service employment. Despite the important differences between marriage
and contracts of paid employment, these similarities mean that the
socialisation of girls prepares them for both kinds of relationship, if it
prepares them for either. Furthermore, though the general gender
ideology which associates femininity with nurturing and servicing does
not in itself *explain* the preponderance of women in servicing occupations,
a convergence between general and occupation-specific gender ideologies
certainly facilitates the legitimation of women's employment in services.

[11]Delphy (1977) has argued that domestic servicing done by women for men within
the marriage relationship is an important component (if not the very basis) of the
social domination of men over women. Although class inequalities result in a minority
of women being serviced by men, and the cash nexus has reduced the importance of
domestic servicing, the association between femininity, servicing and servility remains
and requires further sociological exploration.

The systematic associations between femininity and service work, between relations of gender and relations of service employment, require considerably more investigation before their implications for differentiating among, and classifying, specific occupations can be seen. But such research would bear interesting and valuable fruits.

7.4.2 Occupation and stratification

Occupation is not the only source of social differentiation and inequality among women. Marriage, domestic position, and the occupations of other household members are also major sources of inequality among women. The latter also affect women's relations with paid employment and their position in the occupational structure. To include women in a study of occupational stratification sharpens the problem of the relationship between occupation, social standing, and class position. Elsewhere I have argued that it is necessary to include unpaid work within the universe to be stratified, and that closer attention must be paid to the relationship between individuals, households, and families as units of stratification, before women can be adequately included in stratification studies. This eventually necessitates a radical recasting of stratification theory and a shift in the focus of studies of work more generally.

Even if the scope of the discussion is limited, as in this chapter, to differentiating among people who are in full-time employment, a number of problems remain. The relation between income, education, and occupation is different for women than for men. Social origins too have a different relation to occupation, according to sex (see Heath, 1981a), and career patterns are affected differently by sex and marital status, as Greenhalgh (1980) has demonstrated. A dynamic element to stratification studies is necessary if these factors are to be taken into account. The relation between occupation and social standing is clearly sex-dependent, and gender itself affects prestige. A ranking exercise of the kind undertaken by Hope and Goldthorpe (1974), for example, could in theory be performed quite easily, substituting women for men, but the meaning and value of such ordering is problematic. Indeed it is not clear that *any* unidimension ranking of men and women according to their occupations would be readily interpretable. An index of the kind constructed by Duncan (1961) could not incorporate the different relationships between income, education, and occupation that pertain for men and for women. Similarly a scale constructed on the basis of patterns of friendship would contain a host of ambiguities[12].

---

[12]For example, Stewart et al (1980) produced an occupational scale, one basis of which involved a sample of male white-collar workers stating the occupations of four people with whom they associated, as friends. From the mention of women (page 84), it would seem that some of the friends cited were female. Stewart et al do not state this explicitly, neither do they say that women were excluded from this operation, although they were in all the other parts of their empirical research. If it is true, this gives rise to a number of problems of interpretation.

Occupational scales have generally been constructed on the basis of a set of assumptions about the relation of people's occupations to their positions in the stratification scheme more generally. Whereas the assumptions already have many limitations where it is only men that are considered, the problems are multiplied disproportionately if women are also included. If occupational scales are to be constructed for the purpose of studying stratification, it is crucial that the ambiguities associated with gender are minimised. One course that might be taken would be to construct independently a pair of occupational scales, one for males and one for females. These could then be analysed in combination, and hypotheses about the effects of gender could be tested instead of assumptions being made. If the scales are being constructed as an index (à la Duncan), a factor for segregation might be imputed, as might one indicating career prospects (or another indicator of labour-market prospects). If they are built from de facto social behaviour (such as patterns of association) these factors may be expected to be incorporated as intrinsic elements contributing to 'social standing'. Either way, the importance of, and relation between, different features which differentiate among men and women in terms of social stratification might thereby be assessed (see Murgatroyd, 1984, for further development of this argument).

7.5 Conclusion

In this chapter, I have addressed some of the problems which need to be resolved before stratification studies may include both women and men among the population studied. As I mentioned above, this is important in a number of fields of planning and policymaking, for the information available to and the concepts used by planners often ignore the crucial dimension of gender as a result of its omission in the past from the core of social sciences more generally. At best, this gives rise to inefficiency in the provision of relevant information, and at worst to misinformation, and hence to unrealistic and ineffective planning.

The different relationships borne by women and men to the labour market, and the high degree of sex-segregation in the labour force, require that gender be assigned a central place in any such analysis and planning framework. I have argued that the social relations of gender have had a crucial role in determining the occupational structure and the position of individuals within it. Occupations have largely become defined as 'male' or 'female', and where an occupational group contains a mixture of men and women at national level, the degree of segregation increases as the group is broken down, be it by rank, by region, or by employer, so that segregation is high at the level of the workplace. Sexual divisions obtained in this static picture are accentuated when career paths are taken into account. When the labour process at the workplace is investigated, it becomes apparent that occupational segregation and sex-typing are products of a particular set of social relations, in which gender plays a central part. The interests of different groups are pursued through a variety of mechanisms, including normative and institutional ones.

Traditionally, stratification theory has paid little attention to these matters. It has generally focused on males, and has been riddled with ambiguities concerning gender and the extension of conclusions drawn from studies of men to cover society as a whole. Meanwhile, economists and planners have often made assumptions about gender-differentiated behaviour (if women have been considered at all), without taking much account of the processes and the social relations which give rise to it.

In ignoring gender, such studies draw only a very partial analysis of stratification even among men; and the omission of women from studies of stratification precludes the validity of drawing conclusions with regard to the division of labour as a whole. This has repercussions in a wide range of applied social science and planning fields which incorporate concepts developed within the sociology of stratification. I have made some suggestions as to possible ways of pursuing these problems, but these are as yet only embryonic. It is, however, to be hoped that these may be refined and built upon in the future.

Theories of women, work, and unemployment

Sylvia Walby

8.1 Introduction

Gender relations are an important component of social stratification, and any analysis of locality and social relations must take them into account. In this chapter, I pursue this theme, common to all the contributions in this book, by exploring the various theorisations of women, work, and unemployment. Such theoretical understanding is a crucial preliminary to consideration of policy issues; yet existing work in this area is inadequate. Neglect by policymakers of the problems unemployment causes to women has frequently been underpinned by highly dubious theoretical arguments as to the place of women in the division of labour. Theoretical fallacies have had the effect variously of denying the true extent, significance, and causes of women's unemployment.

The explanations of gender differences in unemployment, which will be considered here, have been developed in a variety of theoretical frameworks, including neoclassical economics, institutional labour-market analysis, radical labour-market analysis, Marxism, and radical feminism. Though it would be possible to divide the consideration of existing theories according to the theoretical framework from which they derive, that is not the most useful approach. The key issues on which approaches to women's unemployment and employment divide do not coincide with the theoretical divisions between neoclassical economics, institutional labour-market analysis, Marxism, and radical feminism. The main difference is rather the degree of centrality which is accorded to the family or to labour-market structures in explaining women's movements into and out of paid work. It is on the question of whether the family is seen as the chief determinant of women's participation in paid work, or whether structures within the labour market are held to be key, that the most significant differences emerge. Many of the problems in existing approaches stem from an inadequate analysis of gender divisions. Some ways of overcoming this will be suggested.

In most Western industrialised countries the rate of unemployment among women is greater than that of men. The United Kingdom is exceptional in that the rates for men and women are roughly equal. Any adequate theory of gender and unemployment must be able to handle such empirically varied phenomena. Yet rarely do theorists in this area take notice of such internationally varying rates of male–female unemployment.

I shall start the review of explanations of gender differences in unemployment and employment by looking at the work of Mincer and

Beechey, who are among the most important writers on the topic. Both writers stress the importance of the family in structuring women's participation in paid work [although Beechey's (1983) more recent work has a much wider focus, taking labour-market structures much more into account]. The fact that Mincer (1962; 1966) and Niemi (1980) operate within a neoclassical economic framework, and Beechey (1977; 1978) within a Marxist–feminist approach, has not prevented them from having a very similar emphasis upon the centrality of the family in determining women's participation in paid employment.

8.2 Family-focused theorists
8.2.1 Mincer

Mincer (1962) explains women's labour force participation in terms of women's commitment to the domestic sphere and its interaction with variations in the level of the economy. Women are seen as marginal workers because of their position in the family. He sees women's participation in paid employment as 'flexible' because of the alternative forms of work which are open to them in the household. It is the availability of these alternative forms of productive activity that are the explanation of married women spending only part of their time in paid work. Women, according to Mincer, choose the best time to participate in the economy according to the ups and downs of the business cycle. Those people who spend only a portion of their working lives in paid work choose these times to coincide with the periods of the business cycle when the most work is available with the best conditions of employment. The import of this is that the periods outside the labour force are seen as voluntary. This means that they do not count as involuntary unemployment.

A major concern of Mincer's is the question of whether wives are encouraged or discouraged from working by particular wage levels of the husband. This has become known as the issue of the income or the substitution effect. The question is whether wives work more in times of economic expansion because jobs are available (income effect), or whether they work more in times of economic recession when there is likely to be less income from a husband who might be unemployed (substitution effect). Mincer is able to show that both effects operate. He separates out the importance of the wife's level of earnings, the husband's expected income, the husband's actual income, and the education levels of the wife and the husband. This enables him to argue convincingly that in early postwar USA the increase in married women's paid employment was largely the result of the increase in the level of their wages, which outweighs the negative effect of the increase in the husband's income. (However, we should note that Mincer was working before the impact of the current recession.)

Mincer's model assumes that the choice is not between paid work and leisure, but a threeway one between paid work, leisure, and unpaid

housework. The recognition that the wife does productive work in the
home is important. In this, his early model-building work, Mincer (1962)
does not build unemployment into his analysis of women's activities.
This is unfortunate and a major source of his problems. In this way
Mincer has constructed a model for women's participation in paid
employment which is different from that of men. He has defined
unemployment out of existence for married women, whereas it is a crucial
part of any account of male participation in employment. In his later
work, Mincer (1966) does discuss the question of unemployment among
married women and other secondary workers. It is discussed in relation
to the question of whether discouraged workers are really unemployed,
and whether the lack of jobs among these secondary workers is an issue
of any significance. Here Mincer effectively denies the existence, let
alone social significance, of disguised unemployment among secondary
workers, by suggesting that they engage in nonmarket work when they do
not engage in market work, and that at these times they would only
accept employment at better-than-prevailing conditions: "The fact that
60 per cent of his time is spent outside the labour force *means* that other
than 'gainful' activities are important" (Mincer, 1966, page 102; my
emphasis). Mincer does explicitly state that he is not ruling out the
existence of involuntary unemployment, but I would contend that this
denial is contradicted by his analysis.

A second major problem in Mincer's analysis is his neglect of patriarchal
structures within the labour market. Like most neoclassical economists
Mincer assumes that the labour market works smoothly and perfectly
competitively. Inequalities in the wages and participation rates between
people in the labour market are conceptualised as merely reflecting the
inequalities of human capital they bring to it. Consequently Mincer can
have no explanation of such central features of the labour market as the
segregation of the sexes and ethnic groups into different occupations with
unequal wages and conditions of job security. This general point will be
discussed more fully later.

A third problem in Mincer's analysis is his assumption that the
household rationally decides on its labour-market activities so as to
maximise its income and leisure as a unit. This ignores the inequality in
power within the family, which has important effects on the decisions on
the distribution of paid work, unpaid work, and leisure *between* the
household members. Time budget studies have shown that women do
more work (paid and unpaid) than men and have less leisure (Vanek,
1980). Qualitative studies have shown that husbands sometimes exert
considerable influence over their wives' decision to take paid work (see
Scharf, 1980). This may not be to the advantage of the household as a
unit, but is done in order that the man retains a position of authority.
The family should be analysed as a patriarchal structure, not as an
egalitarian unit.

8.2.3 Niemi

Niemi (1980) takes a neoclassical economist's position on women's participation in paid work, which, unlike Mincer's, does recognise the conceptual existence of married women's unemployment. She tries to explain why women, in the early postwar USA, had consistently higher rates of unemployment than men. She concludes that the main reason is that women have higher rates of frictional unemployment because of their greater number of moves into and out of the paid work force. She suggests that these moves are a result of married women's domestic commitments and consequential intermittent pattern of participation in the labour force. Each move is seen to result in an associated period of frictional unemployment at the point of reentry to the labour market. In this way women's position in the family is seen as the cause of women's higher rate of unemployment. Like Mincer she regards these moves into and out of paid work by married women as essentially voluntary. Women have other things to do and, since women typically have less skills or human capital than their husbands, it is they who stay at home to do housework. This is seen as the voluntary decision of a rational unit. Hence the unemployment which stems from such choices is seen as essentially voluntary also. Niemi considers the impact of women's lesser training and their lack of geographical and occupational mobility (because of their husbands) on their unemployment chances. She argues that the latter are much less significant.

The problems with Niemi's analysis are similar to those of Mincer in her neglect of labour-market structures and patriarchal relations. Women's mobility into and out of paid employment and between jobs may be as much a product of the structures of the job market and the occupational slots open to women as it is the result of their domestic situation. Women tend to be concentrated in jobs which have high rates of turnover attached to them. Thus the high rate of turnover is a product of the nature of the occupational slot rather than of the characteristics of those who fill the slot. Niemi has ignored the significance of the structuring of the labour market. Like Mincer, Niemi also ignores the patriarchal structuring of family relations which influence women's participation in paid work.

8.2.4 Beechey

Beechey's account of women as a reserve army of labour is based upon Marx's (1954) general concept of reserve army as developed in *Capital*. So it is appropriate to consider Marx's non-gender-specific account before moving on to Beechey's application of this to women.

Marx argues that capital calls into being a relative surplus population which serves to support the extraction of profit by capital from the workers. The relative surplus population acts as a reserve army of labour which depresses the level of wages. The existence of a supply of labour which is greater than the demand for it reduces the ability of those in employment to demand higher wages.

> "The industrial reserve army, during the periods of stagnation and average prosperity, weighs down the active labour-army; during the periods of over-production and paroxysm, it holds its pretensions in check" (Marx, 1954, page 598).

The existence of a reserve means that in times of expansion there are people whose labour capital can draw upon without the necessity of offering high wages to attract people already employed elsewhere. Marx sees this not merely as advantageous to capital, but as necessary. He says that it is essential for it to be possible to employ people rapidly in newly profitable ways without damaging the existing branches of industry. An industrial reserve army from the relative surplus population is the way in which this is achieved.

After showing the function the industrial reserve army fulfils for capital, Marx moves on to an account of the three ways that this is supplied. The first is the 'floating' form of the industrial reserve army. This results from the expansion and contraction of capitalist industry and consequent attraction and expulsion of workers. The second is the latent form of the reserve army, which is composed of workers who have not been employed in capitalist industry, but who are underemployed in their current jobs as a consequence of capitalist expansion. Marx provides the example of agricultural workers affected by the penetration of capitalism into the countryside. Their wages are severely depressed as a result and thus they are ready to move into industrial employment at the first opportunity. The third form is termed the 'stagnant'. This is composed of workers who are in irregular employment for long hours at low wages. Marx gave the example of workers in decaying branches of employment such as 'domestic industry'. Marx also refers to pauperism, which is the lowest layer of the relative surplus population, which, in addition to including some who seek paid work, includes some who are not able to take on such employment; for example, the sick and crippled.

Although Marx did not refer to the gender of the members of the industrial reserve army, Beechey (1977) does argue that married women are a preferred source of the industrial reserve army for capital. Married women may be paid low wages and be easily dismissed, according to Beechey, because they are partially supported by their husbands' wages. It is married women's financial relationship with their husbands that differentiates them from other wage labourers and which gives rise to women's particular and distinctive position in the labour market. Married women do not bear all the costs of the reproduction of their labour power because of their dependence on their husbands' wages. Thus they may be paid lower wages than men and may be dismissed more readily because they can fall back on the financial support of their husbands.

Married women are not the only category of potential wage workers whose costs of subsistence are partially borne elsewhere. Semi-proletarianised workers meet part of the costs of their reproduction from subsistence agriculture and hence might be seen to have a similar position to married women. Beechey suggests that we need to analyse political factors to explain why one category is chosen for the role of reserve army rather than another. Married women are thus seen as a latent reserve army of labour, rather than as part of the floating or stagnant forms. They are ready to be drawn out of the family into paid employment in a similar manner to the agricultural workers in Marx's analysis.

The 'flexibility' of married women appears to stem from two sources in Beechey's analysis. First, it is partly because of the support of the husband's wage. Beechey (1977, pages 56-57) states that the advantages for capital of

"... those categories of labour which are partially dependent upon sources of income other than the wage to meet some of the costs of the reproduction of labour power ... are ...
(a) they can be paid wages which are below the value of labour power ...
(b) they provide a flexible working population which can be brought into production and dispensed with as the conditions of production change".

The second reason for flexibility seems to be that married women have somewhere to go and something to do. Thus writing of why they are preferable to semiproletarianised workers as a reserve army, Beechey (1977, page 57) writes:

"One important difference is that married women have a world of their very own, the family, into which they can disappear when discarded from production, without being eligible for state benefits, and without appearing in unemployment statistics (unless they sign on). The existence of the family, and of the fact that the married woman also performs domestic labour within it, differentiates the position of the married woman within the metropolitan society from that of the semi-proletarianised worker who enters into the metropolitan society on a temporary basis".

However, a central problem in Beechey's analysis is her inability to explain why, if women's labour is so cheap, capital does not continually employ women in preference to men. She argues that capital employs women during economic upturns because their labour is cheaper than that of men; that is, women can be paid less than the value of their labour power, unlike men. There would appear to be no reason, within the logic of capitalism, why they should not be employed all of the time. Beechey suggests that capital wishes to maintain the family and that this puts limits on women's paid employment. However, no suggestion is made that the use made of women workers during economic booms undermines the family, so Beechey is still in need of an explanation as to why it should be so at other times.

I would argue that we should look at patriarchal relations to explain these limits on women's paid employment. They cannot be derived from capitalism alone. There is a need to analyse patriarchal relations both within the labour market and within the household; for instance, the role of male-dominated trade unions in protecting male jobs at the expense of women, and the role of other male-dominated organisations including that of the state. Beechey's later work (1983) does place greater stress on the significance of practices in the workplace; however, these are not analysed as patriarchal practices.

Beechey (1977; 1978) also notes the processes whereby employers attempt to utilise women's relatively cheap labour in their strategies of deskilling the labour process. This point is more fully developed by Humphries (1983) and Braverman (1974), who have each argued that there is a long-run secular tendency for women to enter paid work as capitalism develops and that there is a concomitant decline in male paid labour. Whereas Braverman's emphasis is both upon the movement of tasks from the domestic economy to the capitalist factory and upon the newly deskilled nature of the labour processes in which women are engaged, Humphries's focus is upon the substitution of women for men within the market economy. These writers thus note the interest of capital in the employment of women because women may be more easily paid lower wages. Their arguments thus run directly counter to the suggestion that women constitute a cyclical reserve and are the first to be ejected in times of lower demand for labour. In one case women are preferred to men as workers, in the other men are preferred to women.

The major problem with the arguments of Braverman and Humphries is that they are unable to explain why employers have not substituted cheap women workers for men a long time ago. Yet the logic of their argument would lead to the supposition that this is what employers would already have done. Their argument is flawed by its neglect of patriarchal forces which restrict women's access to paid work. It is now a standard criticism of Braverman that he did not take account of worker organisation (Friedman, 1977b; Rubery, 1978; Wood, 1982). Here I want to emphasise the problem of his neglect of specifically patriarchal forms of worker organisation. This criticism also applies to Humphries. Male workers have fought long and hard to exclude women from many forms of paid work, especially that which is well paid (Braybon, 1981; Drake, 1920; Summerfield, 1984; Walby, 1983c, 1985). The history of women's employment and unemployment cannot be understood without this important factor being considered.

8.3 Labour-market structures
All the writers discussed so far have emphasised the importance of the family in the explanation of women's participation in paid work, and have almost completely ignored patriarchal (or other) structures in the labour market.

A greater emphasis on labour-market structures rather than the family is to be found in the writings to be considered in this section. Many early writers on gender and labour-market structures drew their inspiration from the work by radical US economists on the disadvantaged position of blacks in the US labour market. These writers analysed the barriers to the free movement of labour and the privileges whites derived from certain institutional structures. In Britain, Barron and Norris (1976) applied these ideas to sexual divisions in the labour market.

8.3.1 Barron and Norris

The dual labour-market approach of Barron and Norris (1976) focuses on the imperfect workings of the labour market and its institutional structure in order to explain patterns of employment. Barron and Norris contribute to the understanding of sex differences in unemployment through their analysis of how women come to be found occupying jobs which are themselves unstable and which lead to high turnover. Instability of jobs and a high rate of turnover are important contributors to unemployment. Barron and Norris suggest that women are more likely to be in jobs which are unstable and lead to a high turnover of workers because of the way women fit into the secondary sector of the dual labour market. Their analysis is in two parts: first, an explanation of why the labour market is segmented into primary and secondary jobs; and, second, why it is women who tend to fill the secondary slots. Instability rather than stability of jobs is one of four characteristics which, according to Barron and Norris, differentiate primary and secondary jobs. Unstable jobs are also characterised by low pay, whereas stable jobs typically have high pay. There is little mobility across the boundary between these two sectors, and, finally, primary sector jobs are generally tied into long promotional ladders, unlike secondary jobs (Barron and Norris, 1976, page 49).

Barron and Norris suggest that the structure of the labour market is a consequence of, first, attempts by employers to retain workers whose skills they need, and second, an attempt by employers to buy off the best-organised workers. So, on the one hand, it is a consequence of directly economic factors which make employers seek to retain those key workers who have skills that the employer would find hard to replace; and, on the other, a result of political and organisational factors which make the employer seek to structure the work force in a hierarchical manner in order to control the work force.

Barron and Norris argue that secondary jobs are primarily occupied by women, if pay is taken as evidence of the secondary status of a job. Barron and Norris suggest that women are primarily secondary workers because of five characteristics: dispensability, clearly visible social difference, little interest in acquiring training, low economism, and lack of solidarity. These characteristics are partially the result of the individual's labour-market experience and partly the result of aspects of the social structure outside the labour market. Barron and Norris are keen to point out the distinction between the characteristics an individual possesses independently of the labour market and those that they acquire as a result of labour-market experiences. They argue that it is often incorrectly supposed that a person's labour-market attributes are a consequence solely of themselves rather than merely of the slots they have occupied in the labour market. It would appear that employers hold unsubstantiated beliefs that women possess these five characteristics of secondary workers. Employers perceive women as conventionally set apart from men and with less commitment to advancement at work because of women's orientation to their domestic situation and as a result of their socialisation. Women are seen as reluctant to struggle to obtain, or even to seek, high monetary rewards. Thus the characteristics of women at work are seen to fit with those required from secondary rather than primary workers.

This approach has come under criticism for overemphasising the importance of labour-market processes at the expense of a proper consideration of the underlying relations. For instance, Beechey (1978) argues that labour-market processes are not very important. She argues that we should concentrate our efforts on the relations of production rather than on the workings of the market. She suggests that in practice this is what Barron and Norris come back to in their argument. She says that four out of their five reasons why women constitute the secondary part of the labour force are to do with factors external to the labour market. Hence she says the labour market is not important to the analysis of the position that women hold in paid work. I shall come back to this debate later.

A major problem with Barron and Norris's analysis is, ironically, their lack of appreciation of, and analysis of, patriarchal structures in the labour market. Despite their emphasis on the importance of the labour market, much of their article is taken up with merely a description of the characteristics that women bring, or are believed by employers to bring, to the labour market. They describe the structuring of the labour market into two sectors in non-gender-specific terms and, I would suggest, mistakenly ignore the structuring of the market by sexual divisions (compare Murgatroyd, chapter 7 above). They treat sexual differentiation as determined largely outside the labour market in the sexual division of labour in the household. It is then incorrectly treated as a given which is unmodified by the workings of the labour market. There are two ways in which they approach the problem of patriarchal structures, but fail to complete their analysis. The most important is the discussion of women's supposed lack of solidarism. This is always seen in terms of women not managing to organise; never in terms of men being organised against women in the labour market. The nearest they get to men being an opposing force is to suggest that male trade unionists do not assist women trade unionists, to the point of being obstructive. They never mention men actively organising against women, although I would argue this is very important (see my chapter 9 below; Andrews, 1918; Braybon, 1981; Hartmann, 1979a; Oakley, 1976; Scharf, 1980). Barron and Norris do refer to general attitudes of hositility to women working, both in general and in relation to particular jobs, but this is seen as relatively diffuse rather, than as I would suggest is the case, as politically organised. In fact much of their article is about attitudes; it refers to ideological intervention in the labour market more than to political and organisational interventions. I would argue that they are mistaken to see patriarchal intervention in the labour market as so confined to the level of ideology.

8.3.2 Other forms of segmentation

Another problem with Barron and Norris's work is to be found in the incorrect assumption that the primary and secondary division in the labour market extends across all jobs in the United Kingdom. For instance, clerical work does not fit into this division very well. Rather it seems more appropriate to limit this division to manual jobs in manufacturing, for which it was originally developed. I would suggest that 'dualism' is not the best way to characterise the institutional rigidities of the labour market, although it is clearly an advance on the traditional neoclassical model of a smooth, open, and competitive labour market. Other writers have suggested a variety of alternative approaches, such as the internal labour market (for example, Doeringer and Piore, 1971); segmentation into several parts (for instance, Edwards et al, 1975; Loveridge and Mok, 1979); and occupations (Hakim, 1978; 1979). On the one hand, Bosanquet and Doeringer (1973) suggest that there is a distinction between open and structured labour markets in the United Kingdom. On the other hand, Mackay et al (1971), in a study of 75000 manual workers in sixty-six UK engineering plants, suggested that there was not a significant distinction between the two and that there was not an easier route to promotion through internal ladders. However, Mackay's analysis was for a seven-year period only, which might have been too short a period to pick up the effects of labour-market structures on individual career mobility. Sloane (1980) suggests that the empirical evidence is inconclusive, although he notes that most studies are confined to male workers and do not take sexual divisions into account.

Further support for my argument that Barron and Norris's division of the labour market into primary and secondary sections is too crude comes from Hakim's (1978; 1979) analysis of horizontal and vertical segregation of occupations by sex. She suggests that horizontal occupational segregation occurs when men and women work in different types of occupations, and vertical segregation when men are working in higher grade occupations than women. She argues that, in the United Kingdom during the twentieth century, horizontal segregation has slightly declined, with men entering occupations which were previously exclusively female, while women have not entered male-dominated occupations to the same extent. Vertical segregation, on the other hand, has increased during the twentieth century, with women being increasingly concentrated in the least-skilled jobs.

Hakim does not consider the division between full-time and part-time jobs to be pertinent to the forms of occupational segregation. She argues that, since part-time workers are distributed across the majority of occupations, it is not a significant factor in occupational segregation. Although this is a correct statement, it should be noted that Hakim has seriously limited the import of her analysis by confining herself to looking at very particular forms of occupational segregation and by omitting to consider other types of labour-market structures which act as barriers to women's advancement in paid work. Hakim discusses in detail the formidable methodological problems entailed in such an analysis, especially the difficulties of consistent occupational classification, rather than attempting an explanation of these changes and lack of changes. Thus we are still left with questions as to the nature of the barriers to the movement of women and men into different occupations.

Other writers have also suggested the need to take into account more divisions than that between primary and secondary and have characterised the labour market as 'segmented' rather than 'dualistic' (Edwards et al, 1975) or as composed of a 'vertical mosaic' (Kreckel, 1980). One major division between labour-market theorists is whether the divisions are seen to be based on skill, such as employers' attempts to keep workers who have learned valuable firm-specific skills (for instance, Doeringer and Piore, 1971), and those who see the segmentation based on power struggles between different groups (Edwards et al, 1975; Gordon, 1972; Rubery, 1978). The latter group of radical labour-market theorists can be differentiated again according to whether gender divisions are seen as by-products of struggles between capital and labour (Humphries, 1977; 1981), or whether they are seen as a central feature of analysis (Hartmann, 1979a), or whether indeed, they are effectively ignored altogether (Kreckel, 1980). Still others (Edwards, 1979) see sexism as being somewhat independent of capitalism, although Edwards does not follow his analysis through.

Hartmann (1979a) argues that the attempts to exclude women from certain occupations were a deliberate attempt by male workers to better their own position at the expense of female workers. Hartmann argues that a patriarchal division of labour existed long before the advent of capitalism. This division of labour was perpetuated, however, by male workers in industrial capitalism and exploited by capitalist employers for their own benefit. The most important aspect of this process for Hartmann was the active organisation of male workers seeking to exclude women workers from their trades. Hartmann substantiates her argument with a considerable amount of historically detailed information, about both the USA and the UK, during the nineteenth and early-twentieth centuries. She describes the movement to restrict the hours that women

were able to work in factories, quoting from their proponents' stated
views about the place of women being in the home. Her evidence about
the USA concentrates on cigarmaking and the Cigarmakers International
Union and on the case of printing and the National Typographical Union.
Thus she argues that the organisation of male workers has been instrumental
in the exclusion of women from many sectors of skilled work. She is not
specifically concerned with unemployment, though we might presume
that expelling women from paid work would have the immediate effect of
raising unemployment among women.

Humphries (1977) argues that the pressures on women to withdraw
from paid work were not the result of a division of interests between male
and female workers. She argues that this was merely a differentiation of
tasks which was in the interests of the working class as a whole in its
struggle against capital. She has argued this in relation to at least two
examples drawn from nineteenth-century UK history: the family wage
(Humphries, 1977) and the 1842 Mines Act (Humphries, 1981). The
alternative to paid employment is not seen as unemployment, however,
but rather greater involvement with unpaid domestic work.

Kreckel (1980) attempts to pull together the writings on the labour
market and to relate them to structured social inequality. He reviews the
literature and, after determining that the main asymmetry is between
capital and labour, arrives at a typology of eight levels of labour-market
structuration based on five strategies of closure of labour submarkets. His
five strategies are demarcation or horizontal divisions; exclusion, which is
directed against potential competitors; solidarism, which is pressure
upwards against a more privileged group; inclusion, which is a process of
encirclement of skilled workers by employers; and, last, exposure, which
is the employers' strategy of removing any protection the workers might
have against the pressures of the open market of supply and demand. The
eight submarkets for labour which stem from these forms of closure are,
first, that of workers who are criminalised and have no legal rights, such
as illegal immigrants; second, that of marginal and stigmatised unskilled
or dequalified workers; third, 'normal' unskilled workers; fourth,
specialised or semiskilled workers; fifth, submarkets for general
occupational qualifications threatened by devaluation; sixth, submarkets
for general occupational qualifications which are in demand; seventh,
submarkets for revalued qualifications; and eighth, those with academic,
managerial, and professional qualifications who are able both to make
themselves indispensable and to keep alternative options open. Kreckel
can be considered more sophisticated than other writers on labour markets
both in that he recognises the complexity of the organisational strategies
which are available to workers and employers and in his attempts to
systematise these. However, his lack of explicit consideration of gender
divisions, given their importance in the organisation of the labour market,

is a problem for his own terms of reference. For instance, the 'horizontal' occupational segregation of the sexes that Hakim describes is not neutral for the relations between the sexes in the way his concept 'demarcation' (which is the nearest one) would suggest. Another limitation with Kreckel's schema is that it is concerned only with divisions between labour submarkets and not with the boundary between paid work and unemployment or between paid work and housework. Unemployment is not a matter of bumping down the job hierarchy and falling out at the bottom (although more people in the bottom categories do become unemployed). There are institutionalised practices for ejecting people from paid work, and Kreckel like many other labour-market analysts has not really looked at these and how they differentially affect different social groups. The boundaries around the labour market are as important for gender divisions as are barriers within it.

8.3.3 Occupational segregation

Some labour-market theorists have noted the defects of theories of women as a reserve army of labour which do not take labour-market structures into account (Bruegel, 1979; Connelly, 1978; Milkman, 1976; OECD, 1976). The most important of the labour-market structures noted by these writers is that by which the sexes tend to be segregated into different occupations. These writers suggest that occupational segregation has protected women from higher rates of unemployment, thus negating the tendency for women to be pushed out of paid employment in recessions more than men. They argue that women are protected during recessions from worse unemployment rates than men by their location in the service industries, which are less affected by unemployment than manufacturing industries in which more men are concentrated. The OECD produced evidence in support of this thesis to explain women's lower rate of unemployment than men during the 1974–1975 recession among OECD member countries. Milkman has argued this same thesis in relation to the 1930s depression in the USA. Milkman suggests that women were concentrated in the low-unemployment service sector. However, the data she presents from the 1930 Census show that women's unemployment rates were lower than men's in almost all occupations, and this does not support her argument. So the examination of the occupational distribution of women is not significant for women's lower rate of unemployment. The overall lower rate remains in need of explanation, and Milkman's suggestion that occupational segregation is an important factor is not, in this instance, of much importance.

  Indeed, Bergmann (1980a; 1980b) has argued that sex-segregation in employment is the cause of consistently higher rates of unemployment among women than men in the postwar period in the USA. Bergmann argues that women are more likely to be unemployed than men because they are crowded into a small number of occupations which do not provide sufficient employment for the number of women who seek it.

Men, however, are able to enter a greater number of occupations proportionate to their number and hence do not suffer such high unemployment as women. She suggests that women are confined in this way as a consequence of the hiring practices of employers. She argues that employers discriminate against women in certain occupations, thus preventing their entry. She goes on to suggest that, although the number of women seeking paid employment in the postwar period in the USA has substantially increased relative to the number of men, the number of occupations to which women are allowed entry has not increased. However, Bergmann provides no explanation as to why employers should discriminate against female workers, except to hint that it is part of a wider attempt by men to control women. Neither does she provide any substantiation of her assertion that it is employers alone who act to prevent women's entry to certain jobs in opposition to their interests in employing women who could be paid lower wages than men. I would suggest that her failure to consider the interests and actions of male workers is a serious omission in her analysis.

Bruegel (1979) has also looked at the question of whether the concentration of women in the service sector protected women from becoming an unemployed reserve army during the recession of the mid-1970s in the UK. She suggests that, at the level of the entire economy, women's concentration in services did protect women's employment as a whole from higher rates of unemployment. However, she argues that a different and more complex picture emerges if the figures are disaggregated further. She suggests that individually women are more vulnerable to redundancy than are men in similar circumstances, whereas collectively women's employment does not suffer as much as men's. Thus she suggests that, in manufacturing, women lose their jobs proportionately more than men, in a manner which fits the reserve army thesis. She suggests it is useful to differentiate between full-time and part-time women workers. It is predominantly part-time workers who have lost their jobs, rather than full-time workers, and part-time workers are usually married women. It is then part-time married women workers whose employment fluctuations most fit the reserve army model. However, Bruegel's analysis, though a much needed testing of the reserve army theory against empirical evidence, is limited by the fact that it does not go on to explain why part-time workers should be sacked first.

Connelly (1978) attempts to test the reserve army thesis against data from Canadian history. She suggests that three conditions must be met if the reserve army theory is to be confirmed: that women are cheap labour; that women are available labour; and that women provide a source of competition with other workers. Connelly is easily able to show that the first two conditions hold in twentieth century Canada. She notes that the existence of occupational segregation might be held to preclude the possibility that women could be a source of competition which would affect the conditions of employment of male workers, since women would not be directly competing with men for jobs. However, she argues that there is competition, but that this is indirect. It exists because there is the possibility of reclassification of male jobs as female jobs under pressure from female competition. However, although this last point is very important, Connelly is not able to muster more than one anecdotal piece of evidence in its support. Thus, I would suggest, her confirmation of the reserve army theory must be somewhat in doubt.

Rubery and Tarling (1982), on the basis of a statistical analysis of unemployment rates, argue that women have not been a reserve army of labour in postwar Europe. They suggest that this is partly because employers prefer to employ women for certain jobs, since they can be paid lower wages and given worse conditions of employment than men, and partly because of occupational segregation. However, their analysis of job segregation is rather inadequate. They refer to it as "traditional" (1982, page 150), with only passing reference to "historical, social or technological reasons" for the exclusion of women from certain paid jobs (page 54). I would suggest that this incorrectly ignores patriarchal organisation in the labour market, which is a highly significant force for the sexual segregation of the work force.

8.4 Conclusion
I have argued that the level of women's unemployment vis-à-vis men's cannot be understood without an analysis of patriarchal as well as capitalist relations and of the articulation of the two. Most existing attempts to analyse women's unemployment and employment have focused almost entirely upon capitalist relations and the workings of the market. The existence of systematic attempts by men to protect their paid jobs at the expense of women tends to be underplayed, if not ignored, in these analyses (for instance, see Beechey, 1977; 1978; Bruegel, 1979; Connelly, 1978; Gardiner, 1975; Mincer, 1962; 1966; Rubery and Tarling, 1982).

As I have shown, many of these existing debates, both within neo-Marxian and neoclassical economics, on changes in women's employment focus upon the question of whether women constitute a reserve army of labour. Though Beechey (1977; 1978), Braverman (1974), McIntosh (1978), and Connelly (1978), drawing on Marx's analysis of the industrial reserve army, presumed that the overriding importance of capital and family structure would lead to women being used in this way, Milkman (1976), Bruegel (1979), the OECD (1976), and Rubery and Tarling (1982) have stressed the importance of occupational segregation and other factors which seriously qualify the thesis. Mincer (1962; 1966) argued that married women were secondary workers who participated in paid work only when booms in the economy made it particularly worthwhile. At other times, he suggested, they would have other activities to perform in the household. Milkman (1976), however, argued that occupational segregation was too rigid to allow the substitution of women for men, or vice versa, and that women's employment was thereby protected in the recession of the 1930s in the USA. Similarly, Rubery and Tarling (1982) argue that women have not functioned as a reserve army of labour in postwar Europe, but more as a consequence of employers preferring to employ women who can be paid lower wages and given worse conditions of employment than men because of occupational segregation.

These divergences in the employment and unemployment of men and women are generally seen as an effect of the capitalist organisation of production. Very little attention is paid to the noncapitalist patriarchal causes of horizontal and vertical occupational segregation. Furthermore, some of these accounts have limited appreciation of historical and spatial variation. The temporal dimension is quite often restricted to a notion of fluctuations around an equilibrium point (see especially Beechey, 1977; McIntosh, 1978; Mincer, 1966), although some attention has been paid to twentieth-century increases in women's paid employment (see Braverman, 1974; Mincer, 1962), whereas those of Connelly (1978), Milkman (1976), and Rubery and Tarling (1982) contain quite sophisticated analyses of particular conjunctures. The spatial dimension is more lacking and, though crossnational comparisons of women's unemployment have been attempted by OECD (1976), Rubery and Tarling (1982), and Walby (1983b), there is little analysis at the subnational level.

Many of those few existing writings which do examine the relation between patriarchy (or gender inequality) and the capitalist mode of production assume that there is a harmonious articulation between the two. It is a common presumption that capital benefits from the subordination of women by men and that men utilise capitalist relations in the subordination of women. This model of a neat fit between the interests of capitalists and men underlies many of the discussions on the use of women as a reserve of labour. Here the subordinated position of women on the periphery of the labour market is held to benefit capitalists, whereas the temporary nature of women's participation in paid work prevents such employment from undermining gender inequality in the family. I would argue that this position underestimates the conflict between patriarchy and the capitalist mode of production and presents an inaccurate picture of historical stasis. Rather, the relations between patriarchy and capital should be seen as historically and spatially variable and riddled with conflict.

In this chapter, I have sought to isolate the strengths and weaknesses of existing theorisations of gender relations in employment and unemployment; in the next one, I will attempt to apply the conclusions arrived at to spatial and historical variations in women's unemployment and employment in the United Kingdom.

Spatial and historical variations in women's unemployment and employment

Sylvia Walby

9.1 Introduction

The wide spatial and historical variations in women's unemployment pose questions both for the analysis of gender relations and for regional studies. The ratio of women's to men's unemployment rate varied by degrees from 0.7 to 1.7 in the United Kingdom in 1979, and has varied from 0.7 to 1.3 in the United Kingdom as a whole between 1973 and 1981 (see table 9.1).

In this chapter, I shall argue that gender differences in rates of unemployment are the result of three processes. First, there are different rates of decline of employment in industries and occupations in which different sexes predominate. If male-typed forms of employment decline at different rates than female-typed forms, then this produces different rates of employment loss for each sex and differential unemployment rates. Second, there is the ejection of one sex more than the other from any particular type of employment. Historically, this has been seen in instances of well-organised men making women bear a disproportionate amount of employment loss. Third, there is the possibility of uneven

Table 9.1. Unemployment rates and ratios of female to male unemployment rates by region, 1973–1981 (sources: calculated from Eurostat, 1980, table VII/3; 1981, table 60; OPCS, 1982, table 4.16).

Region	Year[a]				
	1973	1975	1977	1979	1981
North	3.6(0.3)	6.3(0.9)	6.2(1.0)	8.1(0.9)	12.2
Yorkshire and Humberside	2.2(0.7)	4.5(1.5)	4.2(0.9)	5.6(1.5)	9.8
North West	2.8(0.5)	5.1(0.9)	5.4(0.8)	4.3(1.2)	11.8
East Midlands	1.7(0.7)	4.4(1.4)	3.8(0.9)	4.1(1.6)	8.7
West Midlands	1.7(0.9)	4.0(1.4)	4.5(0.9)	3.5(1.3)	12.7
East Anglia	1.1(1.1)	4.0(1.5)	4.5(1.1)	4.7(1.7)	8.7
South East	1.3(1.0)	3.7(1.4)	3.8(1.0)	4.9(1.6)	7.0
South West	1.9(0.7)	5.4(1.3)	4.0(0.9)	6.3(1.4)	7.0
Wales	2.1(0.5)	5.1(1.3)	4.8(0.8)	6.5(1.4)	11.7
Scotland	3.7(0.9)	5.5(1.2)	6.5(0.8)	7.2(1.2)	12.0
Northern Ireland	4.6(0.8)	7.1(1.4)	8.5(0.9)	8.6(0.7)	15.4
United Kingdom	2.1(0.7)	4.6(1.2)	4.7(0.9)	5.2(1.3)	0.7(0.9)

[a]Numbers represent total unemployment rates (%); those in brackets the ratio of female to male unemployment rates.

rates of increase in employment for women and men. All three processes were operating historically and indeed today, and they should be seen as interrelated though distinct processes. When women's conditions of employment are depressed beneath those of men by patriarchal forces, it is to be expected that employers developing new products will endeavour to devise forms of labour process and locational policies to take advantage of women's labour. The restructuring of gender relations takes place in the context both of patriarchal and of capitalist struggles. In this chapter, I trace the historical and spatial variations in these processes. I draw on the theoretical arguments developed in the preceding chapter and apply them to concrete historical and spatial events. Current patterns of gender rates of unemployment must be seen as the result of the accumulation of rounds of restructuring of gender relations.

9.2 Patriarchy and capital

Many existing writings which do examine the relation between patriarchy and capitalism, or between gender inequality and capitalism, assume that there is a harmonious articulation between the two. It is a common presumption that capital benefits from the subordination of women by men and that men utilise capitalist relations in the subordination of women. This model of a neat fit between capital and gender inequality underlies many of the discussions on the use of women as a reserve of labour. Here the subordinated position of women on the periphery of the labour market is held to benefit capital, and the temporary nature of women's participation in paid work prevents such employment from undermining gender inequality in the family.

I intend to argue that this position underestimates the conflict between patriarchy and capital and presents an inaccurate picture of historical stasis. Rather, the relations between patriarchy and capital should be seen as historically and spatially variable and riddled with conflict.

The most important basis of this tension lies in rival interests in the exploitation of women's labour. Patriarchal relations depress the level of wages that women are able to command in the labour market. This makes women's labour particularly attractive to employers looking for cheap unskilled labour. This can threaten to undercut men's wages and could lead to the employment of women and the unemployment of men. This would threaten that base of patriarchal power which lies in women's subordination in the family to a male wage earner. Historically, tendencies for women's paid employment to grow at the expense of that of men have usually been met by a political reaction from patriarchal forces which have restored the status ante. Patriarchal power in a capitalist society thus depends upon restricting women's access to paid work. This has been partially achieved, although with historical and spatial variations. The consequences of these patriarchal struggles have been on occasions the rise of unemployment among women rather than men and the forcing of women back into domestic relations. The actual struggles can only be understood in the context of both disputes, within capitalist relations over the level of the wage as well as within this patriarchal context. Organised male labour is simultaneously fighting upwards against capital and downwards against women. These struggles have structured women's access to paid employment and consequently to unemployment for the last couple of centuries, and so have played a part in structuring the contemporary situation in women's unemployment.

9.3 Regionalism and gender relations

Most of the existing regionalism literature is unsatisfactory in its approach to gender relations. Though some analyses note the differentiation of female and male wage labour and its effects, this is rarely developed, and others ignore gender altogether. So although such analyses are not always totally blind to gender relations, this is rarely treated as a serious issue. The focus of analyses on capital–labour relations has tended to preclude any understanding of the connections between different aspects of gender relations. Gender relations tend to be introduced into the analysis in a relatively ad hoc manner, rather than being systematically analysed. Some writers have noted the typical differences in wages and job security that women and men workers are able to command (for instance, Donnison and Soto, 1980; Gregory, 1980; Marquand, 1980; Massey, 1978a; 1978b; Massey and Meegan, 1982; Urry, 1981b; 1982). These differences between men and women are usually treated in isolation from other aspects of gender relations and with little analysis of their causation. So though these analyses note that new forms of employment which are low waged, insecure, and in the service sector are taken primarily by women, there is little explanation of why women should take these jobs rather than men, or even why there is such a pool of female labour available. The analyses thus implicitly assume that the determination of these occurrences lies outside their field of study; that is, that women are constituted as workers with few skills and prepared to work for lower wages in a relatively timeless sort of way. Even the varying increase in women's participation in paid work since World War 2 usually calls forth little more than descriptive acknowledgement (compare Donnison and Soto, 1980, chapter 5). There are limits to these analyses, in that the causation of women's disadvantaged labour-market position is sited in the family and outside the field of vision of regionalist analyses as a consequence of the assumed unvarying spatial and historical functioning of the family under capitalism. The problem with many of these analyses is a lack of an understanding of patriarchal relations.

9.4 Rounds of restructuring of gender relations

I shall argue for the necessity of a historical dimension in any explanation of spatial variations in female activity rates. Current patterns are in some

ways continuations and accumulation of patterns which were fixed at
earlier times. The ratio of female to male employment in any particular
industry is remarkably constant through time. Thus an explanation of
female/male ratios of employment in any industry must examine the point
at which that industry developed and its particular sex ratio of employment
was fixed. Current employment patterns for women can be seen as the
result of the accumulation of one pattern on top of another. Spatial
variations in women's employment are then the outcome of the spatial
distribution of different industries which developed and had their sex
ratios fixed at previous points in time. It is the accumulation of these
rounds of gender restructuring that leads to distinctive spatial patterns of
women's employment and unemployment (compare Massey, 1978a).

9.5 Methodological issues

The definition and measurement of women's unemployment present
difficult and important questions. In addition to the general problems
surrounding the definition and measurement of unemployment, there is
the issue of where and how to draw the line betweem married women
whose position as housewives conventionally precludes them from the
status of unemployed and that of married women without paid jobs who
are actively seeking one. Though it is assumed that men of working age
will be unemployed if they do not have a paid job (apart from the sick,
the early retired, and those in education), women have a third major
status open to them: as housewife. Indeed some conceptual schemata of
women's economic activity discussed earlier suggest that married women
move between paid work and housework and do not become unemployed
on the loss of a *paid* job (for example, Mincer, 1962; 1966). These
models provide next-to-no conceptual space for the possibility of
unemployed married women. They tend to do this in two ways. First,
they confuse the existence of tasks to do in the home with the lack of
availability for paid work. However, since most married women do
considerable amounts of housework while having a paid job, there is no
logical reason why this should necessarily preclude their readiness to take
paid work if this were to be available. Second, it is sometimes assumed
that women's financial position with a husband to 'support' her precludes
her from the possible status of unemployed. These assumptions are built
into social policy and make the identification of the actual level of
women's unemployment through time and space very difficult.

In the United Kingdom the official measure of unemployment is based
on the number of unemployed people who register for both work and
benefit. The level of women's unemployment indicated by these official
statistics of those so registered significantly undercounts the number of
women who are unemployed. Many married women are not elegible to
claim unemployment benefit because of an insufficient national insurance
contribution record, and are prohibited from claiming social security in

their own right, as indeed is any woman cohabiting with a man. Thus official unemployment figures for women cannot be reliably used in any research. Historical research based on trade union records of the unemployed undercount both sexes, but especially women, since women were less likely to be members of unions and thus less likely to report as unemployed in order to claim any benefit.

Many countries, including the USA, gather the data for unemployment statistics through a regular sample survey. The UK Census, with a 100% sample and the longest historical reach of the surveys, might have been considered an ideal source of information on women's unemployment in the United Kingdom. However, it too seriously undercounts unemployed women, for instance, in 1961 returning less married women as unemployed than did even the Ministry of Labour figures on registered unemployed. The most likely explanation is that unemployed married women are often entered as 'housewife' on the Census form by the 'head of household' who sought to enhance his own status thereby. The more detailed questions of the General Household Survey makes its figures on women's unemployment more reliable. However, its sample size is too small to allow any satisfactory analysis of regional variations and, since the first survey was not conducted till 1971, the time span is seriously limited.

The EEC Labour Force Survey does provide a figure for women's unemployment on a regional basis. However, since the Survey was not conducted in the United Kingdom until 1973, and is carried out only biennially, the historical dimension is rather limited. Nevertheless it is the best available source.

However, survey methods of measuring unemployment do have a problem in that they rely upon self-definitions as unemployed and these are open to a range of interpretations. For instance, people who would take a job if one were offered, but do not actively search for one because they do not expect to find one, may be omitted. These 'discouraged workers', who are not actively seeking work, would probably not appear in the General Household Survey as unemployed, since it asks questions about job-*seeking* activities. However, such 'discouraged workers' are undoubtedly part of a labour reserve. Research from the USA (Shiskin, 1976) suggests that a higher proportion of women than men fall into this category of 'discouraged workers'. However, even surveys which ask about discouraged workers may underestimate the number of people actually prepared to take a job if one presented itself (see Swedish evidence in OECD, 1976; also see Finegan, 1981). That is, people who do not consider themselves as seeking work may nonetheless take paid work if it suddenly became available. Thus the use of self-definitions of unemployment may lead to an underestimate in the size of the labour reserve. We see here the difference between the concepts of 'the unemployed' and 'the labour reserve'.

An alternative to using measures of unemployment is to analyse variations in levels of employment instead (compare Bruegel, 1979; Shiskin, 1976). Figures on employment are much more reliable and are available over a longer time span and with accurate regional rates. It can be argued that any fall from an employment peak indicates an equivalent increase in labour reserve and thus that regional variations in female employment indicate inverse regional variations in unutilised women's labour.

Where data on women's unemployment are missing, then the best procedure available is to use data on women's employment and to analyse drops in these data as representing equivalent increases in women's unemployment (and regional rates beneath the national average similarly). This may or may not be self-defined unemployment, but at a minimum it must be considered a reserve of female labour available for paid work. A reserve of labour here differs from conventional definitions of unemployment, primarily in that it does not require subjective definitions of unemployment by those involved, whereas the latter does.

9.6 Regional variations in women's activity rates

Although there has been little attempt to analyse spatial variations in women's unemployment, there have been some attempts to explain spatial variations in women's activity rates. Industrial structure appears to be the most important factor correlating with women's activity rates. Bowers (1970) demonstrates that almost all the regional variation in women's activity rates in 1961 and regional changes in women's activity rates during the period 1954–1964 could be accounted for by regional variations in industrial structure. A secondary effect was that a region with an industrial structure conducive to female employment was likely to have an even higher rate of female activity. Bowers attributed this to a demonstration effect and also to the increased likelihood of support facilities for women in paid work. Allin (1982) also points both to the significance of industrial structure in explaining variations in female activity rates and to a similar secondary effect. However, along the lines of Enersley and Gales, he argues that a 'tradition' of paid work is the most important correlate, even more significant than current industrial structure. Elias and Molho (1982) argue that the most important impact on women's rising participation rates in the period 1968–1977 was the rise in real earnings, rather than changes in the number of children, or changes in the rate of husbands' unemployment. However, they did not analyse changes in industrial structure. The rise in real earnings might in fact be a consequence of a change in industrial structure which involves an increase in job opportunities for women and offers relatively high wages to attract women.

These studies are limited by their discussion of little other than correlations. These surface phenomena are treated as the causes of variations in women's activity rates in classic positivist manner. There is little attempt to identify the structures which generate such correlations. It is the identification of these structures and their interrelationships that are needed for an adequate explanation.

A major issue that is little discussed by these writers is why industries have a particular ratio of female to male employment and why this is relatively fixed over time. Unless this question is answered, it explains little to say that regional variations in female activity rates are accounted for by the industrial structure of that region. Allin's (1982) use of the notion of tradition begs more questions than it answers. The fixation of certain patterns of female economic activity at one point in space through time requires explanation, as does the original patterning.

9.7 Sex-typing of industries
The fixing of the sex ratio of employment in an industry is thus of crucial importance to the questions under consideration. The availability of different types and sex of labour available at that moment is one of the relevant factors. Davies (1979), for instance, argues that the large number of literate women available at the turn of the century, who were barred from entering the professions because they were women, was a crucial factor in the sex-typing of the newly expanding clerical sector as female. In this situation the supply of and demand for female labour appeared to enable the change of clerical work from a small male-dominated occupation to a large female-dominated occupation to occur with very little, if any, social struggle. A very different situation occurred in the development of the medical profession as a male preserve (Ehrenreich and English, 1979; Oakley, 1976). Here there was a prolonged struggle in the political arena between female lay healers and male professionals over the monopolisation of this developing and increasingly lucrative occupation. These two diametrically opposed examples of sex-typing illustrate some of the wide range of possibilities in the changing of sex-typing of occupations. A complete account of the current spatial configuration of women's employment would demand a comprehensive analysis of the sex-typing of every major industrial sector. Though the constraints of time and space obviously make that impossible, a brief sketch of some of the more important contours of women's employment will be attempted (compare Walby, 1983a).

9.7.1 Nineteenth-century textiles
Textiles was one of the first areas of production to be organised under capitalist relations. A high proportion of these textile workers were female, and this continues, with the consequence of high female activity rates in textile towns (Donnison and Soto, 1980) and in the North West.

Women were employed because of the relative cheapness of their labour despite opposition from male operatives and bourgeois philanthropists (Hewitt, 1958; Pinchbeck, 1981; Smelser, 1959). The legislation in the second half of the nineteenth century which restricted the hours of work of adult women and children appeared to stem the influx of women into the mills (Smelser, 1959). The struggle over the factory legislation should be seen as a struggle between patriarchal forces attempting to restrict women's access to paid work and capitalist forces seeking to utilise cheap female labour (for a fuller account, see Walby, 1983c). Nevertheless, the textile industry has employed a relatively high proportion of women workers throughout its history, and these have been spatially concentrated.

9.7.2 Nineteenth-century mining

Mining is currently an almost all-male industry, with consequent depressive effects on female activity rates in the areas where and when it has been a major employer (such as South Wales till very recently). Though it might be assumed that there are certain features of mining which 'naturally' suit it in some way to male workers, the history of its sex-typing shows rather that it is the outcome of particular social processes. Before 1842, women did work in the mines, typically hauling the coal up narrow passages to the surface. The underground working of women in mines was prohibited by the 1842 Mines Act, with consequent unemployment for the women who had been so employed. The unusually low female economic activity in mining areas must be seen as equivalent to high rates of female unemployment which are a result of this legislation. The legislation was passed during a wave of a 'moral panic' about naked and seminaked men and women working together in darkness. It was the outcome of the concern of patriarchal interests in the maintenance of a specific type of gender relations. It was the first of the nineteenth-century Acts to limit the access of adult women to paid work, but was rapidly followed by legislation restricting the hours worked by adult women in textile mills. Together these Acts of Parliament should be seen as attempts both to shore up a patriarchal family structure by limiting women's access to particular sorts of paid work and to reestablish patriarchal relations in paid work in the face of opposition from employers who wanted cheap female labour. The limitation of women's access to paid work logically increases the likelihood of women rather than men being unemployed. The application of those restrictions to some industries and not others (sweated needlework, for instance; see Alexander, 1976; Scott and Tilly, 1980) in the context of spatial variations in the location of those industries produces an uneven spatial distribution of women's lack of access to paid employment.

9.7.3 The interwar depression

The depression of the interwar period saw further conflict of interests between patriarchy and capital. The decline in the number of jobs led to increased competition for those which remained and renewed attempts by patriarchal forces to claim priority for men for the jobs which did exist (Lewenhak, 1977). The reserve army model would predict a drop in female employment. However, female employment remained more or less constant between 1921 and 1931 (UK Censuses of 1921 and 1931; see OPCS various). It is clear that patriarchal forces were not successful in prioritising men's claims to employment over women in the first part of the depression over the economy as a whole. However, there were significant variations between industries, occupations, and regions (see tables 9.2 and 9.3). For instance, although the South East had an increase of 2.6% in its female activity rate, the North West had a decrease of 1.5%. These regional changes appear to be partly the result of the growth and decline of employment in specific industries. Thus textile employment for women showed a significant decrease and this was concentrated in the North West, whereas the growth of the personal service sector, commerce and finance, and the professions was concentrated in the South East (Lee, 1979).

However, there was a further gender-related aspect to this restructuring. In the declining occupations the percentage decrease in women's employment was usually greater than that of men's, whereas in the expanding occupations women's employment increased more rapidly than did that of men (see table 9.4). So although women were being expelled from declining occupations more rapidly than men, they were drawn more rapidly into the growing ones. Women were not ejected from the work force during this part of the depression, but their position in it was substantially restructured. This suggests that there were occupational and regional variations in the strength of patriarchal organisation. Male workers were organised in trade unions more in the traditional occupations which were declining than in the newly expanding occupations (Lewenhak, 1977). It would appear that in the occupations, and hence regions, where male-dominated trade unions were strong, women were more likely to be ejected from paid work and hence to become unemployed than in jobs and places where they were not so well organised.

Table 9.2. Changes in women's employment by industry, 1921–1931 (source: calculated from industry tables of the UK Censuses for 1921 and 1931; see OPCS, various).

Industry[a]	Change in women's employment	
	Numbers	%
Fishing	−229	−14.0
Agriculture	−29363	−34.4
Mining	−1667	−15.4
Bricks, pottery, and glass	310	+0.6
Chemicals and paints	−34	−0.1
Metal	13554	+5.5
Textiles	−106879	−16.1
Leather	1447	+6.5
Clothing	−7100	−1.4
Food, drink, and tobacco	6609	+3.3
Wood and furniture	3591	+14.8
Paper and publishing	14192	+11.2
Building	1328	+14.7
Other manual	−5422	−7.6
Gas, electricity, and water	2220	+48.3
Transport and communications	−606	−1.5
Commerce and finance	92215	+12.4
Public administration and defence	−351	−0.1
Professions	31450	+13.0
Entertainments and sport	7243	+17.7
Personal services	94720	+6.2
Other	−59162	−88.3
Total	+57647	1.1

[a]Categories have been adjusted, where necessary, to enable comparison across the two Censuses.

Table 9.3. Changes in women's employment, by region, 1921–1931 (source: calculated from Lee, 1979).

Region	Change in women's employment (%)
South East	2.6
East Anglia	0.9
South West	−0.7
West Midlands	1.0
East Midlands	0.9
North West	−1.5
Yorkshire and Humberside	−0.4
North	1.1
Wales	0.3
Scotland	1.3
Great Britain	−0.4

Table 9.4. Changes in men and women's employment, by industry, for England and Wales, 1921–1931 (source: calculated from occupation tables of the UK Censuses for England and Wales for 1921 and 1931; see OPCS, various).

Industry[a]	Change in employment (%)	
	Men	Women
Fishing	−6.5	−51.8
Agriculture	−4.7	−33.0
Mining	−9.0	−23.9
Mine products	−10.0	−36.1
Bricks, pottery, and glass	−21.8	−39.5
Chemicals and paints	−33.2	−73.1
Metal workers	−12.4	−11.9
Precious metals	−20.8	−24.4
Electrical apparatus	+29.4	+39.4
Watches and clocks	−14.4	−35.9
Leather	−16.1	+13.2
Textiles	−18.9	−5.0
Clothing	−4.1	−0.9
Food, drink, and tobacco	−13.2	−25.6
Wood and furniture	+0.8	−25.8
Paper and publishing	+12.6	−7.2
Construction	+37.5	−55.5
Painters and decorators	+27.5	+1160.6
Other materials	−9.7	−20.6
No comparison possible		
Gas, electricity, and water	+38.5	+3714.7
Transport and communications	+10.2	+8.4
Commerce and finance	+36.1	+21.9
Public administration and defence	−34.4	−96.0
Professions	+19.2	+7.4
Entertainments and sport	+36.2	−20.1
Personal services	+7.7	+14.9
Clerks and draughtsmen	+40.0	+35.0
Warehouse and packers	+14.7	+21.0
Stationery engine	+0.5	+20350.0
Other comparison not possible		

[a]Categories have been adjusted, where necessary, to enable comparisons across the two Censuses.

9.7.4 Postwar

The postwar period has seen a significant increase in the proportion of women in paid employment, rising from 26.9% in 1951 in Great Britain (Lee, 1979) to 33.4% in 1979 (Eurostat, 1981), which has only started to fall off since 1979. However, this overall increase of 6.5% hides wide regional variations, ranging from an increase of 10.8% between 1952 and 1979 in East Anglia to one of only 2.3% over the same period in the North West (see table 9.5).

There has been a narrowing of regional variations in women's employment rate, with the difference in percentage points between the highest and lowest employment regions in Great Britain falling from 13.0% in 1951 to 6.1% in 1979 (see table 9.6).

We may take the wide regional variations in the early 1950s as indicative of substantial hidden unemployment among women in the regions with low female employment rates, and the increase in these low rates as indicative of the reduction of women's unemployment in these areas.

Table 9.5. Changes in women's employment rate, by region, 1951–1979 (source: calculated from Census data in Lee, 1979, and in Eurostat, 1981).

Region	Change in women's employment (%)[a]
East Anglia	+10.8
North	+10.6
Wales	+10.2
South West	+10.1
Scotland	+8.3
East Midlands	+7.4
South East	+5.7
West Midlands	+5.2
Yorkshire and Humberside	+5.0
North West	+2.3

[a]This is the employment rate and not the activity rate, and therefore excludes the growth in 'unemployed' women.

Table 9.6. Women's employment rates, by region, 1951 and 1979. Source: 1951 figures calculated from Lee, 1979 (hence based on Census data); 1979 figures calculated from Eurostat, 1981, table 60, using the restricted labour force definition. The rates are calculated on a base of the total female population, not merely those of working age.

Region	Women's employment rates (%)	
	1951	1979
Wales	18.5	28.7
East Anglia	21.0	31.8
South West	21.7	31.8
North	21.2	41.8
Scotland	25.1	33.4
East Midlands	25.8	33.2
Yorkshire and Humberside	27.8	32.8
South East	28.9	34.6
West Midlands	29.6	34.8
North West	31.5	33.8
Northern Ireland		27.4
Great Britain	26.9	33.4
Range	13.0	6.1

There are two reasons for this narrowing of regional differences in female employment rates. First, there has been a relatively more even spatial distribution of the increase in some of the types of service sector jobs in which women predominate. For instance, health, education, and retailing became an increasingly important source of employment for women in all regions. Second, this convergence in regional employment rates for women is related to the overall changes in regional employment. The regions with the fastest growing employment (see table 9.7) are among the regions with the lowest rates of female employment at the beginning of the period (see table 9.6). Wales, East Anglia, and the South West had particularly low rates of female employment and have experienced above average rates of employment growth.

Table 9.7. Regional employment change, 1952–1979 (source: Fothergill and Gudgin, 1982, table 2.1).

Region	Employment change (%)
East Anglia	+43.5
South West	+29.6
Northern Ireland	+22.4
East Midlands	+21.0
South East	+14.4
Wales	+10.0
North	+9.4
West Midlands	+8.3
Yorkshire and Humberside	+5.8
Scotland	+1.5
North West	−5.2

9.7.5 The current recession

An understanding of women's unemployment and employment in the current recession requires an examination of the same three processes as were examined for the interwar depression. These were: the differential rate of job-loss among men and women in the same industries and occupations; the differential rate of employment decline in industries and occupations in which one sex or the other predominates; and last, the differential rate of increase in new employment opportunities for men and women.

The current recession and high levels of unemployment might have been expected to set off similar patriarchal pressures on women's employment as in the interwar depression. Yet, although there have been some similar statements from men advocating that married women should leave the labour market, there has not been such a direct attack on women's right to paid work as happened before. However, to conclude from this that a spirit of equality of the sexes reigns would be a mistake.

One of the recent developments in the structuring of the labour
market has led to the reduction in the disproportionate loss of jobs by
women without much explicit patriarchal action. The massive increase in
part-time work has served to differentiate a large number of women from
the rest of the work force in terms of job security. Part-time workers
lack many of the protections against dismissal that full-time workers now
have under recent legislation such as the Employment Protection Act.
They are often the first to go in a situation of job-loss, either through
wastage or through short contracts, or the first to be dismissed in a
redundancy. This differentiation and vulnerability of part-time jobs is
supported both by trade unions and by the state and is embodied in
various forms of legislation such as National Insurance as well as
Employment Protection. As Bruegel (1979) has noted, insofar as women
are used as a reserve army, it is part-time women workers who are made
to play the part. Part-time work only developed on a large scale during
World War 2, when it was introduced so as to get some war work out of
women whose domestic responsibilities it was thought prevented their
working full-time (Summerfield, 1984). It was a solution to the
government's dilemma of working to increase the availability of women
for war work while not disturbing the privatised domestic arrangements of
the reproduction of labour power by socialising the performance of this
work to any great extent. Part-time work represented the new form of
the compromise between patriarchal and capitalist interests. The expansion
of part-time work and the consolidation of the distinction between it and
full-time work during the postwar period saw the continuation of this
patriarchal and capitalist accommodation. Women's labour was made
available to capital, but on terms which did not threaten to disrupt the
patriarchal status quo. However, although part-time workers may be
individually more vulnerable to losing jobs than full-time workers, overall
their numbers have not rapidly diminished, because employers elsewhere
have created part-time jobs.

A further way in which women typically lose their jobs more easily
than men arises because of the particular forms of job-loss which may be
negotiated. Most forms of negotiated job-loss attempt to prioritise the
claims of the longest serving workers. The 'last-in first-out' selection
procedure in redundancy situations is the classic example of this, and
typically involves more women than men leaving at that time (Walby and
Green, 1982). Thus women may lose their jobs more often than men in
situations of job-loss, because of their vulnerability as part-time workers or
because of their lack of seniority or negotiating power.

The proportionate changes in employment for each sex in each industry
grouping has been remarkably even (see table 9.8). The only significant
differences are the greater decrease of female employment in 'other
manufacturing industries'; the greater decrease of male employment in
'construction' and 'transport and communications'; and the female

employment increase in 'distribution, hotels and catering, repairs'.
However, these are sufficient for the decrease in female employment to be
substantially less than the decrease in male employment. Thus although
some, for example, Huws (1982), have suggested that women are
particularly likely to lose their jobs because of the new technology, this
has not yet happened—at least in 1981.

Regional differences in changes in female activity rates are quite
marked as in the earlier postwar period (see table 9.9). Again those
regions which had the lowest female activity rates are among the ones
with the highest percentage increases during the period 1979–1981,
leading to a further diminution of the differences between regional female
activity rates, indicating an evening of employment openings for women.
Despite the problems women face in keeping hold of jobs, their overall
employment rate has not been affected by the recession as much as has
men's, falling by only 1% as compared with 6% for men. This further
indicates that it is newly developing areas of employment that are
important in protecting women from greater unemployment. The
evidence suggests that women are not substituted for men, but rather that
they take a higher proportion of new jobs in expanding industries in
locations where their activity rate was previously relatively low.

Though high rates of unemployment are often held to push women
back into the home, this does not appear to have happened in the period
1979–1981. Despite the 1% fall in women's actual employment,
women's activity rose by 1% in this period.

Table 9.8. Changes in men's and women's employment by industry group, 1979–1981
(source: calculated from Eurostat, 1981, table 60; OPCS, 1982, tables A3 and A4).

Industry group		Change in employment[a]	
		Women	Men
0	Agriculture, forestry, and fishing	11 (12)	50 (12)
1	Energy- and water-supply industry	6 (6)	44 (7)
2	Extraction of minerals, manufacture of metals and chemicals	−92 (−30)	−307 (−30)
3	Metal goods, engineering, and vehicle industries	−163 (−21)	−530 (−19)
4	Other manufacturing industries	−105 (−9)	−61 (−4)
5	Construction	−7 (−6)	−202 (−12)
6	Distribution, hotels and catering, repairs	144 (7)	0 (0)
7	Transport and communications	−8 (−3)	−142 (−11)
8	Banking, finance and insurance, business services, and leasing	81 (11)	89 (10)
9	Other services	−1 (0)	−12 (−1)
NK	No reply or inadequately described or working outside United Kingdom	84 (68)	124 (70)
	All industries	−52 (−1)	−945 (−6)

[a]Numbers represent actual changes in employment in thousands; those in brackets
percentage changes.

Table 9.9. Regional changes in women's activity rates, 1979–1981 (sources: calculated from Eurostat, 1981, table 60; OPCS, 1982, table 4.5).

Region	Number of economically active women (1000)		Changes in number of economically active women, 1979–1981	
	1979	1981	(1000)	(%)
North	550	563	13	2
Yorkshire and Humberside	889	916	27	3
North West	1240	1248	8	1
East Midlands	682	714	32	5
West Midlands	969	972	3	0
East Anglia	323	348	25	8
South East	3182	3274	92	3
South West	760	778	18	2
Wales	452	470	28	6
Scotland	994	954	−40	−4
Northern Ireland	224	244	20	9
Great Britain	10044	10237	193	2
United Kingdom	10268	10481	213	2

9.8 Conclusion

Spatial and historical variations in women's unemployment cannot be understood by finding correlations between the official figures for women's unemployment and other phenomena. Since official figures and surveys both underestimate the extent of hidden female labour reserves, it is essential to examine figures on women's employment as well as on unemployment. An explanation of any configuration of gender rates of employment and unemployment at any point in time and space requires an analysis of the rounds of gender restructuring which preceded the period under study. Accretions to preexisting patterns of gender relations take place in varying ways according to the particular relations between patriarchal and capitalist forces at that time and place. These rounds of gender restructuring are fixed in the sex-typing of particular occupations and industries, which is remarkably rigid over time. The market for women's labour is divided into lumpy submarkets which are relatively fixed in time and space. A new balance of forces at the time of the next round of employment change will fix at a new point the sex-typing of those new jobs. Those rounds of accumulation and gender restructuring give rise to the spatial patterns we now find in women's employment and unemployment. The dominant pattern of the postwar period has been the reduction of those regional differences in employment, and hence unemployment, of women which were created in previous rounds, in particular in nineteenth-century patterns of capitalist industrialisation.

Capitalist and patriarchal relations at work: Preston cotton weaving, 1890-1940

Mike Savage

In this chapter, I will examine the relationship between men and women within capitalist production in an historical study of cotton weaving in the North Lancashire town of Preston between 1890 and 1940[13]. In 1901 there were 15360 workers in the weaving sector, 25.85% of the occupied population and the largest single industry in Preston. The vast majority of these weavers, 12393, were female, and, along with the two other major weaving centres of Blackburn and Burnley, Preston had a very high proportion of women in paid employment, 30.5%. I will argue that this relatively high engagement of women in the capitalist economy does not mean, however, that Preston was somehow less patriarchal than other towns, and that it is necessary to examine patriarchal relations between men and women within the capitalist workplace, as well as in the family and in other areas.

I closely follow Hartmann's (1979b) definition of patriarchy as "a set of social relations between men, which have a material base, and which, though hierarchical, establish or create interdependence and solidarity among men, that enable them to dominate women", where that material base, most crucially, is "men's control over women's labour power" (page 11). I will focus on the privileged position of the loom overlooker (or tackler) and show how it rested on this basis. The development of a very strong Overlookers' Union also helped to buttress this authority against management.

The recognition of these patriarchal structures within the capitalist workplace problematises any historical account of changes in the labour process which fails to take these into account. Braverman's (1974) work is rightly regarded as being of seminal importance as an analysis of changes in the capitalist labour process in the twentieth century. In a highly simplified form, Braverman's argument is that the skilled artisan-craftsworker was of central importance in premonopoly capitalist enterprises, but the need for continued capital accumulation has led to a growing managerial control of work and the deskilling of these craftworkers. There are three main respects in which Braverman's arguments are deficient when patriarchal divisions in the workplace are borne in mind.

---

[13]This is a much compressed summary of a longer paper (Savage, 1982); for reasons of space, many important issues discussed in that paper, especially the role of employer paternalism and the Weavers' Union, have been omitted here.

First, Braverman overidentifies skill with a particular manifestation of it, in the person of the male craftworker (on this, see Phillips and Taylor, 1980). This gives the unfortunate impression that the female weaver is unskilled at any historical period, and hence makes it difficult to analyse changes in the labour process where craft skills never existed. This is especially problematic bearing in mind that craftwork was not the only, or indeed main, type of production in the nineteenth century (see Littler, 1980; 1982).

Second, Braverman sees capital as the almost exclusive agent of change in the labour process. As has been pointed out on many occasions, he ignores the way in which worker resistance can affect the structure of the labour process (Elger, 1982; Friedman, 1977a; 1977b; Penn, 1982). The focus on capital as instituting changes at the workplace overlooks the extent to which certain features he discusses are the result of more indirect factors. The decline of the craftworker, for instance, may simply be because of cyclical fluctuations in the economy (see Lee, 1981; 1982). From our point of view the most important point is that he does not examine how conflicts between male and female workers may significantly affect the structure of the labour process, regardless of capitalist intent.

Finally, Braverman tends to see changes in the labour process as being entirely intrinsic to the workplace. There is therefore no indication of how changes outside the workplace may affect changes in the capitalist workplace. This is especially important in the context of women's paid labour, since their entry into the labour market will be critically affected by, among other things, the nature of domestic labour (see Beechey, 1982). I will try to show how state intervention in the labour market indirectly helped to undermine the authority of the overlooker.

Littler's (1980) recent account avoids many of these problems. He argues that, in the United Kingdom, the male craftworker was not particularly common in the days before scientific management. He argues that there was a diversity of forms of labour control and management, and focuses particular attention on internal contracting, a system whereby capitalists contracted with a worker who would actually supervise and be responsible for production. Typically the contractor would be responsible for seven functions: hiring and firing; discipline and supervision; wage payment and determination of other terms and conditions; training; task allocation; work methods; and production planning. This usefully draws attention to the heterogeneity of the work force and to possible conflicts between workers. In addition, it allows us to break from the false antinomy between workers' control or capitalist control which exists in much Marxist writing, especially in Braverman. To point to the lack of capitalist control at work need only mean that other modes of control existed, based on internal contractor-type figures, although Littler's (1982, chapter 6) reference to 'traditional modes of control' here is rather imprecise.

It should be made clear at the outset that overlookers were not internal contractors, since they were waged workers, generally paid on commission (or poundage as it was called) depending on the output of the weavers whom they supervised[14]. Nonetheless, they possessed several of the functions Littler assigns to them. I will examine first the overlooker's authority in the period before 1914 and try to indicate how it was patriarchally based. In the latter part of the chapter, I will look at the decline of the overlooker's authority attendant on change in the labour market and on expanded capitalist control at work.

10.1 Patriarchal control, circa 1890–1914

The overlooker had three main tasks. First, he supervised the weavers in his section. He would usually have about eighty looms and about twenty-five to thirty weavers. These would include perhaps fifteen adults working four looms each (four-loom weavers), eight teenage two-loom weavers, and seven tenters, who were assistants to the weavers and earned a small wage in learning the job and performing the more routine tasks, such as fetching weft and sweeping the loom. The weavers were mainly female[15]; out of the thirty weavers, perhaps two would be adult men and two or three others boys. The remaining twenty-five were female, about ten or eleven being over twenty-five years of age. The overlooker took on new weavers and fired old ones. He was also responsible for deciding when tenters were competent enough to be put on two looms, and when two-loom weavers were able to be put on a full complement of four looms. He could move weavers onto different looms and move tenters around the shed. More generally, he was responsible for maintaining discipline in the weaving shed.

The second main task was that of being a loom mechanic. When a loom broke down the overlooker was supposed to repair it, and he was generally responsible for ensuring that the loom was turning out cloth of adequate quality. Finally, the overlooker was responsible for 'gaiting' the loom—preparing a loom for weaving by putting the new beams with fresh warp into the loom. He also performed odd jobs, the most important of which was to carry finished cloth to the warehouse and to carry the fresh beams from the sizing room to the loom.

The overlooker was, then, a supervisor, mechanic, and general labourer rolled into one. This fusion of tasks is most interesting, bearing in mind that capitalist production tends to a separation of these functions, and

[14]Indeed, Littler's (1982, page 71) belief that internal contract was widespread in textiles is perhaps unfounded. It did not exist in the preparatory process, and, though a form of subcontract existed in mule spinning, the wage lists negotiated by the Spinners' Union from the 1850s laid down in agreement with employers the wages to be paid to the spinners' assistants (see Jewkes and Gray, 1935; Savage, 1984).

[15]The extent to which weaving was a female occupation varied immensely among the cotton towns. Preston had one of the highest proportions of female workers. For the implications of this, see chapter 11 below.

bears testimony to the gendered nature of the work[16]. Power, skill, and strength were all regarded as being distinctly men's work. On the other hand, certain odd jobs, most notably cleaning and sweeping, which were seen as linked to forms of domestic labour, predominantly remained the work of the female weavers. The ethos of masculinity in a productive process employing large numbers of women is best revealed in the autobiography of William Holt, an eccentric one-time Communist weaver, talking of his experiences as a young learner:

> "How I admired the tackler for his strength, his aloofness, his skill, his almost mystical knowledge of the looms ... I admired his masculine gruffness as he scowled at the weavers ... at that time he was my ideal of perfect manhood and I could scarcely contain my admiration for his prodigious strength when he lifted in the new beam full of warp ..." (Holt, 1939, pages 33–34 and passim).

Managers, though reserving to themselves the ultimate say in supervising affairs, generally accepted this division of labour and the large amount of authority overlookers possessed over their weavers. "Managers often found themselves powerless to interfere. The response 'I leave it to the tackler' from managers was said to be typical" (Healey, 1977, page 13). In one case a weaver complained to the manager about her tackler's conduct and asked him what she should do. The manager told her to work her notice and work in a different shed (WC, 6 March 1907)[17]. When another weaver complained that a tackler had not come to mend her looms, "the manager said the tackler had told him that I had been giving him too much impudence" and refused to take any notice (WC, 27 February 1912; also see WC 25 May 1907). In some cases overlookers were even allowed to impose their own fines on weavers (WC, 30 March 1913).

[16]The 'despotic foreman', a common figure in industry at this time, generally took no part in the work process (see Williams, 1969, for one example). Craftworkers, though they sometimes supervised their own labourers, made a sharp distinction between craftwork and labouring work.

[17]WC stands for the Preston Weavers' Union Complaints Book. Other abbreviations adopted in this chapter for manuscript sources are, in alphabetical order: DDHs, Horrockses Records; ECO, Preston Employers' Correspondence with Overlookers' Union; ECW, Preston Employers' Correspondence with Warehouseman's Union; EJM, Preston Employers' Joint Meetings with Operatives; ERT, Elizabeth Roberts's Oral History Transcripts; JH, John Hawkins and Sons' Records; OCJB, Preston Overlookers' Union Correspondence with John Bibby's Union; OM, Overlookers' Union Minutes; OSJ, Overlookers' Union Secretary's Journal; PUR, Preston Union Rules; SM, Preston Spinners' Union Minutes; TTF, Preston Textile Trade Federation Minutes; WM, Preston Weavers' Union Minutes; WR, Preston Warehousemen's Union Reports; WRM, Preston Weavers' Union Minutes of Meetings of Mill Representatives; and WSB, Preston Weavers' Union Scrapbook. All these sources are located in the Lancashire County Record Office, Bow Lane, Preston, with the exception of SM, which is located in the Harris Library, Preston, and of ERT, which is to be found in the Library, University of Lancaster, Lancaster LA1 4YW.

On what basis did the overlookers' autonomy lie? One explanation might be that the degree of skill needed to manage looms made the overlookers indispensable to capital. Contrary to some opinion (Burgess, 1975, pages 236–237; Turner, 1962), weaving was a highly skilled job, since looms were not automatic and needed constant attention to ensure smooth production (see CFT, 1929a; 1929b; 1930a, for an extensive list of weavers' duties). The precise demarcation between weavers' work and overlookers' work was never clear. Most experienced workers were able to repair looms on most occasions, and overlookers were not especially skilled over and above weavers, except insofar as they had access to spare parts and tools. One old weaver, interviewed by Elizabeth Roberts, an oral historian, recalled:

"... my selvedges had broken so I thought I'll have to go and tell him [the tackler] ... at 8 o'clock he hadn't been so I thought 'blow this!' He had fetched these new heels so I get them on the loom and fastened them to this broad tape and ties them up and hooks them up like I had seen them doing and I flattened it and I thought now they are level and I pushed them right back and the bottom one has to be on the sleigh on the other top and then when it goes over that has to be on the sleigh or else it stitches underneath ... then about half-past ten he comes, a great big fellow, he says 'Where is it?'. I said 'I thought you started when we did. I've done it. It's been weaving 2 hours'. He took a deep breath and cleared off" (ERT, Mrs HIP).

This instance, among others, shows that weavers were able to do most of the skilled jobs associated with loom repair perfectly adequately. There was no reason why managers should rely on overlookers specifically. The most distinctive overlooker's task, that of 'gaiting up' a loom, was not one which weavers normally performed, but it was relatively easy and on certain occasions overlookers allowed weavers to gait their own looms (though see page 184 below for a discussion of the changing attitudes of overlookers).

The real importance of the overlooker lay in his ability to find labour, more specifically female labour, and especially skilled female labour. Weaving was a skilled job, yet it was not one learnt through apprenticeship, so employers could not assume that a 'time-served man' with a union card was competent. Nor were there any other formal qualifications. The only way by which skilled weavers were known was through personal knowledge and acquaintanceship. Here managers were badly off. Many Victorian managers were sons of employers (Joyce, 1980, pages 162–163) who had little knowledge of individual workers. For those managers who had risen through the ranks, a move to the middle-class suburbs of Fulwood and Penwortham was often in store, which cut them off from working-class neighbourhoods.

The need for neighbourhood contact was essential, especially for female labour in cases where women had taken time off for childbirth or domestic affairs and they wanted to come back to work. There was no developed labour market which could find such women a job. As one old cotton worker remembered:

> "It wasn't easy to be employed. Again I think in those days as today it was who you knew ... this was a bush telegraph, good, bad and indifferent. If you were a good weaver you got a job but if you were a careless weaver or you forgot to come to work or this kind of thing or domestic problems stopped you coming to work then nobody wanted you" (ERT, Mr T.Z.P.).

The tackler was of pivotal importance here. It was he who knew old weavers who might be persuaded to work, and it was to him that informal inquiries would be made about restarting work. And, of major importance here, it seems that it was often male family heads who would make contact through pub, club, and church. In short, the labour market was mediated by male contacts, even though it was female labour being offered for sale.

The most obvious manifestation was the way in which the overlooker could call on the labour of his own family members. To examine how common this was, I looked at the Census enumerator's schedules for three areas of Preston for the year 1881, the most recent available (full details in Savage, forthcoming). Of the thirty-two overlookers (about 6%–7% of the total number in Preston) in my survey, twenty-eight had coresiding wives, of whom eleven were weavers. They had thirty coresiding daughters of working age, of whom twenty-two were weavers, and twenty male coresiding relatives (nineteen of whom were sons) of working age, eight of whom were weavers. Altogether the thirty-two overlookers had forty-one immediate family members who worked as weavers, and, if this is a representative sample, perhaps 750 weavers (out of about 14 000) would have been directly related to overlookers. The practice may in fact have been increasing towards the end of the century, for in 1898 the Overlookers' Union claimed that 1000 weavers were family members of the overlookers (WRM, 18 September 1898).

Clearly the direct family members of overlookers represented only a small proportion of the labour force, though the number would no doubt increase significantly if the extended family was included. The male relatives of other weavers were often instrumental in getting work for them later through contact with the tackler. In one case a weaver slept in one morning and appealed to the manager that she should not lose her work:

> "The manager said he would leave it entirely with the tackler. She then went to the tackler and told him what the manager had said, the tackler said he had arranged for the clothlooker's wife to go on the looms: he told A. Ashcroft to go to the clothlooker's house to tell his wife not to come, it seems after this the clothlooker went to the tackler and said it seemed strange to him" (WC, 7 December 1908).

And, indeed, the clothlooker's wife was finally put on the looms. It was frequently the case that fathers of young weavers (even if they did not work in the cotton industry) intervened to decide on working conditions. In one case where a manager told a weaver she would be moved from three looms to two:

"She came home at night and told her father and he advised her to take notice ... [later] she informed me that her father thought it would be best for her to go on two looms" (WC, 9 June 1904).

In another case when a tackler wanted to move a weaver onto different looms her father successfully intervened to prevent this (WC, 22 January 1913; for other similar instances, see WC, 16 July 1904; 29 January 1907).

It was common for parents of young weavers, and even for husbands of women weavers, to visit the tackler at home to discuss grievances or to arrange time off for female relatives to attend to pressing domestic commitments. On one occasion "her husband went to the tackler at his own home to ask off for her for a fortnight, he said it would be right" (WC, 3 February 1908). This system whereby male family heads could informally arrange with tacklers for time off meant that the domestic division of labour remained patriarchal, with women taking time off when domestic circumstances demanded (for example, WC, 23 January 1904; 13 February 1905; 24 August 1905). Thus, despite the extent of female paid labour, women were still responsible for domestic labour (for a contrast with another weaving town, Nelson, see chapter 11 below). The fact that overlookers were active within working-class neighbourhoods therefore allowed informal collaboration between male family heads and the overlookers over the conditions of female employment (for the associational practices of overlookers outside the workplace, see Savage, forthcoming). One result of this was that supervision in the workplace was not only concerned with efficient production, but also involved a policing of female morals, with managers and tacklers acting, in a sense, as surrogate fathers. One manager told a weaver to tell another to return to work, adding "don't forget to tell her that they are too fond of a boy from Preston" (WC, 7 February 1910). On another occasion a weaver was sacked for being "with Joe on Saturday night" (WC, 14 July 1909), and at one shed a young female weaver was discharged for apparently passing an 'indecent' book around the shed (WC, 14 March 1912).

The most important way by which male family heads sought to preserve their control was through refusing to allow weavers in their family to join the Weavers' Union, despite the irony, frequently noted by the Weavers' Union, that the family heads themselves were amongst the most ardent Union supporters (CFT, 1890, and passim). The Overlookers' Union was particularly notorious here, and in 1898 boasted that, out of the 1000 weavers related to overlookers, only fifteen were members of the Weavers' Union (WRM, 18 September 1898). The spinners also had large numbers of relatives working as weavers. The Weavers' Union frequently appealed for support (SM, 5 December 1901), yet when some spinners proposed the motion that "no members of this Association [the Spinners' Union] be eligible for any office in this society whose wife or any member of his family under the age of 21 years does not pay to the trade union attached to whatever calling they may follow" there were only three who voted for the resolution, which was lost "by a great majority" (SM, 4 April 1907).

The Overlookers' Union, founded in 1875, had by 1890 recruited nearly all overlookers, and it set about strengthening the overlookers position still further. The main loophole to the overlookers' authority was that, as I have shown, there were plenty of skilled weavers who would have made competent overlookers, and the overlookers' knowledge and control over the local labour market could have been matched by most adult male weavers. This had allowed employers considerable flexibility in promoting weavers of their choice to become new overlookers. The Overlookers' Union set about changing this by enforcing learner rules whereby only weavers nominated by a majority of overlookers in the shed were entitled to become learner overlookers. Effectively this meant that only the sons of overlookers stood any chance of promotion. This was tied in with a strict policy of preventing male weavers from repairing their own loom or doing their own 'gaiting', so that they could not learn the skills of tackling. This effectively tied the employers hands, for, when vacancies arose, only one weaver, the 'recognised learner', had been given the general experience necessary to take on the job. In fact the work of male weavers was to some extent deskilled as the overlookers allowed them less and less discretion; yet this was a form of deskilling which capital did not institute. Conflict between male weavers and overlookers consequently rose in the period leading up to World War 1 (for example, WC, 8 May 1912). The overlookers also attempted completely to control their labour market by refusing to allow overlookers to be sacked without union consent and by insisting that any vacancies be filled by unemployed Union nominees.

These controls were so effective that by 1910 the overlookers were effectively self-recruiting. Many observers felt that this increased their autonomy from management. One critic wrote to the trade union newspaper, the *Cotton Factory Times* (CFT, 1911), that

"It is not only unfair but it is absolutely unjust to both weavers and employers that a shed should be filled with tacklers who are all relatives to each other ... . The Manager is face to face with a body of men who will on many occasions do their own, irrespective of instruction".

As with internal contract (compare Littler, 1982, page 67), patriarchal control may have served capital well in the nineteenth century as it took away the burdens of management. By 1914, however, the degree of control exercised by overlookers had increased to the extent that the employers had virtually no say at all over labour recruitment and promotion.

10.2 The decline of patriarchal control
10.2.1 The labour market

I have argued that it was the lack of a well-developed labour market which gave tacklers a pivotal position in recruiting adequate labour. The increased state intervention in the labour market went some way to providing means by which employers could bypass tacklers in finding skilled weavers. Employers could use Labour Exchanges (Preston's was opened in 1910) as a means of finding labour. Furthermore, for a worker to qualify for unemployment benefit under the National Insurance Acts of 1911 and 1920, they had to be prepared to take on work anywhere. In the interwar years, workers were often forced to go round to different mills to get the manager's signature to show that they had been seeking work.

In itself the onset of mass unemployment made the problem of finding new skilled weavers less acute. After a short postwar boom in 1919, unemployment rose to 42% among cotton workers by March 1921, and then fluctuated between 7% and 20% until 1930 (Clay, 1929). There was next a dramatic increase in unemployment and, in September 1930, 40.7% of all cotton workers were unemployed. The level remained high until the mid-1930s, with 30.6% of cotton workers unemployed in 1932 and 10.9% in 1937 (Glynn and Oxborrow, 1976).

The weaving centres of Burnley, Blackburn, and Preston were all badly affected. The 1931 Census, which almost certainly underrecorded unemployment, found that in Preston 18.9% of the adult population were unemployed, 17% of men and 20.9% of women. Most of these were weavers. What is especially important was that unemployment was short-term. Hence in Blackburn, where 33.5% of the population was unemployed in 1931, 70% of the insured male population and 87% of the insured female population signed on at some time in 1930 (Industrial Survey, 1932, page 111). Hence large numbers of workers were prone to be asked to find work elsewhere. One of Elizabeth Roberts's respondents was forced to go to the village of Longridge several miles from Preston to take on a weaving job (ERT, Mrs AIP). Employers could rely, therefore, on Labour Exchanges to provide weavers, and the tackler's role became much less important (see CFT, 1930b).

A further consequence of the 1911 National Insurance Act should be mentioned. It provided insurance cards for the workers, so that if they left work they would collect these cards from their old employer and give them to their new employer. This was a severe blow to the tackler's informal right to hire and fire. Whenever he dismissed a weaver the weaver always had to go to the office to collect her cards, and thus the manager would be able to overrule the decision if he felt so inclined. The informal 'weeks off' which tacklers sometimes allowed were also more difficult to continue since regular insurance payments were essential. Hence the informality upon which the tackler's authority had depended was seriously undermined by the introduction of regularised insurance and unemployment benefits.

The development of Employment Bureaux in the 1930s was also significant here. Previously, nearly all learner weavers were taken on by tacklers on the personal recommendation of parents or friends. The Employment Bureaux, however, provided alternative ways of finding work, which, once again, bypassed the tackler. A survey by Jewkes and Jewkes (1938) between 1934 and 1936 revealed that by this time only 34.3% of boys got jobs through the recommendation of parents and friends, whereas Employment Bureaux found work for 23.6%, and 38% stated that they found work through applying at the factory or workplace, sometimes under the direction of the Employment Bureaux. For girls, a lower proportion, 28%, obtained work through family and friends, whereas 34% were placed by the Employment Bureaux and 33% applied at the factory direct (1938, page 34).

State intervention in the labour market, then, had considerable ramifications inside the workplace also, as it undercut the tackler's pivotal position as one who knew about and could employ good skilled weavers. It replaced this with a more formalised system by which labour was marketed, allowing employers to find workers by using the Labour Exchange and allowing young workers to be directed to the industry through institutional channels. In itself these changes did not lead to an automatic decline in the autonomy of the tackler at work; this had to be wrested from him. Nonetheless it provided an alternative means of securing labour which reduced the indispensibility of the overlookers.

10.2.2 Managers and clothlookers

Throughout much of the Victorian period, managers were of relatively minor importance in directing the labour process. They lacked the detailed knowledge of the tacklers about the individual abilities of the weavers, and were in many cases sons of the employers who knew relatively little of the practical aspect of weaving (Joyce, 1980, pages 162-163). There was usually only one manager responsible both for internal operations and for marketing, a fact which prevented detailed acquaintanceship with the intricacies of the labour process. By 1900 this was beginning to change, as, particularly in the larger firms, the career manager became more common, a man who had worked for one firm all his life as weaver, overlooker, and manager (for one instance, see PG, 1930). These managers had a greater knowledge of individual weavers and some took a more active role in hiring and firing, insisting on having the last word on these matters (though there appears to be considerable variation between firms here). The emergence of the limited company was especially important here (see Joyce, 1980, Epilogue).

In 1892, six of Preston's forty-three cotton firms were limited companies, but, by 1913, over twenty of fifty firms were limited companies [a very small number of these firms (three to four) were spinning-only firms; figures

derived from various trade directories]. The main period of transition was
1918–1919, and by 1922, fifty-eight out of sixty-one firms were limited
companies. The implications of this can be seen by examining the records
of the firm John Hawkins and Sons, which was taken over as a limited
company in 1899. The main shareholders were the Eccles family, who
possessed 2360 of the 6000 original shares, and the Birtwistle family, who
owned 1250 shares. The Eccles family were Liverpool merchants, and the
Birtwistles were Blackburn cotton manufacturers who took over the
everyday running of the business. The latter were mainly involved,
however, in marketing and appear to have left the internal running of the
mill almost entirely to the manager. In most limited companies managers
were given much more autonomy from the employers and this allowed
them to use much more discretion in reorganising working practices when
they felt fit. Unlike directors of limited companies, managers were
locally based (whereas directors frequently lived nowhere near their mills),
were linked to one firm only (whereas directors often had interests in a
wide number of firms), and were concerned only with production
(whereas the directors became more responsible for selling, or could
appoint salesmen and outside managers to do this). As the *Cotton
Factory Times* (CFT, 1930c) remarked:

"In Lancashire the limited liability company is predominant, and as far
as the latter is concerned this means that the manager is to all intents
and purposes the employer".

The manager's position was also enhanced by the fact that management
was not bureaucratised. There was still only one manager for each shed,
with occasionally a head manager if it was a large firm with several sheds.
The largest cotton firm in Preston, Horrockses, which employed 3000
when in full production, employed only twenty-two salaried staff in 1922,
of whom thirteen were responsible for shipping, retail, stock, and
consignment (DDHs, 1922, file 115). Within each shed, therefore, the
manager's discretion was not hindered by bureaucratic procedure.

The increasing homogeneity of the managers' occupations also facilitated
the emergence of a Mill Managers' Association, which generated a degree
of occupational loyalty. Formerly managers had been linked by family or
career to particular firms, and no sense of occupational solidarity developed.
The Preston Mill Managers' Association had been formed some time in the
early twentieth century and, in 1917, an industry-wide amalgamation of
Mill Managers' Associations was formed. One of the main concerns of
this group was to stress the need for impartial leadership in industry.
Mr Watson told the Preston Mill Managers' Association in 1921 that:

"... real success cannot be reached unless this varied spirit of enthusiasm
is widely grasped by a leader and appreciated by taking into consideration
the views of those amongst whom he works sympathetically encouraging
the true road to co-operation before giving his final decision (and this
final decision must rest with the leader ...)" (JTWMA, 1922).

This leadership involved a much more stringent watch over the tacklers. There were attempts by individual managers to overlook the overlooker. In 1929 one manager tried to force overlookers to go to each loom at a certain time twice a week "to tighten spindles, replace buffers, pick spindle sticks etc" rather than allowing overlookers to do this at their own discretion (OSJ, 6 March 1929). Another manager asked the overlooker to give him details of the number of beams they gaited each day (OSJ, 12 March 1932). At Queen's Mill in 1923 the manager introduced a 'clock system' whereby times taken for weaving cloth were to be recorded (OSJ, 19 February 1923). One overlooker at Ashton shed had to report to the manager twice a day because of his "insubordination and defiance" (OSJ, 11 January 1934). One index of increased management interference is the increased number of complaints overlookers made to their Union about management[18]. In the period 1903–1905, seven were made, mainly concerning the attitude of managers. In the period 1929–1931, there were nineteen complaints, and these would often be about managerial actions.

Managers took over many of the tackler's supervisory jobs. In one case the manager declared himself responsible for the number of looms a weaver worked, previously the overlooker's responsibility (WM, 24 November 1930; 30 May 1932). Managers would also organise the handing out of beams to weavers (OSJ, 6 June 1930; WM, 29 December 1931), and might also decide what technical procedures should be used (WM, 16 June 1924; 19 December 1930), in one case (OSJ, 27 November 1931) causing the over-lookers to complain that the manager was interfering with their looms at weekends. Hiring and firing, it appears, were almost completely taken over.

Managers could not, however, be everywhere at once. Their increased authority was linked to the changing function of the clothlookers. Clothlookers checked the finished cuts of woven cloth to ensure it was of adequate quality and would reckon up the weavers' wages and sometimes pay them. The clothlooker before 1914 had, like the tacklers, considerable autonomy from the manager and could fine weavers for bad cloth, and in exceptional cases could even dismiss them, without referring to the manager (for example, WC, 11 July 1905; 28 May 1906; and see the account of Brooks, 1950, pages 123–126). Generally, however, the clothlooker's job was not felt to be of great importance, and firms often gave it to old and loyal workers in need of a less-strenuous life. The Warehouseman's Union complained that at Broomfield Mill.

"The warehouse foreman at this firm is MINUS ONE ARM and the other 2 clothlookers are men of 70 and 80 years of age, these are assisted by 2 females. What the results are from such a staff it is difficult to understand, but you will have at least some idea of OUR difficulty in organising cripples" (ECW, 5 March 1925).

[18]These are defined narrowly and exclude complaints about discharges, putting on nonunion members, etc. The figures are taken from the Overlookers' Union minute book and the Overlookers' Secretary's Journal.

As better quality cloth was needed in the interwar years, and firms competed more intensely on the contracting market, clothlooking became a more serious affair. The *Cotton Factory Times* (CFT, 1929c) noted that

> "... clothlooking methods have certainly undergone a revolutionary change since the war ended and apparently gone for ever are the old slipshod methods of looking and hooking pieces ... [new methods] carry a great deal more responsibility for the clothlooker".

Alongside this the manager usually took over decisions as to whether to fine weavers. It became less frequent for clothlookers to be older weavers, and they were more likely to be recruited from the general warehouse staff. The Weavers' Union complained in 1927 that 90% of clothlookers had never been weavers (WSB, 20 May 1927). The warehouse staff also increased in size and several women were employed to repair slightly damaged cloth, the previous practice being to tell the weaver to repair her own. This indicates a move to rely less on the weaver's skill and to settle for more shoddy production which could be repaired in the warehouse. Thus by 1930 the older, easy going, autonomous clothlooker had been replaced by specialised workers under managerial control. In Horrockses the Bedaux system of scientific management was even used to rationalise warehouse work (TTF, 5 May 1933; WR, March 1933). This managerial control over the warehouse also meant that it was easy to learn of the competence of weavers without actually watching them, simply by looking at their finished product in the warehouse. The manager thus had a mode of supervision which bypassed that of the overlooker.

In two firms these general changes were supplemented by a more thoroughgoing reorganisation of the labour process. At Horrockses, 700 automatic looms were introduced in 1929. For a time it was agreed that weavers should work six looms each (the maximum for the ordinary Lancashire loom being four), but in 1930 they suddenly increased this to twenty-five looms per weaver. Overlookers supervised sixty looms, so that they now had only three weavers under them. The tasks of beam-gaiting and camping were hived off onto a separate grade of labour, and tacklers were now more or less entirely loom mechanics. The commission system of payment was ended and overlookers got £4 for being '70% efficient', with a bonus of 1/8d for every percentage of efficiency above this. This type of payment sounds very much like that used in the Bedaux system which was being widely introduced at this time (see Littler, 1982; chapters 8 and 9). The overlookers were aware that this gave the firm considerable discretion in determining wage rates, and in 1930 the overlookers complained that "they had no guidance as to the reckoning of their wages and were entirely at the mercy of the office" (OSJ, 19 July 1930; also see 26 June 1931; 16 February 1932). Indeed, in 1932 the basic efficiency level was raised from 70% to 85%, so reducing the amount of bonus to be earned (OSJ, 24 October 1932). Similar forms of payment were used for the weavers, replacing traditional piece rates. By 1936, forms of time and motion study were being used in other Horrockses sheds (WM, 23 January 1936).

The other firm which carried out far-reaching changes was that of Carrington and Dewhurst, who owned a mill in the small village of Eccleston, near Preston. In 1933 they put their 1479 looms on a more-looms basis, with weavers working six to eight looms each (the impact of the more-looms dispute is dealt with in greater detail in Savage, 1982). The weaver's job was greatly simplified, as a new grade of labour, the weaver-helper, was created to carry out certain tasks such as to fetch the weft. The weaver was only meant to change shuttles and to draw ends in. The supervision of labour was also formalised. Each loom was given a card on which all breakage of weft had to be recorded and this allowed managers to keep an exact record of each weaver's performance at their looms (WC, 11 May 1933).

It should be made clear, however, that these two firms were exceptional. As I have argued, this does not mean that there were no changes in other firms, but that generally these took place in a less-dramatic and gradual way.

10.2.3 The attack on the Overlookers' Union

The declining indispensability of overlookers to employers led to an increased willingness to undermine the various regulations the Overlookers' Union had built up to buttress the overlookers' authority at work. By 1918 the Overlookers' Union not only effectively controlled its labour market, but also regulated the work tasks of its members (by, for instance, disciplining members who allowed weavers both 'to run among their looms' and informally to carry out some of the overlooker's tasks). It had also succeeded in undermining the system of paying wages on commission by securing a full back wage of 85% of normal wage and by drawing up a list of extra payments to be made for extra duties (which, in fact, had always been their responsibility).

The first signs of a managerial attack on the overlookers was in 1915 when the management at Victoria Mill told the overlookers that they would not be able to employ their own family members as weavers: this provoked a strike supported by the Overlookers' Union, and the firm eventually gave in (TTF, 15 December 1915; 6 January 1916). It was with the growth of unemployment after 1919 that the employers were better placed to get their way. In 1920 the Employers' Association issued a statement that they would

> "reserve to themselves the right to engage or discharge loom overlookers employed by them, and adding that in future the employers intend to exercise this right without binding themselves to seek the consent of the Loom Overlookers Association" (ECO, 16 October 1920).

This aggression led to a large number of disputes in the early 1920s about whether employers could discharge overlookers without Union consent (for example, EJM, 4 August 1920; 5 December 1921; OM, 23 November 1921; 29 September 1924; OSJ, 5 October 1921; 11 November 1921; 1 November 1922). The pressure on the Union was such that though it formally continued to uphold its right to sanction dismissals, it preferred to avoid strikes and increasingly put pressure on incompetent overlookers to leave work. The reluctance to strike was not simply because of expense and organisational problems, but also because in 1922 there had been a strike at Queen's Mill when the mill apparently worked normally although the overlookers were on strike (EJM, 12 December 1922). This revealed the declining importance of the overlooker as supervisor, and made the Union aware that any further strikes would only reveal to employers that the overlookers were not as vital to smooth production as they once were.

The Overlookers' Union therefore increasingly refused to support overlookers who the management wanted to remove. In one case the Union Secretary

"was shown a piece of cloth and the clothlooker said complaints were pretty general. I sent for [the overlooker] and told him I was convinced he would never be a success at Ashton Shed and advised him to go away. He handed in his notice" (OSJ, 3 April 1922).

Indeed the Union Secretary appears to have become some sort of troubleshooter, responding to employers' complaints about their overlookers by visiting his mills and telling his members "that it was very necessary that they should pull themselves together" (OSJ, 28 October 1922; also see OSJ, 5 April 1922; 18 April 1922; 13 October 1922). The employers began to recognise the value of the Union as a policing agent, and would often call the secretary in whenever there was trouble (for example, OSJ, 22 January 1929; 24 October 1929).

Another main line of attack was over the Union's control of promotion. From the early 1920s, various firms began to ignore the Union's regulations and made weavers of their own choosing learners, and later overlookers (for instance, OSJ, 20 April 1922; 10 May 1922; 19 May 1922; 23 June 1922; 10 August 1922; 29 September 1922). Though the Union maintained its policy of having the sole right to select learners, it became decreasingly able to enforce it. Its usual sanction against firms which chose their own learner was to stop the other overlookers from helping the learner, which severely affected his ability to do his job, beam-carrying, for instance, always requiring two people to carry the heavy load. The growth of unemployment and the possibility of being laid off made overlookers less likely to defy management in this way. (For examples of firms promoting weavers, see OSJ, 27 February 1931; 4 August 1931; 7 September 1931; 19 September 1931; 19 December 1932; 10 January 1933; OCJB, 26 November 1935; 30 November 1935.)

The Union also lost much of its power to regulate working conditions. Its insistence that the overlookers' sections (that is, their looms) could not be changed without Union consent was put to the test in a dispute at Queen's Mill in 1922 when the firm cut the number of looms under each overlooker from eighty-four to seventy-two. This led to a strike, but eventually the Union had to give in (EJM, 9 November 1922; 20 November 1922; 12 December 1922; OSJ, 31 October 1922; 4 November 1922; 6 November 1922; 19 December 1922).

The decline of the overlookers as supervisors forced the Union to find new grounds on which to legitimise their claims to high wages and security. As late as 1923, the Union rule book emphasised the authority of the overlookers:

"The overlookers hold permanent and important positions. As overseers they are in some degree bound to set an example to the working men and women under their charge, not only of sobriety, industry and integrity of character but of economy, providence and forethought" (PUR, 1923, page 2).

Increasingly the Union played this down and presented the overlooker as a skilled mechanic, as a technician necessary for the modernisation of the industry. The *Cotton Factory Times* (CFT, 1929d) stressed that

"the many contrivances which overlookers are now called upon to cope with test their skill and patience to the uttermost ... I do not think that a tackler's skill is properly appreciated by masters and their managers".

Tom Shaw, for many years Preston's Labour MP and a former Weavers' Union official, stressed also that the tackler "is a very highly skilled workman indeed—though you will never get a weaver to admit that there are many good tacklers" (Jackson, 1930, page vi).

The final twist to this did not come until after World War 2 when the industry attempted to 'modernise' itself. The tacklers insisted that they should not be left out. As the vice-chairman of the Preston Overlookers wrote:

"If those in authority in the cotton trade would try to free themselves of their silly prejudice against tacklers and consult the man at the bench a little more the work of reorganising the cotton trade would proceed more smoothly" (ECO, 21 June 1949).

The Overlookers' Union was, he declared,

"a progressive body, most willing to help in any reasonable and just measure of reform ... several members of the executive are voluntarily undertaking instruction in time and motion study" (ECO, 6 July 1949).

The overlookers who thirty years previously had fought any attempts to undermine their patriarchal authority at work, now presented themselves to the world as the bringers of technical efficiency.

10.3 Conclusion

One important point which emerges from this discussion is that the notion of 'deskilling' is much too simple to be of any use. Littler's (1982, chapter 1) distinction between skill as discretion and skill as task range is much more helpful. The attacks on the autonomy of the overlooker did not in themselves have any implications for the work tasks in weaving. Changes in modes of control at work do not necessarily link with changes in the work itself. And, indeed, the main changes in the work tasks, the attempts by overlookers to limit the weavers' task range so that they were disqualified from promotion, were not the result of a changed mode of control at work, but were the culmination of a particular form of patriarchal control. The two firms which used scientific management (of sorts) were in fact rather special, as their strategies involved a simultaneous attack on overlookers, with a subdivision of weaving jobs. Furthermore, though overlookers lost their authority at work, it is difficult to say with confidence that they were 'deskilled'. Although some of their tasks, such as beam-carrying, were hived off to different grades of labour, increasing technical complexity of the looms may have made their mechanical tasks more 'skilled'.

The real significance of the growth of managerial control in the weaving industry was not that it allowed the work tasks to be reorganised with the result of greater efficiency in production and increased capital accumulation. Indeed, one index recorded that productivity per head dropped from 100.0 in 1924 to 93.1 in 1929 (Industrial Survey, 1932, page 129). The development of managerial control was not because of the needs of capital accumulation, but because of structural changes in the nature of the capitalist firm and as a result of the struggle of managers themselves (see Stark, 1980).

The effect of this was to allow control at work to be generated entirely within the workplace. Patriarchal control, I have argued, involved the importation of patriarchal modes of domination within the family and neighbourhood into the workplace. The overlooker did not hire and fire and supervise labour because of his place in the weaving shed. Rather he was made an overlooker because of his ability to find labour in working-class neighbourhoods and because he could discipline workers on the basis of his place in working-class life. Management control managed to dissociate the capitalist workplace from its environment. One of the interesting points to arise out of this study is that state intervention in the labour market was of major importance here.

Hartmann (1979b, page 16) has argued for the importance of looking at the "hierarchy between men and the solidarity between them" in examining the development of patriarchal structures. There is perhaps a danger in overconcentrating on formal male organisations and expressions of solidarity—such as trade unions, campaigns over state regulations over women's work, etc. These formal organisations were never frequent enough in the nineteenth century to explain the pervasiveness of patriarchy. It is the informal neighbourhood contacts between men that appear to be of major importance in sustaining their hold over women's labour power in Preston. Arguably it is the decline of this distinctive male-controlled labour market which leads to the emergence of more formal organisations, attempting to gain state intervention or to force employers to employ men. This clearly leads on to the fascinating question of the effect of the change in work control on the overlooker's political behaviour. The extent to which the emerging Labour Party was concerned not only to struggle against the capitalist class, but also to shore up patriarchal control within the working class, clearly would repay examination (this is dealt with in the chapter that follows, and is the subject of continuing research).

Gender and local politics: struggles over welfare policies, 1918-1939

Jane Mark-Lawson, Mike Savage, Alan Warde

The study of urban politics was revitalised by the work of Manuel Castells. His argument, that the organising principle of modern urban systems is a need for the provision of adequate means for collective consumption, led to the identification of a new form of urban politics in which urban social movements and the state provision of services were central (Castells, 1977; 1978). Subsequent work in the field has produced something of a theoretical impasse. The central concept, collective consumption, has been found wanting: more-orthodox Marxists, feminists, and neo-Weberians have made withering criticisms. Yet the explanatory problems identified by Castells remain, recognised as important but unresolved. The currently dominant Anglo–Saxon position, for instance, acknowledges that we need to know what determines the levels and content of urban services, but rejects Castells's theoretical presuppositions. The result has been a definition of urban politics in terms of a special, but ill-defined, category of 'consumption issues', concerned roughly with the (re)production of labour power. Analysis is directed towards explaining political system outputs regarding such issues (for example, Cawson, 1982; Dunleavy, 1980; Saunders, 1979). Such a mode of inquiry is essentially atheoretical, losing completely Castells's impressive, if contestable, grounding of urban politics in what Hindess (1976) would call its social conditions of existence. Though not wholly convinced that the concept of collective consumption is beyond redemption, we avoid its use in this chapter because it is sufficient for our purposes to refer to the public provision of welfare services—to what O'Connor (1973) designated as social provision and social expenses—with a view to casting further light on the general issues raised originally by Castells.

Our chapter is concerned with the role of social movements and class struggle in the determination of local state policies on 'consumption issues'. We thus pursue the problems identified by Castells, with our principal focus being upon his empirical generalisations rather than upon his abstract theoretical propositions. We explore the development of urban politics in three towns in the northwest of England in the interwar period, our initial aim being to explain differences in the levels of services provided by the local authorities of Nelson, Preston, and Lancaster. In the process, however, we expose some lacunae in Castells's theoretical edifice. Most obviously, by showing that the political organisation of women is central to an explanation of local variation, we draw attention to the inadequacy of any study of urban politics which ignores gender.

In this omission, Castells is regretfully not alone, it having become almost routine for urban politics and urban political economy to ignore gender divisions.

It should be stressed that there is nothing uniform or inevitable about the extension of local state services, for, although there may be some diffusion effect deriving from central government directives, variation is considerable. The benefits of the public provision of services are unevenly distributed. Not only are there spatial variations, but there is also a significant dimension of inequality between men and women. Although recent work on the effects of cuts in welfare spending has revealed that women are disproportionately affected, little awareness of the sexual divisions of welfare has filtered into work on urban social movements and struggles over services.

Gershuny and Miles (1983), in a recent volume *The New Service Economy*, make the point that there are several modes of provision of a 'service function'—a given final service to a consumer:

"service functions involve individuals in service work, but this need not take place within the money economy (and thus be directly reflected in the statistics of service industries, occupations or products): voluntary associations, households and individuals may produce their own final service functions informally in their 'free time' (1983, page 4).

One might add that the final provision of a service is typically fulfilled under different social arrangements at different points in time.

Provision for education, child care, food preparation, medical attention, etc may be obtained in a number of ways. At least five can be distinguished. First, there is the labour of wives working within what Delphy (1977) calls the domestic or family mode of production. Second, services may be provided through the market by capitalist firms. Third, they may be secured within a neighbourhood 'informal economy', for money or through reciprocal agreements. Fourth, services may be provided by voluntary or charitable organisations. And finally, they may be provided by the state. In historical practice the extent to which an individual or group of persons has a realistic choice between agencies is highly constrained by other structures and processes. But over time there has been considerable change concerning which services are delivered by which agencies. It is, for example, a commonplace that, between the eighteenth and twentieth centuries, the function of teaching children to read and write shifted from the domestic and informal spheres, through the market and voluntary spheres, into the state sphere. The consequences of shifting activities from one sphere to another are not predictable: there is no line of transfer which universally guarantees the greatest happiness of the greatest number. But consequences there are in abundance, as is evidenced by current concerns with the effects of the fiscal crisis of the state, the growth of the informal economy, or the pressure placed upon women by the present government's policy of returning the primary responsibility for 'caring' back to the family as a result of expenditure cuts.

It is our argument that in the interwar period women in particular stood to gain from the transfer of certain service functions from the domestic mode of production and from the market into the sphere of state provision. Many of the areas of state provision of welfare developed since the beginning of the twentieth century have been of direct concern to women; the shift of responsibility to the state for maternity and child welfare, child allowances, and nurseries are obvious examples. There are many other less-apparent instances. Oren (1979) has pointed to a rigid division of resources in the pre-1939 working-class household. The wife would receive a fixed amount of housekeeping money, which remained surprisingly inelastic, and she would be expected to provide the material essentials of the household—food, housing, clothing, etc—out of this sum. Extra expense, such as the birth of a child, would be balanced by the wife. Moving to cheaper accommodation, letting a room, or simply cutting back on food expenditure would be ways of achieving this. Where women worked, payment for covering additional burdens, such as child care, largely remained her responsibility. Hence such developments as state provision of housing or, more importantly, the introduction by Arthur Greenwood, Labour Minister of Health 1929-1931, of a workable system of subsidised rents, could have a major impact on the standard of living of women. During periods of economic depression and unemployment the health and welfare of the primary wage earner and of children (especially male children) were literally balanced physically against the health of women. Even the Ministry of Health, which throughout the interwar period ignored all evidence to the contrary and insisted that unemployment had little effect upon health, was forced to admit that women in the depressed areas were suffering from anaemia and debilitation. There is little doubt that for many women in the period the margin between real poverty and a 'standard of living' was a very slim one (see Webster, 1982). Thus any measures which transferred domestic or financial responsibility to the state, from free or subsidised feeding of school children, through rent rebates, to free state nursery schools, materially benefitted women.

Furthermore, state provision of services should be recognised as important in any analysis of the changing position of women because of the element of redistribution involved in welfare services. In the interwar period, Exchequer grants on many services redistributed resources from taxpayers to nontaxpayers (that is, away from middle-class salaries and property income). It has been pointed out that class redistributive elements are no longer present in the post-1945 welfare state, since resources now move only within the working class. This is largely because the working class has only fallen into the tax bracket since this date. But it would seem that, as low or nonwage earners, women as a group have

most to gain from the 'social wage' and most to lose by welfare cuts
(CPAG, 1980; Edgell and Duke, 1983). Moreover, since their domestic
labour is considered 'free' and elastic, in the sense that it may be almost
endlessly intensified to cover services reduced in other spheres, women
have a large 'stake' in struggling over such services and, by and large, in
preferring state provision to that by domestic or market channels[19].

If Castells is correct that "traditional inequality in terms of income,
which is inherent in capitalism, is expressed in new social cleavages related
to the accessibility and use of certain collective services" (Castells, 1978,
page 16), and if we are not mistaken in thinking gender a major
'consumption cleavage', the question arises under what structural conditions
are women able to organise effectively to pursue their common interests.
Libraries do not appear to stock books on this subject. One reason for
this scholarly neglect has been an almost universal proclivity for treating
welfare solely as a class issue and the mobilisation of women solely as an
aspect of feminist politics. The conventional assumption has been that
the extension of state provision has been a function of the strength of
local Labour Parties. However, since we know that Labour Parties have
also frequently exhibited strongly patriarchal tendencies, we should be
wary of accepting such a view. Indeed, our study suggests that Labour
Parties' strategies vary. Where women are relatively weak there is a
tendency for trade-union sectionalism and economism to be the
fundamental strategy; active pressure from women is required to challenge
and to replace that strategy with one promoting state provision of services.
The relationship between class and gender is complicated, here as elsewhere,
and our study could not reach simple conclusions. Still, we believe we
can specify some of the conditions under which women's interests may be
advanced within the realm of institutionalised reformist urban politics.

Our empirical study breaks some new ground. There is very little work
done on urban politics in the interwar period in the United Kingdom; the
Victorian era and the postwar periods are much more widely explored.
The studies that are available for the period 1918–1939 are almost
entirely concerned with class structure and class conflict, which has
perhaps fostered the misleading impression that urban movements, based
upon 'nonclass cleavages', are an explicitly contemporary phenomenon.

_____

[19] This is not, of course, to claim that welfare services, *as they are actually
experienced* by individual women, are universally welcome. There is a well-
documented process of transmutation which takes place between struggles over services
and their actual implementation; between demand and service. As various writers
have pointed out (for instance, Lewis, 1980; Ross, 1983; Wilson, 1977), the
'policing' aspect of some welfare services often brought unwelcome intrusions into the
lives of women, and, furthermore, the extension of state welfare has sometimes served
to reinforce the notion of male breadwinner and dependent wife. However, these
patriarchal facets of welfare services are not a necessary part of the relationship
between women and the state.

Nor has there been much by way of comparative analysis of urban politics. Although local variation is a distinctive feature of UK development, it has been largely overlooked. Whereas significant 'statistical explanations' have been offered for variability in urban public spending in some other countries in the postwar period, students of the UK case have failed in similar endeavours. Neither the social characteristics of the population nor the party political histories of local authorities seem to correlate well with spending on public services (for example, Newton, 1981b; Sharpe, 1981). The need for adequate explanation and further exploration is considerable. In the absence of comparable work our arguments are necessarily tentative. But even if they are treated as no more than hypotheses based on a comparison of limited scope, they should nevertheless shift the grounds of discussion on urban politics.

Public services and the Labour Party

The three towns we examined all lie within forty miles of each other in North Lancashire (see figure 11.1). In the interwar years an outside observer would probably have felt that Lancaster, Nelson, and Preston were quite similar, except for the greater size of Preston. All were

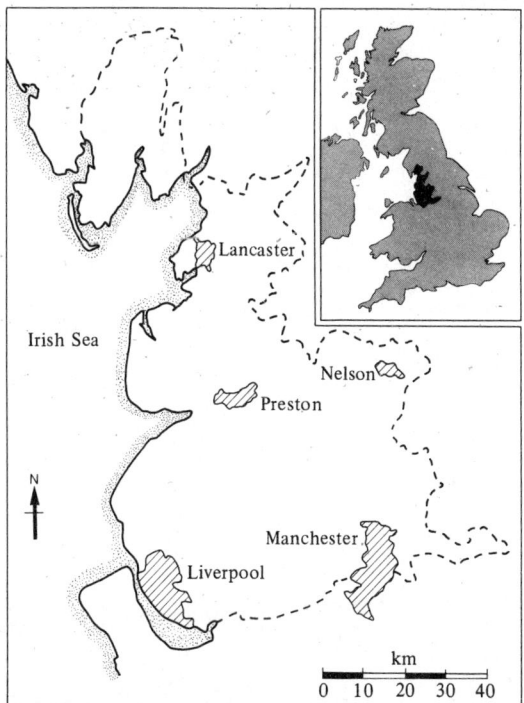

Figure 11.1. The County of Lancashire in the interwar period showing the towns of Lancaster, Nelson, and Preston.

predominantly working-class towns based on factory production; cotton in the case of Nelson and Preston, and linoleum in Lancaster.

It is therefore initially surprising to observe discrepancies between the three towns in their public provision of services. Using the Treasurer's Reports for the three towns in financial years 1924–1925 and 1935–1936, we compared spending on three areas of public services: education; maternity and child welfare; and parks, baths, libraries, and recreational facilities. In both years, Nelson was much the most generous local authority, Lancaster spent least, while Preston fell in between on each of the expenditure heads (see table 11.1). In the earlier year the differences were extremely large, with Nelson spending ten times as much as Lancaster on maternity and child welfare, per head. Even in education, where there was the least divergence, Nelson spent half as much again as either Lancaster or Preston. Between 1925 and 1936, the differential between the towns altered, with Preston's expenditure catching up to some degree with that of Nelson, especially in education. Lancaster, however, remained niggardly.

Such evidence must be used with caution given the difficulties experienced by political scientists trying to explain variations in recent local authority spending (for example, see Sharpe, 1981). In our case the differences in expenditure are so great that technical problems involved in obtaining precisely comparable figures and estimating exactly the number of people eligible for the use of services seem insignificant, as does the reservation that the amount of money spent may not reflect the quality of the services. Previous studies have been divided as to whether expenditure is significantly correlated with local political behaviour (see Newton, 1981b). We hope to show that, for the interwar years at least,

Table 11.1. Approximate per capita net expenditure on some services in financial years 1924–1925 and 1935–1936

Service	Financial year	Lancaster	Preston	Nelson
Education (per child under 15 years of age)	1924–1925 1935–1936	£2 13s 8d £3 8s 1d	£2 17s 7d £4 13s 10d	£4 1s 4d £5 1s 8d
Maternity and child welfare (per woman of 15–44 years of age)	1924–1925 1935–1936	7d 4s 1d	8d 5s 6d	5s 11d 8s 2d
Parks, baths, libraries, and recreation facilities (per head of population)	1924–1925 1935–1936	8d 2s 9d	3s 4d 4s 7d	4s 11d 6s 8d

local politics are of great importance, though it is necessary to look at a number of often neglected political forces.

The most obvious way of explaining these differences would be to look at the strength of the Labour Party in the three localities, the assumption being that a strong Labour Party would be most likely to support extensive public services. This argument is to some extent borne out. Lancaster, with the lowest expenditure on public services, had a notoriously weak Labour movement. No Labour MP was elected for Lancaster until 1966, and the Liberal Party remained an important force throughout the interwar years, winning the seat in a three-cornered contest at a by-election in 1928. Even in 1935, when the Liberal Party elsewhere had lost virtually all its working-class support to the Labour Party, the Liberals pushed Labour into third place at the General Election with a paltry 18% of the votes.

This was reflected in the performance of Labour in municipal elections. Of eighty-seven persons elected to the town council between 1913 and 1939, only thirteen were Labour candidates and five of these were elected between 1936 and 1938. Out of a possible 120 contests in local elections between 1921 and 1935, Labour contested only eleven. The Lancaster Labour Party was based in the local Trades Council, dominated by engineers, public employees, railwaymen, and retail workers, all groups which lacked numerical significance among Lancaster's working class as a whole. Lancaster appears to have deserved a visiting Labour speaker's description of it, in 1930, as 'the black hole of trade unionism'.

In Preston, the Labour movement was rather stronger. In a two-member seat, Tom Shaw, Minister for War in the Labour Government of 1929, held one of the seats between 1918 and 1931. At a municipal level, Labour never won an overall majority, although it came near to doing so in 1929. This partly reflected the presence of nonelected Conservative aldermen in the council chamber, for in many years Labour won a majority of the elected seats. In 1919, 1926, 1928, and 1929, Labour won seven of the twelve seats. The strength of Labour was largely based on extensive unionisation among the town's work force. The Trades Council in Preston was dominated by unions of the engineers, railwaymen, and cotton workers, whose members, unlike Lancaster's, did come from the bulk of the town's working class[20]. The Independent Labour Party (ILP), composed of activists, and the main left-wing force in Labour politics, was, however, quite weak. Despite its frequent insistence that Labour should put up two candidates for the double-member seat, they were easily overruled by the unions on the Trades and Labour Council,

[20]This should not imply that the Trades Council represented all the town's workers. The building trade was never affiliated to the Trades Council, and the general and unskilled unions had various conflicts with the craft unions, especially the Amalgamated Engineering Union in the early 1920s, which led to their temporary exclusion of the general and unskilled unions from the Council.

who refused to risk alienating the Liberal voters by putting up two candidates. Indeed, in the 1920s, Preston was the last constituency in the country where an informal Liberal–Labour alliance operated, with each party only putting up one candidate.

The Nelson Labour Party appears to have been far more radical. Nelson was one of those areas in which a Conservative–Liberal pact arose to fight local elections on an 'antisocialist' ticket. Labour had, briefly, a majority on the local council in the prewar period, but after the war the town council, up until 1927, consisted of equal numbers of Conservative, Liberal, and Labour Councillors. The year 1927 saw a victory for the Labour Party in this town, which was maintained thereafter, in spite of the catastrophic defeat for Arthur Greenwood, the parliamentary Labour candidate, in 1931. Even in that year Labour managed to retain control on the local council. The composition of the local Labour Party in Nelson was significantly different from that of both Lancaster and Preston. The ILP was a far more important political and social force here, with contests within the local party for prospective candidates at parliamentary elections running very close. The Weavers Association was dominant in the local Labour Party, with many local councillors being members.

Expenditure on public services does correspond, at first sight, to the general strength of the Labour Party, as judged by indications of its local membership and electoral success. That Nelson was spending generously in financial year 1924–1925 indicates that it was not solely Labour's control of the council which mattered, since Labour only achieved a majority in 1927, but that local notables of other parties were themselves responsive to pressure from Labour. (Indeed, having a Labour Council did not produce gains for the population of Nelson relative to Preston or Lancaster.) However, it is not necessarily the case that local Labour Parties will always seek to increase spending on municipal services: some local Parties, Preston being an instance, preferred strategies which were, at best, indifferent to such reforms.

A contrast between Preston and Nelson is instructive here. The Labour Party in Preston did not generally support a more active role for the local authority in providing services. In 1921 the *Lancashire Daily Post* (LDP, 1921) observed that in the local election campaign

"the tenor of most of the Labour Party addresses was an indictment of the dominant party for maladministration in the past for unbusinesslike procedure in saddling future ratepayers with the responsibility of long past expenditure and a refutation of the accusations levelled against the Labour Party of having no regard for soaring rates".

This 'ratepayer' perspective led to a conservative approach to public services. Labour Councillors justified their strong advocacy of council house building by arguing that council houses were a sound business investment, since they brought in more rates than it cost to maintain them

(LDP, 1929a). Councillor Morris, the Labour Chairman of the Housing Committee, also expressed his belief that the council houses should be sold off if possible. The Labour Party, he observed, "wished to encourage people who wanted to own their own homes" (LDP, 1925). It was not until the late 1920s that Labour put greater emphasis on the need for low-rent council housing.

Labour's transport policy was also based on 'business principles'. Labour opposed suggestions that the tram service should be financed out of the rates. The 1929 local election seems bizarre to those more accustomed to the recent battle between the Conservative Government and Labour-controlled local authorities over subsidised transport. In 1929 the Conservative candidate in Preston believed that the tram fares should be reduced, and, if necessary, subsidised out of the rates, whereas the Labour Party opposed this, emphasising the need for 'safety first' (LDP, 1929b).

The Nelson Labour Party was entirely committed to the expansion of public and municipal services. The Party took control in 1927 when it found itself with a majority, twenty seats to twelve, and an ILP mayor. In Nelson, as in Preston, the Labour Party also stressed its role as one of service to ratepayers, it having noted that 80% of occupants of houses in the town either owned them or were buying them through building societies (NL, 1928a). However, they were at pains to stress that economy in health, housing, and education was false economy. The existing high levels of health care were to be maintained and plans instigated for the creation of a local hospital. A programme of educational reform was drawn up, which included plans for several nursery schools. Parks were to be provided in the poorer areas of the town. Plans for a municipal bank and systems of rent rebates for poorer tenants were discussed, although these latter two never came to anything. The setting up of a works department and the use of direct labour for the building and servicing of council houses, schools, etc was probably their most contentious local achievement. The *Nelson Leader's* letter column contained a flood of rhetoric about the death of competitive capitalism which was bound to follow from the use of direct labour. Most surprisingly, the Labour Party did reduce the rates, which rather threw the antisocialist candidates. One defeated Liberal complained to a meeting:

"He had just one thing to say about Labour. That Party was going to avoid by hook or by crook raising the rates, so that their opponents would obtain no advantage from them doing that. They had made up their minds that the majority of people owned their own houses or were buying them from building societies, and that meant that they would have to respect the small property owner as well as others" (NL, 1928b).

In power, the Labour Party maintained broadly socialist principles. During lockouts, programmes of assistance and entertainment were provided by the Nelson Council, ranging from feeding centres to cheap bus

trips and free swimming. It campaigned for rises in the rate of
unemployment assistance and poor law assistance, clashing with the
Ministry of Health in 1931 over this issue. It consistently refused to have
military bands at public events, to play the national anthem, would not
celebrate the King's Jubilee, and in the 1930s declared Nelson a 'war-free
zone', all of which helped earn its title of a 'little Moscow'.

In Lancaster the Labour Party was too weak to mount successful
struggles for public service. Lancaster, however, was extensively endowed
with private voluntary provision of services, mainly introduced between
1880 and 1914 at a time when most towns were seeing a decline in this
sort of provision. The leading benefactor was James Williamson, later
Lord Ashton, who owned the major linoleum firm and who provided
Williamson's Park, a town hall, a library, and gave money to local schools
and hospitals. Thomas Storey, also a linoleum employer, provided the
Storey Institute, a technical school, among other gifts.

Whether a direct consequence or not, the Lancaster Labour movement
subsequently developed an ambivalent attitude towards such services. In
one of the few instances of open political conflict during the period
1908-1909 which ensued when Williamson tried to run the nascent ILP
out of Lancaster, his beneficence became an object of debate. Most
Labour activists apparently backed the Trades Council's motion to thank
Lord Ashton for his generosity (Gooderson, 1975; Todd, 1976).

We might, then, characterise the emphases of the three local Labour
movements to public service as follows. Lancaster Labour Party was not
insistent that services should be provided by the state and, in part, gave
support and legitimacy to the initiatives of 'generous' local elite figures.
Preston Labour Party believed that the state had a role to play in the
provision of some services, but that they should be run on business lines
and the 'ratepayer' should be protected. Nelson Labour Party gave
priority to state intervention in various services, implementing ambitious
plans when in control, even while taking account of the fact that most of
their supporters were ratepayers[21].

Public services and women's politics

Why should the orientation of local Labour Parties differ? This is where
the role of women is central. At a national level, writers such as Banks
(1981) and Middleton (1977) have examined the close relationship
between women's movements and welfare campaigns. Many national
women's organisations, such as the Women's Cooperative Guild, exhorted
their members to become involved in local politics as the best way of
pushing forward the women's cause (Webb, 1927). They published lists of

---

[21] We have, for reasons of space, had to ignore changing emphases of the respective
Labour Parties in the interwar years, and we do not want to ascribe a static essentialist
nature to the Labour movement in the three areas. Our accounts are somewhat more
biased towards the 1920s than the 1930s.

the number of Guild members who became Justices of the Peace, Poor Law Guardians, and Councillors, and ran classes to train women for municipal work. During the interwar period, women, perhaps more strongly than any other group, were concerned to retain what they saw as the effectiveness of local autonomy in welfare issues. They campaigned so vehemently over the centralising principles behind the Local Government Act of 1929 that the Minister of Health, Neville Chamberlain, was forced to remove Maternity and Child Welfare services from the terms of the Act. This suggests that women's political activity may be important in explaining local variations in the Labour Party's commitment to public service and 'welfare' in general.

In Nelson, women dominated the town and the voters lists, by sheer force of numbers. Even in 1921, before the extension of the franchise to all women, women voters outnumbered men and, not surprisingly, all political parties were eager to attract the 'women's vote' (seen at this date as qualitatively different from the 'male vote'). Liberals argued the peculiar relevance of their foreign policy to women, while Conservatives stressed the importance to the woman of national economy. There were, by 1921, women's sections of the local Conservative, Liberal, and Labour parties, but the efforts of Conservatives and Liberals seem to have been in vain. As the *Nelson Leader* admitted sadly in 1921 (NL, 1921), "Women are not, as previously believed, a force for Conservatism ... they are the stuff that sentimental socialists are made of".

But this was not simply a question of numbers, for by 1921 there existed in Nelson a thriving women's movement. Before World War 1, Nelson had been a stronghold of the Lancashire suffrage campaign (Liddington and Norris, 1978). Throughout the War, the women in Nelson campaigned for peace, with enormous local support. After the War, however, women largely removed their affiliations from all-women organisations, such as the Nelson branch of the National Union of Womans Suffrage Societies. In the interwar period they worked through membership of other associations to which they belonged, presumably on the assumption, not unwarranted, that having obtained the vote their interests could best be met through democratic representation at central and local government level. In the prewar period, some women had been members of the Marxist Social Democratic Federation and the ILP. After the War, however, the ILP was the most important radical political force, and the number of women in this organisation, at some points, exceeded that of men. They belonged to the two large and active branches of the Women's Cooperative Guild, and probably most importantly, a large proportion of the membership of the Weavers' Association was female (although most committee members were men). By the late 1920s they played an important part in the Communist Party and the 'Rank and File' committees. Membership of these various organisations overlapped, a web of political and social affiliations emerging. The strength of women in the

Labour Party was thus wielded by its constituent associations and, especially, through the numbers of women involved in the Weavers' Association. It was this strength and organisation of women locally that served to politicise women's welfare issues—and allowed broad interpretations as to exactly what were women's issues, housing and education for instance, early in the period.

In Preston the situation was rather different. There was a fairly strong independent women's movement, but the Labour Party was hostile to feminist causes. This cleavage was evident before World War 1 when the leading suffrage campaigner, Edith Rigby, resigned from Preston Women's Labour League to join the militant Women's Suffrage and Political Union. Her explanation for this action focused on the hostility of the Labour movement to the women's cause. She

> "had been very surprised at the little support which had been given the [Women's Labour] League from the Labour sections ... many men in the trade union movement had not encouraged their wives to think politically and to study the political situation. They only considered women important when they could persuade them to vote the other way at a municipal election" (PG, 1908).

Women continued their independent movement after World War 1 by forming the Women's Citizens Association (WCA), which attempted to get women elected to the town council and which pressured the Preston Council over such issues as the compulsory retirement of married council employees and the need for women police. A similar body had been formed in Nelson in the early 1920s, but failed to get off the ground. In Preston the WCA was sufficiently strong to have several of its members elected to the town council in the early 1920s, with unofficial Conservative support, all of them in opposition to Labour candidates. It remains unclear whether the WCA allied to the Conservative Party because the WCA membership was generally in sympathy with Conservatism and the Party's class base, or because the Labour Party proved impervious to women's political objectives.

The Preston Labour Party *was* hostile to women's political activity. In part this reflected the relative weakness of the ILP, always to the fore in feminist campaigns. The Labour Party refused to set up a Women's Section until 1924, and the Women's Cooperative Guild, with only one small branch in Preston, was weak compared with that of Nelson.

In Lancaster there was virtually no political activity by women. Although there is some evidence of suffrage campaigning before 1914, women scarcely appear on the political scene in the interwar period. Indicative of this, perhaps, is the fact that, even though some 1400 women linoleum workers were replaced by men between 1921 and 1931, destroying a principal form of women's employment in the town, there was no sign of protest or resistance (see Warde, 1982).

The importance of women's political organisations, and their effect upon the Labour Party's orientation to public services, can best be indicated by looking in detail at maternity and child welfare provision. Nelson had an excellent service. A municipal maternity and child welfare clinic was provided by 1916, even before the introduction of the Maternity and Child Welfare Act of 1918. The establishment of this clinic came in the wake of a local campaign by women. In 1921 a municipal maternity home was established with eleven beds, and it also ran antenatal sessions. Certainly by the 1930s this provided two sessions a week, with the second session in the evening, so that employed expectant mothers could attend without losing wages[22].

Many of those admitted to the home went on reduced fees or were admitted free, especially after 1931. Almost all births in the town were attended by both doctor and midwife: in 1937, 97.7% of births in Nelson were attended by a general practitioner[23]. The council employed six municipal midwives who undertook confinement, postnatal care, and home visits to children under five years of age. Levels of antenatal care were high. 75% of pregnant women received antenatal care, as compared with 50% in England and Wales and 30% in Lancaster. Nelson also provided, by the 1930s, postnatal care, which, according to the PEP (1937) Report on the *British Health Services*, was almost unique. Generous milk and feeding schemes for expectant and nursing mothers and children were implemented in Nelson after the war, and maintained throughout the period in spite of attempts by the Ministry of Health to curtail them. The maternity home came under pressure from the Ministry of Health on grounds of expense in 1928[24], and was also criticised by several local Councillors, but in spite of these criticisms the service was maintained.

Qualitatively, the maternity and child welfare services in Nelson showed a sympathetic understanding of the needs of working mothers, which elsewhere was absent. All financial assistance was administered through the Council rather than through the poor law as in some other areas. The Chairman of the Health Committee told a meeting of mothers in 1917 that:

"They knew that the expectant nursing mother saw anxious time and extra expense in front of her, and she had to work harder to prepare for it just when she should be resting ... if there was an expectant mother who was not in a position to get the necessities required, if she would make her case known, it would be looked into and the nourishing food necessary would be provided by the committee" (NL, 1917).

[22] Public Records Office, file PRO. MH 661764, page 50; copy available from the office at Ruskin Avenue, Kew, Richmond, London.

[23] Public Records Office, file PRO. MH 661764.

[24] Lancashire County Records Office, file LCRO.MBNe 1/17; copy available from the office at Bow Lane, Preston, Lancashire.

Unlike other areas the practice of mothers working was never condemned by local doctors or Medical Officers of Health. The local Officer was quick to point out that slums, poverty, and overcrowding were the reasons for high infant mortality in other industrial towns with a high rate of female employment. It was not that mothers were any worse off (NL, 1927). Indeed, infant mortality in Nelson was low throughout the period.

In Preston, despite the high level of maternal mortality—well above the average for county boroughs—the Labour Party was remarkably apathetic, especially in the early 1920s, not even pressing for the statutory minimum in maternity and child welfare provision. One Labour Councillor in 1923 remarked that "the Maternity and Child Welfare Committee had brought nothing but bills before the Council" (PG, 1923). Jeremiah Wooley, the first Labour Mayor and Secretary of the Weavers' Union, stoutly "claimed for himself and his trade society ... to have done as much in the interests of maternity and child welfare as any other organisation in his town; his society having loaned a room since 1913" (LDP, 1923a).

This attitude may explain why Preston had a very bad record in its maternity provision. By the early 1930s, Preston had six maternity and child welfare clinics, which a Ministry of Health Report in 1929 criticised for providing "unsatisfactory centre premises", with "too few sessions" at the clinic[25]. Thirty-one maternity beds had recently been provided in the Sharoe Green Hospital, the old Poor Law Infirmary taken over from the Guardians in 1929, but it was felt by the Ministry to be 'inadequately staffed'. All other maternity care was in the hands of private midwives, there being no municipal midwives.

Lancaster's maternity and child welfare service was in a similar state. By the 1930s there was one antenatal clinic and three children's clinics. There were maternity beds in the Infirmary, as in Preston, and about one birth in three took place there.

In the case of this service it is clear that the position of women, their organisation and strength within the locality is reflected, qualitatively and quantitatively, in the provision of services. The relationship between women and the Labour movement is central. It is not, of course, the case that the Nelson Labour movement was simply more 'open' to women's pressure. Women in Nelson were well-organised and able to exert pressure, whereas in Lancaster and Preston they appear to have been unable to do so.

The relative apathy of the Preston Labour Party to public provision of services can be contrasted with their much greater enthusiasm for measures likely to improve the money wages of the working class. They were extremely active in supporting unemployment relief schemes for male workers. Great concern was shown that all council work should be done in the towns to provide as much work there as possible. In 1927 a Labour candidate stressed the need that "every municipal undertaking

[25]Public Records Office, file PRO. MH 66.

should be so managed to bring trade to the town and so relieve the ratepayers instead of being a burden to them" (LDP, 1927). When, in 1925, Preston Corporation gave a contract to build an electric turbine to the local engineering firm of Dick, Kerr and Co, Councillor Ellison, speaking for the Labour Group, "could not let that opportunity pass without saying how pleased they were with the committee's action in securing a guarantee for the firm that Preston would get the full benefit of the contract" (LDP, 1923b). The concern surfaced again during the prolonged negotiations in the late 1920s to encourage Courtaulds to build a new factory in Preston, with the Labour Party keen advocates of the Corporation and doing anything necessary to attract it.

In Nelson these concerns were less prominent. It was not until 1932 that the Labour-controlled Council set about trying to advertise Nelson to prospective employers, and even then the approach was distinctive. A booklet produced in that year for prospective new employers described a well-dressed, well-fed, well-paid, highly unionised, and skilled work force as the main attraction. Municipal advantages were also stressed. Nelson offered the advantage of 'a modern town'. "No slums can be found in the whole town. There are wide clean streets and the new housing sites are a revelation, with the graceful curves of their avenues and well-constructed roads" (NL, 1932). Lancaster also made attempts to attract new industry. It was very successful, and actually persuaded Amos Nelson Ltd, the principal employer in the town of Nelson, to locate a new artificial silk mill in Lancaster. Lancaster's town council in the 1930s attributed its general success in such endeavours to having publicised the reliability and flexibility of its work force. Preston's advertising was equally prosaic, drawing attention to the availability of male workers in the town.

Local Labour Parties seem, then, to have pursued rather different objectives. The Preston Labour Party clearly felt that the main way of improving the position of the working class was through increased money wages, and they were aware that the local council played an important role in establishing conditions which might facilitate this. However, they tended to play down the extent to which the local authority could actually intervene directly to improve the position of the working class through an increased 'social wage'. In Nelson, by contrast, there was a much more positive view of the local authority's role in providing services. These different attitudes coincide with differences in the political strength and organisation of women in the respective locations.

Explaining women's political behaviour

Much of the existing literature on women and politics has focused upon national comparisons and international variations in women's political activity, one of the most important explanations of such variation being the participation of women in the labour market (Lovenduski and Hills, 1981). Our work, however, suggests that there are important differences in the workplace experiences of women which affect their political participation, and which only become apparent when local variations are examined. Female participation in the labour market does not appear to be a sufficient condition of women's political activity. The type of work being performed and the precise gender relations involved in the work will also have important effects on the nature and effectivity of women's political activity.

The lack of female political activity in Lancaster could be explained by the relatively low participation of women in paid employment. In 1931, 32.8% of Lancaster's women were economically active, slightly below the national average of 34.8%. Furthermore, those women who did work were distributed among several sectors; only 24% of working women worked in textiles, with 30% in personal service and 14% in commercial jobs, mainly retailing. In Lancaster, women were likely to work outside factory production, in jobs where they would have frequent contact with their employer, a factor known to reduce militancy (Newby, 1977). The relative quiescence of male workers in Lancaster is partly explained by the nature of the linoleum industry in Lancaster. In 1931 it employed 19% of those in work, and many general labourers also worked in it. Unlike the cotton industry, which relied on female labour, by 1931 the work force was overwhelmingly male. 27% of employed men worked in linoleum, compared with only 3% of women. The two major firms were Williamsons, which employed 3000 people, and Storeys.

The linoleum work force was not unionised, and Williamson himself, until his death in 1932, was an authoritarian paternalist. Whereas cotton employers in Preston, Nelson, and elsewhere in Lancashire were among the first employers in the country to engage in collective bargaining with trades unions (Burgess, 1975), Williamson refused to recognise them, except among his skilled engineering workers.

Williamson's paternalism was as a consequence more far-reaching than that of the cotton employer (on which see Joyce, 1980). He traditionally guaranteed a job for life to his workers, and until World War 1 ran his mills even in times of depression to provide full employment. He also paid retirement pensions.

This paternalism aimed at securing the dependence of the town's work force was evidently successful in retaining the loyalty of the working class, even as recently as the 1930s. In Nelson and Preston such paternalist strategies were largely absent. In Nelson the firms were very small, with few employing over 200, and there were no great individual employers who dominated the town. Though Preston had larger firms, such as Horrockses, which employed over 3000, their paternalism was less pervasive than that of Lancaster. Here no cotton firms paid pensions for their workers or ran their mills in depressions.

A final factor cementing the grip of Williamson over Lancaster's working class was the nature of the labour process in linoleum. In cotton weaving the employer left a great deal of discretion to the overlooker (see chapter 10 above), and the work was highly skilled because of the poor machinery. In linoleum making, however, the old craftsmen hand-trowellers (who spread the 'kiver', or linoleum covering, onto the cloth base) had been displaced in the 1880s and the process effectively mechanised (see Christie, 1964, pages 89-94). After this date, necessary skills were largely passed on through 'migration' (More, 1980), whereby a foreman promoted selected workers to learn more difficult processes. The possibility of advancement at work was therefore dependent on conformity and reliability. This was not true of the cotton industry, where there was always a premium on a good weaver. The nature of work in linoleum thus provided a work force receptive to Williamson's paternalist politics. This almost certainly explains the attachment of large sections of the working class to the Liberal Party into the interwar years, Williamson having been the Liberal MP for the town in the 1890s.

It may initially seem more difficult to explain the different political complexion of Nelson and Preston given the role of the cotton industry in both towns. The idea that there is a close correlation between women's participation in the labour market and their increased likelihood of being politically active does not appear to explain the difference. In 1931, 52.7% of Preston's women were economically active, the figure for Nelson being only slightly higher at 57.2%. Furthermore, in both towns, most of the women worked in cotton; 74% of employed women were cotton workers in Nelson, and 51% in Preston. Preston had rather more alternative work for women; 13% of working women were in personal services (6% in Nelson) and 8% were in commercial occupations (6% in Nelson).

More striking than these differences, however, are those between men's employment in the two towns. In Nelson, 49.1% of men were engaged in cotton weaving: there were nearly as many men in weaving as women; 6895 to 7669, respectively. There was no alternative industry of any size for men, the only other substantial employment being in commerce (9%) and general labouring (9%). In Preston, however, only 10% of men worked in cotton by 1931. The engineering industry had become the main source of employment for men (employing 11% of men in 1931), having expanded very rapidly after 1900 with the growth of tram and vehicle building at the works of Dick, Kerr and Co. Preston was also an important transport centre, having a small dock and a large number of railway workers.

The implications of this are considerable. Even though most *women* did roughly the same work in both Nelson and Preston, their work experiences were distinctively different, because in Nelson men were also dependent on weaving. Men and women worked alongside each other and earned similar wages (though some men worked six looms rather than the customary four). A Mrs Abbot, Chairperson of the Open Door Council, visited Nelson in 1930 and told the local newspaper of "the interest with which she had seen men and women cotton operatives working side by side with equal rights" (NL, 1930). Thus the conditions under which men and women sold their labour power were similar in Nelson. As Savage argues, in chapter 10 above, there was a strong patriarchal component to control over weavers in Preston: overlookers were men, weavers women. Such a mode of control could not be appropriate where a large proportion of weavers were men. The structure of authority at work in Nelson was thus one in which men and women were subordinated in identical ways. Furthermore, women were recognised by their male colleagues as genuinely skilled workers. Weaving was regarded as a highly skilled occupation in Nelson, where fine and fancy clothes were manufactured and, in a community where weaving seems to have dominated conversation and social life, women weavers stood to have considerable prestige. If the nature of the labour process affects political mobilisation, then we might expect women under such conditions to be politically active to a similar degree to men.

In Preston the small number of male weavers created a rather different situation. Out of the 4600 male cotton workers, 2000 of these were in the small spinning industry, and many other men worked in the elite jobs associated with weaving as tapesizers, overlookers, clothlookers, or drawers. Weaving itself was a predominantly female occupation. In 1921, 88.15% of weavers were female, and the few male weavers would generally be younger men hoping to be promoted to a better job. The sexual division of labour in weaving was thus linked to the authority structure of the mill, with the men being the managers and overlookers.

The various male cotton occupations were all unionised and had some degree of control over entry, which was used to prevent women being promoted into men's jobs. The Warehousemen's Union which organised clothlookers and ancillary workers in the warehouse did have some female members, but it maintained a differential between male and female wages and ensured that women were not used in men's work. In 1930 the Union complained that at Queen's Mill a woman was doing a man's work when a male worker was sacked and replaced by a female one[26]. The Overlookers' Union also attempted to control entry, and, between 1900 and 1918, only admitted members' male relatives. The tapesizers and drawers had similar restrictions.

During World War 1 the Preston Spinners' Union had to face proposals to use female labour in the spinning rooms because of the shortage of male labour. This it strenuously resisted, and managed to prevent their

[26]See Preston Employers' Joint Meetings with operatives, 1 March 1980 (located in the Lancashire County Records Library, Bow Lane, Preston, Lancashire).

use (Braybon, 1981; Cartmell, 1919). The engineering industry had witnessed similar conflicts. The works of Dick, Kerr and Co had been used as a munitions factory in World War 1, and over 2000 women were employed there in 1917, but, as the Mayor of Preston pointed out, "the numbers would have been even larger but for the opposition of the skilled men's unions to a further extension of what was called dilution" (Cartmell, 1919, page 133).

In Preston, then, women were concentrated in a ghettoised weaving sector. The skilled male workers, who formed a significant part of the local labour force, regarded female labour as a threat and had a history of conflict with women. It was, furthermore, their unions which were well represented in the Trades and Labour Council and hence dictated the tenor of local labour politics.

One reason for the apparent political apathy of women in Preston may thus have been their hostility to a well-unionised grade of workers, active in the Labour Party and marked by their exclusionary practices in the workplace. Although at certain points the local Labour Party appears to have paid lip service to the wider calls for women's equality within the Party nationally, it seems that in the 1920s a very real hostility to women workers existed. Women were not a powerful voice in the Weavers' Union, but were a low-paid ghettoised group. Besides, as we have seen, that union itself was relatively insignificant in Preston politics. The success of patriarchal exclusionary tactics on the part of the unions, and an upholding of the notion of a 'family wage' paid to men, silenced women's voices in local politics. Even women themselves saw a Labour vote as part of defending the wage. Some Preston mill girls, asked why they were supporting the Labour Party, replied,

"women who have left work to take on domestic duties are being compelled to return because their husbands are either unemployed or do not earn enough to ensure a decent standard of living ... Lancashire women are not going back to a 6.00 in the morning start, we are not going backwards at all, we are going forwards" (LDP, 1929c).

Conclusion
We have argued that women have a double interest in the state provision of welfare services, both as nonpaid or low-paid workers and as persons with primary responsibility for domestic labour. For two reasons this was particularly the case in the United Kingdom interwar. First, the system of public finance was redistributive, central grants to local government being funded out of taxation of the middle class. Second, the norms regulating financial responsibilities between men and women in the household meant that any transfer of expenses from the household budget to the state directly benefitted women. Thus the transfer of service functions from the domestic mode of production to public provision could improve the

situation of women, although our work suggests that in many areas, lacking the pressure of organised women, much enabling legislation was never implemented. The extension of such services depended to a significant degree on the local balance of power in the interwar period. In this respect, the cleavages, identified in the literature on collective consumption as a basis for a new politics giving new expression to social inequality (Castells, 1977), seem to have existed in the United Kingdom for a long time. Perhaps 'new' movements in this sphere have developed, deriving from the failure of the state to satisfy promises of universal provision. New areas for struggle have also been opened up since World War 2. However, we suspect that it has been the tendency of the urban politics literature to ignore women which has allowed 'consumption cleavages' to go unnoticed in earlier periods.

Our empirical evidence supports the contention that gender is a principal cleavage to which the state reacts in the extension of welfare provision. Not much is known about the political mobilisation of women, or the conditions under which they come to be an effective social force, except in relation to the feminist movement per se. The 'reformist' politics of women manual workers is untrodden ground. It has generally been assumed that economic participation has been the critical precondition of political mobilisation by women. Thus, for instance, MacIntyre (1980) in *Little Moscows* suggested that women's social position was somewhat better, their political impact somewhat greater, where they were engaged in the formal economy: in the textile-dyeing locality of the Vale of Leven there was less domestic violence and more industrial and political participation by women than in the mining settlements of Mardy and Lumphinnans. Women's widespread participation in the formal economy probably has been a necessary condition of their constituting a political force. However, our comparison between Preston and Nelson suggests that it is not a sufficient condition. The relations between men and women in the production process itself is a critical variable. In Nelson, men and women did the same weaving work, side by side, in roughly equal numbers. This prevented the use of patriarchal modes of control in the workplace by overlookers, which was typical of Preston. The circumstances of, so to speak, equality between men and women in their subordination at work seems to have been conducive to women's political mobilisation, and perhaps also to lower degrees of patriarchal domination in domestic and neighbourhood spheres. That few areas like Nelson have been documented should not lead us to underestimate the importance of this further pernicious effect of labour-market segmentation.

Our analysis of urban politics also casts light on the confused area of the relationship between class struggles and urban, or consumption, struggles. This was one issue over which Castells, for instance, was ambivalent[27]. Although Castells is correct to stress that the relationship between urban and class struggles is important, he gives no explanation of why some local working classes seem to struggle over these issues and others not. Study of the mobilisation of women in the United Kingdom in the interwar period gives some answers. Women intervened in interwar local politics at two levels. They joined urban social movements and voluntary associations specifically for women. They also joined political parties. In the absence of a women's party it was normal for the demands of the movements and associations to be routed through existing political parties. In the case of demands for improved public provision of services directed towards the (re)production of labour power, the Labour Party was the principal conduit. Because of this the independent effect of women as a political force has frequently been overlooked, it being assumed instead that welfare reform and trade-union economism were impulses from the same social bases. In fact, in many instances, these seem to have been competing, if not wholly exclusive, alternative strategies for local Labour Parties. As several writers have documented, male political and industrial militancy does not necessarily coincide with a commitment towards the emancipation of women (Cooke, 1985a; MacIntyre, 1980). The Labour movement has acted as an umbrella organisation within which such strategies have been fought over. The local political strength of women shaped the extent to which policies for social amelioration were pursued. Ironically, then, it might be said that, in the United Kingdom interwar, Castells's political hope for the fusion of urban and class struggles to transform urban life was given a trial, with the growth of a centralised and patriarchal welfare state as its midterm consequence.

[27]Sometimes Castells considers that urban social movements "permit the progressive formation of an anti-capitalist alliance upon a much broader objective basis than that of the specific interests of the proletariat or their contingent political alliances" (1978, page 36). On other occasions he argues that the working class is of central importance within these movements. He insists that "it is the relationship between urban struggles and class struggles and in their concentrated expression as class political struggles that one must seek their different historical roles" (1978, page 149). Castells illustrates this proposition by arguing that the difference between Italian and North American urban social movements is to be found by examining the differing role of the working class in them.

References

Acker J, 1973 "Women and social stratification: a case of intellectual sexism" *American Journal of Sociology* **78** 936-945

Alexander S, 1976 "Women's work in nineteenth century London" in *The Rights and Wrongs of Women* Eds J Mitchell, A Oakley (Penguin Books, Harmondsworth, Middx) pp 59-111

Allin P, 1982 "Women's activity rates and regional employment markets" Office of Population Censuses and Surveys OP 28, St Catherines House, 10 Kingsway, London WC2, England

AMB, 1976 "The ideal secretary—a survey of employers' expectations and requirements" Survey of secretarial and clerical salaries; The Statistical Services Division, Alfred Marks Bureau Ltd, 11 Soho Square, London W1V 5DB

Andrews H F, 1971 "A cluster analysis of British towns" *Urban Studies* **8** 271-283

Andrews I, 1918 *Economic Effects of the War upon Women and Children in Great Britain* Carnegie Economic Studies of the War (Oxford University Press, New York)

Arensberg C, Kimball S, 1968 *Family and Community in Ireland* (Harvard University Press, Cambridge, MA)

Armen G, 1972 "A classification of cities and city regions in England and Wales 1966" *Regional Studies* **6** 149-182

Ball R M, 1980 "The use and definition of travel-to-work-areas in Great Britain: some problems" *Regional Studies* **14** 125-139

Banks O, 1981 *Faces of Feminism: A Study of Feminism as a Social Movement* (Martin Robertson, Oxford)

Barker J, Downing H, 1980 "Word processing and the transformation of the patriarchal relations of control in the office" *Capital and Class* issue 10, 64-99

Barron R D, Norris G M, 1976 "Sexual divisions and the dual labour market" in *Dependence and Exploitation in Work and Marriage* Eds S Allen, D Leonard (Longman, London) pp 47-69

Beechey V, 1977 "Some notes on female wage labour in capitalist production" *Capital and Class* issue 3 (Autumn), 45-66

Beechey V, 1978 "Women and production: a critical analysis of some sociological theories of women's work" in *Feminism and Materialism: Women and Modes of Production* Eds A Kuhn, A M Wolpe (Routledge and Kegan Paul, Henley on Thames, Oxon) pp 155-197

Beechey V, 1982 "The sexual division of labour and the labour process: a critical assessment of Braverman" in *The Degradation of Work?* Ed. S Wood (Hutchinson, London) pp 54-73

Beechey V, 1983 "Reconceptualising women's employment" paper presented to the Sexual Divisions Study Group of the British Sociological Association, Oxford, December, further details available from S Walby

Bell C, Newby H, 1976 "Husbands and wives: the dynamics of the deferential dialectic", in *Dependence and Exploitation in Work and Marriage* Eds S Allen, D Leonard (Longman, London) pp 152-168

Bell D, 1974 *The Coming of Post-industrial Society* (Heinemann Educational Books, London)

Bergmann B R, 1980a "Curing high unemployment rates among blacks and women" in *The Economics of Women and Work* Ed. A H Amsden (Penguin Books, Harmondsworth, Middx) pp 350-358

Bergmann B R, 1980b "Occupational segregation, wages and profits when employers discriminate by race or sex" in *The Economics of Women and Work* Ed. A H Amsden (Penguin Books, Harmondsworth, Middx) pp 271-282

Bertaux D, 1977 *Destins Personnels et Structure de Classe* (Presses Universitaires de France, Paris)

Blackaby F (Ed.), 1978 *De-industrialisation* (Heinemann Educational Books, London)

Blanke B, Jürgens U, Kastendiek H, 1978 "On the current Marxist discussion of the analysis of form and function" in *State and Capital* Eds J Holloway, S Picciotto (Edward Arnold, London) pp 108-147

Bluestone B, Harrison B, 1982 *The Deindustrialization of America* (Basic Books, New York)

BNTR, 1925 and 1936 *Borough of Nelson Treasurer's Report*, Nelson Public Library, Nelson, Lancs.

Bosanquet N, Doeringer P, 1973 "Is there a dual labour market in Great Britain?" *Economic Journal* 83 421-435

Bowers J, 1970 *The Anatomy of Regional Activity Rates* National Institute of Economic and Social Research Regional Papers 1 (Cambridge University Press, Cambridge)

Braverman H, 1974 *Labour and Monopoly Capital* (Monthly Review Press, New York)

Braybon G, 1981 *Women Workers in the First World War* (Croom Helm, Beckenham, Kent)

Brenner R, 1977 "The origins of capitalist development: a critique of neo-Smithian Marxism" *New Left Review* **104** 25-93

Brody H, 1973 *Inishkillane: Change and Decay in the West of Ireland* (Allen Lane, London)

Brooks J B, 1950 *Lancashire Bred* (Church Army Press, Cowley, Oxon)

Broom L, Duncan-Jones P, Lancaster-Jones F, McDonnell P, 1977 *Investigating Social Mobility* (Australian National University Press, Canberra)

Bruegel I, 1979 "Women as a reserve army of labour: a note on recent British experience" *Feminist Review* **3** 12-23

BSO, nd *Historical Record of the Census of Production, 1907 to 1970* Business Statistics Office (HMSO, London)

BSO, 1978a *Report on the Census of Production—Fertilizers* PA 278, Business Statistics Office (HMSO, London)

BSO, 1978b *Report on the Census of Production—Production of Man-made Fibres* PA 411, Business Statistics Office (HMSO, London)

BSO, 1978c *Report on the Census of Production—Weaving of Cotton, Linen and Man-made Fibres* PA 413, Business Statistics Office (HMSO, London)

Buck T, 1979 "Regional class differences" *International Journal of Urban and Regional Research* **3** 516-526

Burgess K, 1975 *The Origins of British Industrial Relations* (Croom Helm, Beckenham, Kent)

Burns S, 1977 *The Household Economy* (Beacon Press, Boston, MA)

Carruthers W I, 1957 "A classification of service centres in England and Wales" *Geographical Journal* **123** 371-389

Carter I G, 1972 "In the beginning was the board: thoughts on the ideology of regional planning" mimeograph, Department of Sociology, University of Aberdeen, Aberdeen AB9 1FX, Scotland

Carter I G, 1974 "The Highlands of Scotland as an underdeveloped region" in *Sociology and Development* Eds E deKadt, G Williams (Tavistock Publications, Andover, Hants) pp 279-311

Carter I G, 1976 "Kailyard: the literature of decline in nineteenth century Scotland" *Scottish Journal of Sociology* **1** 1-13

Carter I G, 1979 *Farmlife in Northeast Scotland 1840-1914* (John Donald, Edinburgh)

Cartmell H, 1919 *For Remembrance: An Account of Some Fateful Years* (Toulmin and Sons, Preston, Lancs)

Castells M, 1977 *The Urban Question: A Marxist Approach* (Edward Arnold, London)

Castells M, 1978 *City, Class and Power* (Macmillan, London)

Castells M, 1980 *The Economic Crisis and American Society* (Basil Blackwell, Oxford)

Cawson A, 1982 *Corporatism and Welfare: Social Policy and State Intervention* (Heinemann Educational Books, London)

Cawson A, Saunders P, 1983 "Corporatism, competitive politics and class struggle" in *Capital and Politics* Ed. R King (Routledge and Kegan Paul, Henley-on-Thames, Oxon) pp 8–27

CEPR, 1980 *Cambridge Economic Policy Review* volume 6, issue 2 (Gower, Aldershot, Hants)

CEPR, 1982 *Cambridge Economic Policy Review* volume 8 issue 2 (Gower, Aldershot, Hants)

CFT, 1890 *Cotton Factory Times* 27 August

CFT, 1911 *Cotton Factory Times* 16 June

CFT, 1929a *Cotton Factory Times* 22 February

CFT, 1929b *Cotton Factory Times* 29 March

CFT, 1929c *Cotton Factory Times* 1 March

CFT, 1929d *Cotton Factory Times* 8 November

CFT, 1930a *Cotton Factory Times* 25 April

CFT, 1930b *Cotton Factory Times* 24 October

CFT, 1930c *Cotton Factory Times* 22 August

Chiplin and Sloane, 1976 *Sex Discrimination in the Labour Market* (Macmillan, London)

Chodorow N, 1978 *The Reproduction of Mothering: Psychoanalysis and the Sociology of Gender* (University of Californian Press, Berkeley, CA)

Chombart de Lauwe M J, Chombart de Lauwe P H, Huguet M, Perroy E, Bissert N, 1963 *La Femme dans la Societe* (Centre Nationale de la Recherche Scientifique, Paris)

Christie G, 1964 *Storeys of Lancaster 1848–1964* (William Collins, London)

CIS, 1974 "Courtaulds, inside and out" report 10, Counter Information Services, 9 Poland Street, London W1V 3DG

Clay H, 1929 *The Post-war Unemployment Problem* (Macmillan, London)

Cockburn C, 1981 "The material of male power" *Feminist Review* **9** 41–58

Cohen A P (Ed.), 1982 *Belonging* (Manchester University Press, Manchester)

COI, 1978 *Chemicals* Central Office of Information (HMSO, London)

Connelly P, 1978 *Last Hired, First Fired: Women and the Canadian Work Force* (The Women's Press, Toronto)

Cooke P, 1981 "Tertiarisation and socio-spatial differentiation in Wales" *Geoforum* **12** 319–330

Cooke P, 1982 "Class relations and uneven development in Wales" in *Diversity and Decomposition in the Labour Market* Eds G Day, D Robbins (Gower, Aldershot, Hants) pp 147–178

Cooke P, 1983 *Theories of Planning and Spatial Development* (Hutchinson, London)

Cooke P, 1985a "Radical regions: a comparison of South Wales, Emilia and Provence" in *Political Action and Social Identity: Class, Locality and Culture* Ed. G Rees (Macmillan, London) in press

Cooke P, 1985b "Class practices as regional markers: a contribution to labour geography" in *Social Relations and Spatial Structures* Eds D Gregory, J Urry (Macmillan, London) pp 213–241

Coombes M G, Dixon J S, Goddard J B, Openshaw S, Taylor P J, 1978 "Towards a more rational consideration of census areal units: daily urban systems in Britain" *Environment and Planning A* **10** 1179–1185

Coombes M G, Dixon J S, Goddard J B, Openshaw S, Taylor P J, 1979a "Daily urban systems in Britain: from theory to practice" *Environment and Planning A* **11** 565–574

Coombes M G, Dixon J S, Goddard J B, Openshaw S, Taylor P J, 1979b "The
    standard metropolitan labour area concept revisited" in *Developments in Urban and
    Regional Analysis. London Papers in Regional Science 10* Ed. M J Breheny (Pion,
    London) pp 140–159

Coombes M G, Dixon J S, Goddard J B, Openshaw S, Taylor P J, 1981 *Appropriate
    Areas for Census Analysis: An Outline of Functional Regions* Centre for Urban and
    Regional Development Studies DP 41, University of Newcastle upon Tyne,
    Newcastle upon Tyne NE1 7RU, England

Coombes M G, Openshaw S, 1982 "The use and definition of travel-to-work-areas in
    Great Britian: some comments" *Regional Studies* **16** 141–149

Coote A, Hewitt P, 1980 "The stance of Britain's major parties and interest groups"
    in *Work and the Family* Eds P Moss, W Fonda (Maurice Temple Smith, London)
    pp 135–159

Corrigan P, 1977 "Feudal relics or capitalist monuments? Notes on the sociology of
    unfree labour" *Sociology* **11** 411–463

Cowling K, 1980 *Mergers and Economic Performances* (Cambridge University Press,
    Cambridge)

Coyle A, 1980 "The protection racket" *Feminist Review* **4** 1–14

CPAG, 1980 "Surveying the cuts" Child Action Poverty Group *Poverty* issue 47, 3–20

Crick B (Ed.), 1981 *Unemployment* (Methuen, Andover, Hants)

Crum R E, Gudgin G, 1977 *Non-Production Activities in UK Manufacturing Industry*
    Regional Policies Series (EEC Commission, Brussels)

CSELWG, 1980 *The Alternative Economic Strategy* Conference of Socialist Economists
    London Working Group (CSE Books, London)

CSEMG, 1980 *Microelectronics* Conference of Socialist Economists Microelectronics
    Group (CSE Books, London)

Daniel W, Stilgoe E, 1976 "Towards an American way of unemployment?" *New
    Society* 12 February, 321–323

Davies D, 1978 "Public and not-so-public relations" in *The Shetland Way of Oil*
    Ed. J Bulton (The Thule Press, Forres, Morayshire) pp 44–60

Davies M, 1979 "Women's place is at the typewriter: the feminisation of the clerical
    labour force" in *Capitalist Patriarchy and the Case for Socialist Feminism* Ed.
    Z R Eisenstein (Monthly Review Press, New York) pp 248–269

Delphy C, 1977 *The Main Enemy* (Women's Research and Resource Centre Publications,
    London)

Delphy C, 1981 "Women in stratification studies" in *Doing Feminist Research*
    Ed. H Roberts (Routledge and Kegan Paul, Henley-on-Thames, Oxon) pp 114–128

Department of Employment, 1978 "Review of travel-to-work areas" *Department of
    Employment Gazette* **86** 815–816

Department of Employment, 1979 *New Earnings Survey* (HMSO, London)

Doeringer P B, Piore M J, 1971 *Internal Labour Markets and Manpower Analysis*
    (Lexington Books, Lexington, MA)

DoI, 1983 *Regional Industrial Development* Department of Industry Cmnd 9111
    (HMSO, London)

Donnison D, Soto P, 1980 *The Good City: A Study of Urban Development and
    Policy in Britain* (Heinemann Educational Books, London)

Drake B, 1920 *Women in Trade Unions* (George Allen and Unwin, Hemel Hempstead,
    Herts)

Drewett J, Goddard J B, Spence N, 1976 *British Cities: Urban Population and
    Employment Trends 1951–1971* research report 10, Department of Environment
    (HMSO, London)

Duncan O D, 1961 "A socio-economic index for all occupations" in *Occupations and Social Status* Eds A J Reiss and others (Free Press, New York) pp 109-138

Dunford M, Geddes M, Perrons D, 1981 "Regional policy and the crisis in the UK: a long-run perspective" *International Journal of Urban and Regional Research* **5** 377-410

Dunleavy P, 1979 "The urban basis of political alignment: social class, domestic property ownership and state intervention in the consumption process" *British Journal of Political Science* **9** 409-433

Dunleavy P, 1980 "The political implications of sectoral cleavages and the growth of state employment. Part 2: cleavage structures and political alignment" *Political Studies* **28** 527-549

Edgell S, Duke V, 1983 "Gender and social policy: the impact of public expenditure cuts and reactions to them" *Journal of Social Policy* **12** 357-378

Edwards R C, 1979 *Contested Terrain: The Transformation of the Workplace in the Twentieth Century* (Heinemann Educational Books, London)

Edwards R C, Gordon D, Reich M, 1975 *Labour Market Segmentation* (D C Heath, Lexington, MA)

Ehrenreich B, English D, 1979 *For Her Own Good: 150 Years of the Experts' Advice to Women* (Pluto Press, London)

Elger T, 1982 "Braverman, capital accumulation and deskilling" in *The Degradation of Work?* Ed. S Wood (Hutchinson, London) pp 23-53

Elias P, Molho I, 1982 "Regional labour supply: an economic/demographic model" OP 28, Office of Population Censuses and Surveys, St Catherines House, 10 Kingsway, London WC2, England

Employment Gazette various, *Department of Employment Gazette* (HMSO, London)

EOC, 1981 "Women and underachievement at work" research bulletin 5, Equal Opportunities Commission, Overseas House, Quay Street, Manchester, England

Eurostat, 1980 *Labour Force Sample Survey 1973, 1975, 1977* (Office for Official Publications of the European Communities, Luxembourg)

Eurostat, 1981 *Labour Force Sample Survey 1979* (Office for Official Publications of the European Communities, Luxembourg)

Ewing A F, 1972 *Planning and Policies in the Textile Finishing Industry* (Bradford University Press in association with Crosby Lockwood Staples, St Albans, Herts)

Filkin C, Weir D, 1972 "Locality" in *Key Variables in Social Research Volume I— Religion, Housing, Locality* Ed. E Gittus (Heinemann Educational Books, London) pp 106-158

Financial Times, 1983 "Regional aid policy to be more selective" 14 December, 1

Finegan T A, 1981 "Discouraged workers and economic fluctuations" *Industrial and Labor Relations Review* **35**(1) 88-102

Flowerdew R, Salt J, 1979 "Migration between labour market areas in Great Britain 1970-1971" *Regional Studies* **13** 211-232

Fothergill S, Gudgin G, 1979 "Regional employment change: a subregional explanation" *Progress in Planning* **12** 155-220

Fothergill S, Gudgin G,1980 "Regional unemployment change: a sub-regional analysis" *Progress in Planning* **12** 155-219 and Appendix 2, 208-209

Fothergill S, Gudgin G, 1982 *Unequal Growth: Urban and Regional Employment Change in the UK* (Heinemann Educational Books, London)

Fothergill S, Gudgin G, 1983 "Trends in regional manufacturing employment: the main influences" in *The Urban and Regional Transformation of Britain* Eds J B Goddard, A G Champion (Methuen, Andover, Hants) pp 27-50

Francis R, 1983 "Symbols, images and social organization in urban sociology" in *Urban Social Research: Problems and Prospects* Eds V Pons, R Francis (Routledge and Kegan Paul, Henley-on-Thames, Oxon) pp 115-145

Frankenberg R, 1966 *Communities in Britain* (Penguin Books, Harmondsworth, Middx)

Friedman A, 1977a *Industry and Labour* (Macmillan, London)

Friedman A, 1977b "Responsible autonomy versus direct control over the labour process" *Capital and Class* issue 1, 43-57

Fröbel F, Heinrichs J, Kreye O, 1980 *The New International Division of Labour* (Cambridge University Press, Cambridge)

Fuchs V R, 1968 *The Service Economy* (National Bureau of Economic Research, New York)

Fulcher M N, Rhodes J, Taylor J, 1966 "The economy of the Lancaster sub-region" OP 10, Department of Economics, University of Lancaster, Lancaster LA1 4YW, England

Gamarnikow E, 1978 "Sexual division of labour: the case of nursing" in *Feminism and Materialism* Eds A Kuhn, A W Wolpe (Routledge and Kegan Paul, Henley-on-Thames, Oxon) pp 96-123

Gardiner J, 1975 "Women and unemployment" *Red Rag* **10** 12-15

Gardiner J, 1982 "Women, recession and the Tories" *Marxism Today* March 3-11

Garnsey E, 1978 "Women's work and theories of class stratification" *Sociology* **12** 223-243

Gartner A, Riessman F, 1974 *The Service Society and the Consumer Vanguard* (Harper and Row, New York)

Gershuny J, 1978 *After Industrial Society* (Macmillan, London)

Gershuny J, Miles I, 1983 *The New Service Economy: The Transformation of Employment in Industrial Societies* (Francis Pinter, London)

Gershuny J, Pahl R, 1979 "Work outside employment: some preliminary speculations" *New Universities Quarterly* **34** 120-135

Gershuny J, Pahl R, 1980 "Britain in the decade of the three economies" *New Society* January, page 3

Gibbon P, 1973 "Arensberg and Kimball revisited" *Economy and Society* **2** 479-498

Giddens A, 1979 *Central Problems in Social Theory* (Macmillan, London)

Glynn S, Oxborrow J, 1976 *Inter-war Britain: A Social and Economic History* (George Allen and Unwin, Hemel Hempstead, Herts)

Goddard J, 1983 "Structural change in the British space economy" in *The Urban and Regional Transformation of Britain* Eds J R Goddard, A G Champion (Methuen, Andover, Hants) pp 1-26

Goldthorpe J, Llewellyn C, 1980 "Class mobility in Britain: three theses examined" in *Social Mobility and Class Structure in Modern Britain* Eds J Goldthorpe, C Llewellyn, C Payne (Clarendon Press, Oxford) pp 38-67

Gooderson P, 1975 *The Social History of Lancaster 1780-1914* PhD thesis, Department of History, University of Lancaster, Lancaster LA1 4YW, England

Gordon D M, 1972 *Theories of Poverty and Underemployment: Orthodox, Radical and Dual Labor Market Perspectives* (Lexington Books, Lexington, MA)

Gorz A, 1982 *Farewell to the Working Class: An Essay on Post-Industrial Socialism* (Pluto, London)

Green B S R, 1971 "Social area analysis and structural effects" *Sociology* **5** 2-19

Greenfield H I, 1956 *Manpower and the Growth of Producer Services* (Columbia University Press, New York)

Greenhalgh C, 1980 "Male-female wage differentials in Great Britain: is marriage an equal opportunity?" *Economic Journal* **90** 751-771

Gregory D, 1980 "Low pay and no pay in Wales" in *Poverty and Social Inequality in Wales* Eds G Rees, T Rees (Croom Helm, Beckenham, Kent) pp 139-155

Gregory D, Urry J (Eds), 1985 *Social Relations and Spatial Structures* (Macmillan, London)

Grieco M, 1980 "Oil related development and Shetland: the institutional framework" in *The Social Impact of Oil in Scotland* Eds R Parsler, D Z Shapiro (Gower, Farnborough, Hants) pp 146-160

Grigor I, 1980 "Local authority accommodation of oil-related developments in East Ross" in *The Social Impact of Oil in Scotland* Eds R Parsler, D Z Shapiro (Gower, Aldershot, Hants) pp 70-86

Guillaumin C, 1981 "The practice of power and belief in nature" *Feminist Issues* **3** 87-109

Haavio-Manilla E, 1969 "Some consequences of women's emancipation" *Journal of Marriage and the Family* February, 123-134

Habermas J, 1970 "Towards a theory of communicative competence" in *Recent Sociology, number 2* Ed. H Dreitzel (Collier-Macmillan, London) pp 114-148

Habermas J, 1974 "The public sphere: an encyclopaedia article" *New German Critique* **3** 49-55

Hakim C, 1978 "Sexual divisions in the labour force" *Department of Employment Gazette* November, 1264-1268

Hakim C, 1979 "Occupational segregation: a comparative study of the degree and patterns of the differentiation between men and women's work in Britain, the USA and other countries" RP-9, Department of Employment, Caxton House, Tothill Street, London SW1, England

Hakim C, 1981 "Job segregation: trends in the 1970s" *Department of Employment Gazette* December, pages 89 and 521-529

Hall P, Gracey H, Drewett R, Thomas R, 1973 *The Containment of Urban England* volume 1 (George Allen and Unwin, Hemel Hempstead, Herts)

Hall S, 1977 "The 'political' and the 'economic' in Marx's theory of classes" in *Class and Class Structures* Ed. A Hunt (Lawrence and Wishart, London)

Harloe M, Lebas E, (Eds), 1981 *City, Class and Capital: New Developments in the Political Economy of Cities and Regions* (Edward Arnold, London)

Harrington T, 1983 "Explaining state policy-making: a critique of some recent 'dualist' models" *International Journal of Urban and Regional Research* **7** 202-218

Hartmann H, 1979a "Capitalism, patriarchy and job segregation by sex" in *Capitalist Patriarchy* Ed. Z R Eisenstein (Monthly Review Press, New York) pp 206-247

Hartmann H, 1979b "The unhappy marriage of Marxism and feminism: toward a more progressive union" *Capital and Class* issue 8, 1-33

Healey D, 1977 "The overlookers" unpublished paper, copy available from D Healey, Manchester Studies Unit, Manchester Polytechnic, All Saints, Manchester M15 6BH, England

Heap S H, 1980 "World profitability crisis in the 1970s: some empirical evidence" *Capital and Class* issue 12, 66-84

Heath A, 1981a *Social Mobility* (Fontana Books, London)

Heath A, 1981b "Women who get on in the world—up to a point" *New Society* February

Hewitt M, 1958 *Wives and Mothers in Victorian Industry* (Greenwood Press, Westport, CT)

Hindess B, 1976 "On 3-dimensional power" *Political Studies* **24** 329-333

Holt W, 1939 *I Haven't Unpacked: An Autobiography* (George G Harrop, London)

Hope K, Goldthorpe J, 1974 *The Social Grading of Occupations* (Clarendon Press, Oxford)

House of Lords, 1972 *Minutes of Evidence and Proceedings of the Select Committee on the Anti-Discrimination (No. 2) Bill* (HMSO, London)

Humphries J, 1977 "Class struggle and the persistence of the working class family" *Cambridge Journal of Economics* 1 241-258

Humphries J, 1981 "Protective legislation, the capitalist state and working class men: the case of the 1842 Mines Regulation Act" *Feminist Review* 7 1-33

Humphries J, 1983 "The emancipation of women in the 1970s and 1980s: from the latent to the floating" *Capital and Class* issue 20, 46-68

Hunt A, 1975 *Managerial Attitudes and Practices Towards Women at Work* (Office of Population Censuses and Surveys, London)

Hunter J, 1976 *The Making of the Crofting Community* (John Donald, Edinburgh)

Huws U, 1982 *Your Job in the Eighties: A Woman's Guide to New Technology* (Pluto Press, London)

Industrial Survey, 1932 *An Industrial Survey of the Lancashire Area Excluding Merseyside. Made for the Board of Trade by the University of Manchester* (HMSO, London)

Interdepartmental Working Party, 1972 *Unemployment Statistics: Report of an Interdepartmental Working Party* Cmnd 5157 (HMSO, London)

Jackson N, 1930 *Lays of Lancashire* (Werner Laurie, London)

Jessop B, 1982 *The Capitalist State* (Martin Robertson, Oxford)

Jewkes J, Gray E, 1935 *Wages and Labour in the Lancashire Cotton Spinning Industry* (Manchester University Press, Manchester)

Jewkes J, Jewkes S, 1938 *The Juvenile Labour Market* (Left Book Club, London)

JHPG, 1968 *The Moray Firth: A Plan for Growth* (The Jack Holmes Planning Group, 62 Kelvingrove Street, Glasgow C3)

Joyce P, 1980 *Work, Society and Politics* (Harvester Press, Brighton, Sussex)

JTWMA, 1922 *Journal of the National Federation of Textile Work's Manager's Associations* (copy in Harris Library, Preston)

Kapp Howe L, 1978 *Pink Collar Worker* (Putnam, New York)

Keeble D, 1976 *Industrial Location and Planning in the UK* (Methuen, Andover, Hants)

Keeble D, 1980 "Industrial decline in the inner city" in *The Inner City Employment and Industry* Eds A Evans, D Eversley (Heinemann Educational Books, London) pp 108-129

Kerr C, 1954 "The Balkanization of labour markets" in *Labor Mobility and Economic Opportunity* Eds E W Bakke, A Hauser (MIT Press, Cambridge, MA) pp 92-110

Knight A, 1974 *Private Enterprise and Public Intervention: The Courtaulds Experience* (George Allen and Unwin, Hemel Hempstead, Herts)

Kreckel R, 1980 "Unequal opportunity structure and labour market segmentation" *Sociology* 14 525-550

Lancaster City Council, 1977 *Industrial Strategy for Lancaster* research paper, Lancaster Town Hall, Dalton Square, Lancaster, England

Lancaster City Council, 1980 *Population Change in Lancaster District* monitor report 1, Lancaster City Council, Lancaster, England

Lazonick W, 1979 "The self-acting mule" *Cambridge Journal of Economics* 3, 231-262

LCBTR, 1925 and 1936 *Lancaster County Borough Treasurer's Report*, Lancaster Public Library

LDP, 1921 *Lancashire Daily Post* 14 November

LDP, 1923a *Lancashire Daily Post* 25 October

LDP, 1923b *Lancashire Daily Post* 29 October

LDP, 1925 *Lancashire Daily Post* 29 October

LDP, 1927 *Lancashire Daily Post* 28 October

LDP, 1929a *Lancashire Daily Post* 29 October

LDP, 1929b *Lancashire Daily Post* 31 October

LDP, 1929c *Lancashire Daily Post* 4 May

Lee C H, 1979 *British Regional Employment Statistics 1841–1971* (Cambridge University Press, Cambridge)

Lee D, 1981 "Skill, craft and class: a theoretical critique and a critical case" *Sociology* **15** 56–78

Lee D, 1982 "Beyond deskilling: skill, craft and class" in *The Degradation of Work?* Ed. S Wood (Hutchinson, London) pp 146–162

Lever W F, 1979 "Industry and labour markets in Great Britain" in *Spatial Analysis, Industry and the Industrial Environment: Volume 1, Industrial Systems* Eds F E I Hamilton, G J R Linge (John Wiley, New York) 89–114

Lewenhak S, 1977 *Women and Trade Unions: An Outline History of Women in the British Trade Union Movement* (Ernest Benn, London)

Lewis J, 1980 *The Politics of Motherhood: Child and Maternal Welfare in England, 1900–1939* (Croom Helm, Beckenham, Kent)

Liddington J, Norris J, 1978 *One Hand Tied Behind Us: The Rise of the Women's Suffrage Movement* (Virago, London)

Lipietz A, 1980 "The structuration of space, the problem of land and spatial policy" in *Regions in Crisis* Eds J Carney, R Hudson, J Lewis (Croom Helm, Beckenham, Kent) pp 60–92

Littler C, 1980 *The Bureaucratisation of the Shop Floor: The Development of Modern Work Systems* PhD thesis, Department of Sociology, London School of Economics and Political Science, Houghton Street, London WC2, England

Littler C, 1982 *The Development of the Labour Process in Capitalist Societies* (Heinemann Educational Books, London)

Littlewood P, Newby H, Rees G, Rees T, 1984 *Restructuring Capital* (Macmillan, London)

Llewellyn C, 1981 "Occupational mobility and the use of the comparative method" in *Doing Feminist Research* Ed. H Roberts (Routledge and Kegan Paul, Henley-on-Thames, Oxon) pp 129–158

Local Socialism, 1980

Lovenduski J, Hills J (Eds), 1981 *The Politics of the Second Electorate: Women and Public Participation* (Routledge and Kegan Paul, Henley-on-Thames, Oxon)

Loveridge R, Mok A L, 1979 "Theories of labour market segmentation" WP-166, Management Centre, University of Aston, Gosta Green, Birmingham B4 7ET, England

Lovering J, 1978 "The theory of the 'internal colony' and the political economy of Wales" *Review of Radical Political Economics* **10**(3), 55–67

LRG, 1982 "Control at work: North Lancashire cotton weaving 1890–1940" WP-7, Lancaster Regionalism Group, University of Lancaster, Lancaster LA1 4YW, England

Macafee K, 1980 "A glimpse of the hidden economy in the national accounts" *CSO Economic Trends* February, 81–87

McIntosh M, 1978 "The state and the oppression of women" in *Feminism and Materialism* Eds A Kuhn, A M Wolpe (Routledge and Kegan Paul, Henley-on-Thames, Oxon) pp 254–289

MacIntyre S, 1980 *Little Moscows: Communism and Working-class Militancy in Inter-war Britain* (Croom Helm, Beckenham, Kent)

Mackay D I, Boddy D, Brack J, Diack J A, Jones N, 1971 *Labour Markets Under Different Employment Conditions* (George Allen and Unwin, Hemel Hempstead, Herts)

MacKay R, Thomson L, 1979 "Important trends in regional policy and regional employment—a modified interpretation" *Scottish Journal of Political Economy* **2** 233–260

Mackinnon C, 1979 *Sexual Harrassment of Working Women* (Yale University Press, New Haven, CT)

Mackintosh M M, 1979 "Domestic labour and the household" in *Fit Work for Women* Ed. S Burman (Croom Helm, Beckenham, Kent) pp 173-191

McNabb R, 1980 "Segmented labour markets, female employment and poverty in Wales" in *Poverty and Social Inequalities in Wales* Eds G Rees, T Rees (Croom Helm, Beckenham, Kent)

McNally F, 1979 *Women for Hire: A Study of the Female Office Worker* (Macmillan, London)

Mandel E, 1972 *Late Capitalism* (New Left Books, London)

Marquand J, 1980 *Regional Policy Series Number 19: The Role of the Tertiary Sector in Regional Policy* (EEC Commission, Brussels)

Marquand J, 1983 "The changing distribution of service employment" in *The Urban and Regional Transformation of Britain* Eds J B Goddard, A G Champion (Methuen, Andover, Hants) pp 99-134

Martin R, Fryer B, 1973 *Redundancy and Paternalist Capitalism* (George Allen and Unwin, Hemel Hempstead, Herts)

Marx K, 1954 *Capital: Volume 1* (Lawrence and Wishart, London)

Marx K, Engels F, 1952 *Manifesto of the Communist Party* (Progress Publishers, Moscow)

Massey D, 1977 "Towards a critique of industrial location theory" in *Radical Geography* Ed. R Peet (Methuen, London) pp 181-198

Massey D, 1978a "Regionalism: some current issues" *Capital and Class* issue 6, 106-125

Massey D, 1978b "In what sense a regional problem?" *Regional Studies* 13 223-243

Massey D, 1981 "The UK electrical engineering and electronics industries: the implications of the crisis for the restructuring of capital and locational change" in *Urbanization and Urban Planning in Capitalist Society* Eds M Dear, A J Scott (Methuen, London) pp 199-230

Massey D, 1983 "Industrial restructuring as class restructuring" *Regional Studies* 17 73-89

Massey D, Meegan R, 1982 *The Anatomy of Job Loss* (Methuen, London)

Matthews K, 1983 "National income and the black economy" *Journal of Economic Affairs* III 261-267

Metcalf D, 1980 "Unemployment: history, incidence and prospects" *Policy and Politics* 8 21-37

Mewett P, 1977 "Occupational pluralism in crofting" *Scottish Journal of Sociology* 2 31-49

Mewett P, 1982 "Associational categories and the social location of relationships in a Lewis crofting community" in *Belonging* Ed. A P Cohen (Manchester University Press, Manchester), pp 101-131

Middleton L (Ed.), 1977 *Women and the Labour Movement* (Croom Helm, Beckenham, Kent)

Milkman R, 1976 "Women's work and the economic crisis: some lessons from the Great Depression" *Review of Radical Political Economies* Spring 73-97

Milkman R, 1981 "Changes in the position of women in the US manufacturing industry" paper given to British Sociological Association Industrial Sociology Study Group, October, London,

Miller A (Ed.), 1966 "Standard occupational classification" in *Proceedings, Social Statistics Section, American Statistical Association* (American Statistical Association, Washington, DC)

Miller S M, 1975 "Notes on neo-capitalism" *Theory and Society* 2 1-35

Mincer J, 1962 "Labour force participation of married women: a study of labour supply" in *Aspects of Labour Economics: A Conference of the Universities—National Bureau Committee for Economic Research* National Bureau of Economic Research (Princeton University Press, Princeton, NJ) pp 63-97

Mincer J, 1966 "Labor-force participation and unemployment: a review of recent evidence" in *Prosperity and Unemployment* Eds R A Gordon, M S Gordon (John Wiley, New York) pp 73-112

Monopolies Commission, 1968 *Man-made Cellulosic Fibres: A Report on the Supply of Man-made Cellulosic Fibres* (HMSO, London)

Moore B, Rhodes J, 1977 "The relative decline of the UK manufacturing sector" *Cambridge Economic Policy Review* 3(2)

Moore R S, 1980 "Northern notes towards a sociology of oil" in *The Social Impact of Oil in Scotland* Eds R Parsler, D Z Shapiro (Gower, Aldershot, Hants) pp 21-37

More C, 1980 *Skill and the English Working Class* (Croom Helm, Beckenham, Kent)

Moser C A, Scott W, 1961 *British Towns: A Statistical Survey of Social and Economic Differences* (Oliver and Boyd, Edinburgh)

MSRG, 1980 *Merseyside in Crisis* Merseyside Socialist Research Group, 23 Glover Street, Birkenhead, Merseyside, England

Murgatroyd L G, 1979 "Domestic labour in a class society: stratification inside and outside the home" mimeograph: copy available from L G Murgatroyd, Department of Sociology, University of Lancaster, Lancaster LA1 4YL

Murgatroyd L G, 1981 "De-industrialization in Lancaster: a review of the changing structure of employment in the Lancaster district" WP-1, Lancaster Regionalism Group, University of Lancaster, Lancaster LA1 4YW, England

Murgatroyd L G, 1982a *Gender and Class Stratification* DPhil thesis, University of Oxford, Oxford OX1 2JD, England

Murgatroyd L G, 1982b "Gender and occupation stratification" *The Sociological Review* 30 574-602

Murgatroyd L G, 1983 "Domestic labour and the production of people revisited" *Socialist Economic Review* 3 85-98

Murgatroyd L G, 1984 "Women, men and the social grading of occupations" *British Journal of Sociology* forthcoming

Murgatroyd L, Urry J, 1983 "The restructuring of a local economy: the case of Lancaster" in *Redundant Spaces* Eds J Anderson, S Duncan, R Hudson (Academic Press, London) 67-98

Newbould G D, 1970 *Management and Merger Activity* (Guthstead, Liverpool)

Newby H, 1977 *The Deferential Worker* (Allen Lane, London)

Newton K, 1981a "Central places and urban services" in *Urban Political Economy* Ed. K Newton (Frances Pinter, London) pp 117-133

Newton K (Ed.), 1981b *Urban Political Economy* (Frances Pinter, London)

Niemi B, 1980 "The female-male differential in unemployment rates" in *The Economics of Women and Work* Ed. A H Amsden (Penguin Books, Harmondsworth, Middx) pp 325-349

NL, 1917 *Nelson Leader* 10 August

NL, 1922 *Nelson Leader* 27 January

NL, 1927 *Nelson Leader* 10 August

NL, 1928a *Nelson Leader* 12 October

NL, 1928b *Nelson Leader* 22 November

NL, 1930 *Nelson Leader* 28 March

NL, 1932 *Nelson Leader* 24 March

Norris G, 1978 "Industrial paternalism, capitalism and local labour markets" *Sociology* 12 469-489

Norris R, 1980 "Towards a sociology of labour markets" paper presented to the Social Science Research Council Workshop, Crawley, further details available from A Warde

Oakley A, 1972 *Sex, Gender and Society* (Maurice Temple Smith, London)

Oakley A, 1976 "Wise woman and medicine man: changes in the management of childbirth" in *The Rights and Wrongs of Women* Eds J Mitchell, A Oakley (Penguin Books, Harmondsworth, Middx) pp 17-58

O'Connor J, 1973 *The Fiscal Crisis of the State* (St Martin's Press, New York)

OECD, 1976 *Measuring Employment and Unemployment* (Organisation for Economic Cooperation and Development, Paris)

Offe C, Hinrichs K, 1977 "Sozialokonomie des Arleitmarktes und die 'benachteiliger' Gruppen van Arbeitnehmern" in *Opfer des Arbeitsmanktes* Ed. C Offe (Luchterhand, Darmstadt)

OPCS, various *Census of Population: 1921, 1931, 1951, 1961, 1966, 1971, 1981* (HMSO, London)

OPCS, 1971a *Classification of Occupations* (HMSO, London)

OPCS, 1971b *General Household Survey* (HMSO, London)

OPCS, 1979a *General Household Survey, 1977* report SS457F, Social Survey Division, Office of Population Censuses and Surveys (HMSO, London)

OPCS, 1979b *Labour Force Survey* Office of Population Censuses and Surveys (HMSO London)

OPCS, 1980 *Labour Force Survey 1973, 1975, and 1977* (HMSO, London)

OPCS, 1982 *Labour Force Survey 1981* number 3 (HMSO, London)

Oren L, 1979 "The welfare of women in labouring families: England 1860-1950" in *Clio's Consciousness Raised* Eds M Hartman, L W Banner (Harper and Row, New York) pp 226-244

Pahl R, 1980 "Employment, work and the domestic division of labour" *International Journal of Urban and Regional Research* **4** 1-20

Pahl R, 1985 "The restructuring of capital, the local politicai economy and household work strategies: all forms of work in context" in *Social Relations and Spatial Structure* Eds D Gregory, J Urry (Macmillan, London) pp 243-264

Parkin F, 1974 "Strategies of social closure in class formation" in *The Social Analysis of Class Structure* Ed. F Parkin (Tavistock Publications, Andover, Hants) 1-18

Parkin F, 1979 *Marxism and Class Theory: A Bourgeois Critique* (Tavistock Publications, Andover, Hants)

PCBTR, 1925 and 1936 *Preston County Borough Treasurer's Report*

Pelling H, 1967 *Social Geography of British Elections 1885-1910* (Macmillan, London)

Penn R, 1982 "Skilled manual workers in the labour process" in *The Degradation of Work?* Ed. S Ward (Hutchinson, London)

PEP, 1937 *Report on the British Health Services* (Political and Economic Planning, London) pp 99-108

PG, 1908 *Preston Guardian* 30 March

PG, 1923 *Preston Guardian* 23 October

PG, 1930 *Preston Guardian* 26 April

Phillips A, Taylor B, 1980 "Sex and skill: notes towards a feminist economics" *Feminist Review* **6** 79-88

Piepe A, Prior R, Box A, 1969 "The location of the proletarian and deferential worker" *Sociology* **3** 239-244

Pinchbeck I, 1981 *Women Workers and the Industrial Revolution 1750-1850* (Virago, London)

RE, 1974, Introduction to part II of the report of the Drumbuie Public Enquiry Reporter to the Secretary of State for Scotland, Document reference RE 31358/2 TBL, page 172

Redfern P, 1981 "Census 1981—an historical and international perspective: 3, Census geography" *Population Trends* issue 24, 15-25

Regional Trends, 1983 Central Statistical Office (HMSO, London)

Reich M, Gordon D M, Edwards R C, 1980 "A theory of labour market segmentation" in *The Economics of Women and Work* Ed. A Amsden (Penguin Books, Harmondsworth, Middx)

Riley S, 1974 *Tourism, Its Impact on Retail Trade* Tourism Research Unit, Department of Marketing, Unviersity of Lancaster, Lancaster LA1 4YW, England

Robson B T, 1969 *Urban Analysis: A Study of City Structure* (Cambridge University Press, Cambridge)

Rodger J J, 1980 " 'Inauthentic' politics and the public inquiry system" in *The Social Impact of Oil in Scotland* Eds R Parsler, D Z Shapiro (Gower, Aldershot, Hants) pp 121-145

Ross E, 1983 "Survival networks: women's neighbourhood sharing in London before World War I" *History Workshop Journal* **15** (Spring) 5-27

Rothwell R, Zegweld W, 1979 *Technical Change and Unemployment* (Frances Pinter, London)

Routh G, 1980 *Occupation and Pay in Great Britain, 1906-1979* (Macmillan, London)

Rowbotham S, Segal L, Wainwright H, 1979 *Beyond the Fragments* (Merlin Press, London)

RSA, 1983 *Report of an Inquiry into Regional Problems in the United Kingdom* Regional Studies Association (Geo Abstracts, Norwich)

Rubery J, 1978 "Structured labour markets, worker-organisation and low pay" *Cambridge Journal of Economics* **2** 7-36

Rubery J, Tarling R, 1982 "Women in the recession" in *Socialist Economic Review* Eds M Sawyer, K Schott (Merlin Press, London) pp 47-75

Rubin G, 1975 "The traffic in woman: notes on the political economy of sex" in *Towards an Anthropology of Women* Ed. R R Reiter (Monthly Review Press, New York) pp 157-210

Sabel C, 1982 *Work and Politics* (Cambridge University Press, Cambridge)

Sabolo Y, 1975 *The Service Industries* (International Labour Organization, Geneva)

Saunders P, 1979 *Urban Politics* (Penguin Books, Harmondsworth, Middx)

Savage M, 1982 "Control at work: North Lancashire cotton weaving 1840-1940" WP-7, Lancaster Regionalism Group, Department of Sociology, University of Lancaster, Lancaster LA1 4YL, England

Savage M, 1984 *The Social Bases of Working Class Politics: the Labour Movement in Preston, 1890-1940* PhD Thesis, Department of Sociology, University of Lancaster, Lancaster LA1 4YL, England

Scharf L, 1980 *To Work and To Wed: Female Employment, Feminism, and the Great Depression* (Greenwood Press, Westport, CT)

Scott A J, 1980 *The Urban Land Nexus and the State* (Pion, London)

Scott J W, Tilly L A, 1980 "Women's work and the family in nineteenth century Europe" in *The Economics of Women and Work* Ed. A H Amsden (Penguin Books, Harmondsworth, Middx) pp 91-124

Shapiro D Z, 1980 "Oil and Shetland—a comment" in *The Social Impact of Oil in Scotland* Eds R Parsler, D Z Shapiro (Gower, Farnborough, Hants) pp 161-163

Shapiro D Z, 1981 "Industrial relations in the wilderness" in *New Perspectives in Urban Change and Conflict* Ed. M Harloe (Heinemann Educational Books, London) pp 157-178

Sharpe L, 1981 "Does politics matter?: an interim summary with findings" in *Urban Political Economy* Ed. K Newton (Frances Pinter, London) pp 1-26

Shiskin J, 1976 "Employment and unemployment: the doughnut or the hole?" *Monthly Labor Review* February, 3-10

Showler B, Sinfield A, 1981 *The Workless State* (Martin Robertson, Oxford)

Singelmann J, 1978 *From Agriculture to Services* (Sage, London)

Singh A, 1977 "UK industry and the world economy: a case of de-industrialisation" *Cambridge Journal of Economics* 1 113–136

Sloane P J, 1980 *Women and Low Pay* (Macmillan, London)

Smailes A E, 1944 "The urban hierarchy in England and Wales" *Geography* 29 41–51

Smart M W, 1974 "Labour market areas: uses and definitions" *Progress in Planning* 12 241–353

Smelser N J, 1959 *Social Change in the Industrial Revolution: An Application of Theory to the Lancashire Cotton Industry, 1770–1840* (Routledge and Kegan Paul, Henley-on-Thames, Oxon)

Smith H D, 1977 *The Making of Modern Shetland* (Shetland Times, Lerwick)

Smith I J, 1979 "The effect of external takeovers on manufacturing employment change in the Northern Region between 1963 and 1973" *Regional Studies* 13 421–437

Smith R, 1976 "Sex and occupational roles on Fleet Street" in *Dependence and Exploitation in Work and Marriage* Eds S Allen, D Leonard (Longman, London) pp 70–87

Smith R D P, 1968 "The changing urban hierarchy" *Regional Studies* 2 1–19

Spaven M, 1983 *Fortress Scotland* (Pluto Press, London)

Stacey M (Ed.), 1969a *Comparability in Social Research* (Heinemann Educational Books, London)

Stacey M, 1969b "The myth of community studies" *British Journal of Sociology* 20 134–147

Stacey M, 1981 "The division of labour revisited, or overcoming the two Adams" in *Development and Diversity: British Sociology 1950–80* Eds P Abrams, R Deem, J Finch, P Rock (George Allen and Unwin, Hemel Hempstead, Herts) pp 172–190

Stark D, 1980 "Class struggle and the transformation of the labour process: a relational approach" *Theory and Society* 9 89–130

Stewart A, Prandy R, Blackburn R, 1980 *Social Stratification and Occupations* (Macmillan, London)

Stillwell F, 1968 "Location of industry and business efficiency" *Business Ratios* 2 5–15

Storper M, 1981 "Towards a structural theory of industrial location" in *Industrial Location and Regional Systems* Eds J Rees, G Hewings, H Stafford (Croom Helm, Beckenham, Kent) pp 17–40

Storper M, Walker R, 1983 "The theory of labour and the theory of location" *International Journal of Urban and Regional Research* 7 1–43

Summerfield P, 1977 "Women workers in the Second World War" *Capital and Class* issue 1, 27–42

Summerfield P, 1984 *Women Workers in the Second World War. Production and Patriarchy in Conflict* (Croom Helm, Beckenham, Kent)

Taylor J, 1976 "The unemployment gap in Britain's production sector, 1953–73" in *The Concept and Measurement of Unemployment* Ed. G D N Worswick (George Allen and Unwin, Hemel Hempstead, Herts) pp 146–167

The Guardian, 1971 12 April

The Guardian, 1979 2 April

The Guardian, 1981 30 January

The Guardian, 1983 11 June

Thevenot A, 1977 "Les categories sociales en 1975: l'extension du salariat" *Economie et Statistique* 91 (Juillet–Août)

Todd N, 1976 *A History of Labour in Lancaster and Barrow-in-Furness c 1890-1920* MLitt thesis, Department of History, University of Lancaster, Lancaster LA1 4YW, England

Tofler A, 1981 *The Third Wave* (Bantam Books, New York)

Touraine A, 1974 *The Post-Industrial Society* (Wildwood House, London)

Townroe P M, Roberts N J, 1980 *Local-External Economies for British Manufacturing Industry* (Gower, Aldershot, Hants)

Turner H A, 1962 *Trade Union Growth, Structure and Policy* (George Allen and Unwin, Hemel Hempstead, Herts)

Urry J, 1980 "Paternalism, management and localities" WP-2, Lancaster Regionalism Group, Department of Sociology, University of Lancaster, Lancaster LA1 4YW, England

Urry J, 1981a *The Anatomy of Capitalist Societies* (Macmillan, London)

Urry J, 1981b "Localities, regions and social class" *International Journal of Urban and Regional Research* **5** 455-474

Urry J, 1982 "Rurality, restructuring and recomposition" paper presented to the Social Science Research Council–British Sociological Association Rural Economy and Society Study Group; copy available from the Department of Sociology, University of Lancaster, Lancaster LA1 4YW, England

Urry J, 1983 "Some notes on realism and the analysis of space" *International Journal of Urban and Regional Research* **7** 122-127

Urry J, 1984 "Capitalist restructuring, recomposition and the regions" in *Rurality and Locality: Economy and Society in Rural Regions* Eds T Bradley, P Lowe (Geo-Abstracts, Norwich) pp 45-64

Urry J, 1985 "Social relations, space and time" in *Social Relations and Spatial Structures* Eds D Gregory, J Urry (Macmillan, London) pp 19-48

Vanek J, 1980 "Time spent in housework" in *The Economics of Women and Work* Ed. A H Amsden (Penguin Books, Harmondsworth, Middx) pp 82-90

Walby S, 1980 "Services and the Lancaster economy" mimeograph, Lancaster Regionalism Group, Department of Sociology, University of Lancaster, Lancaster LA1 4YW, England

Walby S, 1983a *Gender and Unemployment, Patriarchal and Capitalist Relations in the Restructuring of Gender Relations in Employment and Unemployment* PhD thesis, Department of Sociology, University of Essex, Wivenhoe Park, Colchester CO4 3SQ, England

Walby S, 1983b "Patriarchal structures: the case of unemployment" in *Gender, Class and Work* Eds E Gamarnikov, D Morgan (Heinemann Educational Books, London) pp 149-166

Walby S, 1983c "Women's unemployment, patriarchy and capitalism" in *Socialist Economic Review* Eds M Sawyer, K Schott (Merlin Press, London) pp 99-114

Walby S, 1985 *Patriarchy at Work* (Polity Press, Oxford) forthcoming

Walby S, Green A, 1982 *Women's Unemployment: An Investigation into Discriminatory Practices During Job Loss* mimeograph, Department of Sociology, University of Lancaster, Lancaster LA1 4YW, England

Walker D F, 1980 *Canada's Industrial Space-Economy* (Bell and Hyman, London)

Warde A, 1982 "Changes in the occupational structure of Lancaster, 1901-1951" WP-8, Lancaster Regionalism Group, Department of Sociology, University of Lancaster, Lancaster LA1 4YW, England

Warde A, 1985 "The homogenization of space?: trends in the spatial division of labour in 20th century Britain" in *Restructuring Capital: Recession and Reorganization in Industrial Society* Ed. H Newby (Macmillan, London) forthcoming

Warren K, 1971 "Growth, technical change and planning problems in heavy industry with reference to the chemical industry" in *Spatial Policy Problems of the UK Economy* Eds M Chisholm, G Manners (Cambridge University Press, Cambridge) pp 180–212

Webb C, 1927 *The Woman with No Basket: The History of the Women's Cooperative Guild 1883–1927* Manchester Co-operative Wholesale Society, Manchester

Webber R J, 1977 "The national classification of residential neighbourhoods: an introduction to the classification of wards and parishes" TP-23, Planning Research Applications Group of the Centre for Environmental Studies, 5 Tavistock Place, London WC1H 9SS, England

Webber R, 1978 "Parliamentary constituencies: a socio-economic classification" OP-13, Office of Population Censuses and Surveys, St Catherines House, 10 Kingsway, London WC2, England

Webber R, 1979 "Census enumeration districts: a socio-economic classification" OP-14, Office of Population Censuses and Surveys, St Catherines House, 10 Kingsway, London WC2, England

Webber R, Craig J, 1978 "A socio-economic classification of local authority areas" *Studies on Medical and Population Subjects* number 35 (HMSO, London)

Webster C, 1982 "Healthy or hungry thirties?" *History Workshop* April issue, 110–129

Who Owns Whom, various years (Dun and Bradstreet, London)

Williams A, 1969 *Life in a Railway Factory* (David and Charles, Newton Abbot, Devon)

Wilson E, 1977 *Women and the Welfare State* (Tavistock Publications, Andover, Hants)

Wood S (Ed.), 1982 *The Degradation of Work* (Hutchinson, London)

Zetland County Council Act, 1974 *Public General Acts: Elizabeth II* chapter viii (HMSO, London)

Allin P 166, 167
Althusser L 95, 98
Andrews H 58
Arensberg C 92-93
Armen G 58, 70-74

Banks O 204
Barron R 152-154
Beechey V 146, 148-151, 153, 159
Bell C 140
Bell D 14
Bergmann B 133, 157-158
Bertaux D 131
Blanke B 100
Bosanquet N 154
Bowers J 166
Braverman H 27, 127, 151, 159,
    177-178
Brenner R 79-80
Brody H 92-94
Bruegel I 158, 159
Burns S 23

Cambridge Economic Policy Review 40
Carruthers W 72-73
Carter I 85-88
Castells M 97-98, 195-196, 215
Cawson A 28
Centre for Environmental Studies 59-63
Centre for Urban and Regional
    Development 64-65
Chodorow N 141
Clark I 116
Cockburn C 132
Connelly P 158-159, 160
Cooke P 97-105, 108
Cotton Factory Times 184, 187, 189,
    192
Craig J 59-63

Davies M 167
Delphy C 196
Doeringer P 154
Donnison D 58-59
Duncan O 124, 142, 143
Dunleavy P 28, 61

Edwards R 155
Elias P 166

Filkin C 56
Fotherill S 3, 25, 31, 35-38, 67-70, 74,
    76

Frank G 78, 86
Friedman A 101
Fuchs V 14

Gartner A 14, 27
General Household Survey 21
Gershuny J 6, 15, 17-18, 21, 196
Gibbon P 93-94
Giddens A 54
Goldthorpe J 124, 127, 142
Gramsci A 8, 98, 101
Gray M 85-88
Greenhalgh C 142
Grigor I 110
Gudgin G 3, 25, 31, 35-38, 67-70, 74, 76

Haavio-Manilla E 125, 127
Habermas J 96
Hakim C 8, 124, 128, 154-155, 157
Hall S 99
Hartmann H 134, 155-156, 177,
    193-194
Heath A 127
Hinrichs K 101
Holt W 180
Hope K 124, 127, 142
Humphries J 151, 156
Hunt A 133
Hunter J 85-88
Huws V 175

Jewkes J 186
Jewkes S 186

Kimball S 92-93
Kreckel R 99, 156-157

Lacan J 95
Lancashire Daily Post 202
Lever W 65-67
Littler C 178-179, 193

McIntosh M 159
McIntyre S 214
MacKay D 154
MacKay R 50
MacKinnon C 136
McPhail G 65
Mandel E 27
Mark-Lawson J 12
Marx K 78, 148-149
Massey D 4, 25, 30, 41, 45, 78-79, 98
Matthews K 23

Meegan R 4, 41, 45
Mewett I 85-88, 94-95
Middleton L 204
Miles R 17-18, 21, 196
Milkman R 157, 159, 160
Mill J S 56
Miller A 14
Mincer J 146-147, 148, 159-160
Molho I 166
Moser C 57-58, 60, 62
Murgatroyd L 2-6, 7, 9, 101

Newby H 140
Niemi B 146, 148
Norris G 51, 152-154
Norris R 54, 65, 67

O'Connor J 195
Offe C 101.
Office of Population Censuses and
    Surveys 59-63, 124, 165
Oren L 197
Organisation for Economic Cooperation
    and Development 159, 160

Pahl R 23-24
Parkin F 133
Pelling H 61
Phillips A 127
Prebble I 85-88

Regional Studies Association 3
Riessman F 14, 27
Roberts E 185
Ruberey J 159, 160

Saunders P 28
Savage M 11-12, 212
Scott A 98
Scott W 57-58, 60, 62
Shapiro D 7
Sloane P 154
Smailes A 57, 72
Smith R 136
Smith R D P 72
Soto P 58-59
Stacey M 140
Stewart A 122, 138
Stillwell F 49

Tarling R 159, 160
Taylor B 127
Thomson L 50
Tofler A 23
Touraine A 14

Urry J 2-7, 100

Walby S 9-10, 101, 160
Wallerstein I 78
Warde A 7
Webber R 59-63, 74, 75
Weir D 56

Aberdeenshire 87
Agriculture 13, 80, 85-89, 92-94, 149, 150
Australian National University 140
Automobile industry 24
Avonmouth 43

Barnett J 23
Barnsley 65
Billingham 43
Blackburn 31, 177, 185, 187
Blackpool 60, 64
Bristol 57
Burnley 177, 185

Cambridge 4, 68
Canada 16, 158-159
Capital, 2, 8, 10-13, 27-28, 40ff, 81ff, 210-211
    externally controlled 39-40, 52, 186-188
    local 89-90
Capital accumulation 13, 24, 98-99
Capitalism
    changing social relations in 6, 13-29
    patriarchal relations and 10, 148-162
Cardiff 57, 64
Carrington, Dewhurst and Co. 190
Centre for Environmental Studies 59-63
Centre for Urban and Regional Development 64-65
Chamberlain N 205
Chemical industry 69
Circulation, sphere of 14, 27-29, 81, 98-100
Civil society, 7, 22, 81-84, 88, 90-91, 95, 97 ff
    definition of 22, 98
Clothing and footwear industry 33
Clyde 111
Coal industry 2, 22, 24, 168, 214
'Community' 7, 82, 91-94
Community studies 54
Confederation of British Industry 133
Conservative Party, 3, 61-63, 202, 205, 206
    regional policy of 5-6
Consett 26
Consumption 19, 27-29, 52, 98
Cornwall 25
Cotton industry (see textiles)
Courtaulds (Co.) 39, 44, 51, 209

Crewe 31
Cromarty Firth 106-107

Deindustrialisation, 2, 6, 7, 21-29, 70-71
    definition of 31-32
    in Lancaster 7, 30-53, 55
    politics and 24-29
    services and 13-24
Denmark 8
Dependency theory 77-79, 85-91, 106
Detroit 26
Dick, Kerr and Co. 209, 217
Distributive services 33, 47
Division of labour 88, 89, 101, 137, and passim
Docking industry 5, 24, 211
Domestic labour 9, 90, 142, 146-147, 183, 196, 213
Drumbuie 111-114, 119, 120

East Ross 91
Easter Ross 119
Education services 16, 46, 173, 200, 203
'Engel's Law' 18
Engineering industry 24, 33, 90, 106, 112, 154, 211
Europe, Western 16
European Economic Community 8, 64, 165
Family 10, 86, 92-94, 109, 141-142, 145-148, 150, 182-184, 196, and passim
Fertiliser industry 40, 42-43
Feudalism 79-80
'Fisher-Clark thesis' 16
Fishing industry 22
Fisons (Co.) 43
Floorcovering industry 33, 40, 41-42, 209-211
Food processing industry 90
Formal economy 6, 14, 22, 23, and passim
France 15
Functionalist theory 93, 97
Fylde, the 31, 68

Gender, passim
    class relations and 10, 121-144
    division of labour and 90-91, 101, 121, 137
    households and 22, 121
General Household Survey 21

Germany 16
Gladstone W 8, 108
Gloucester 57
Grampian region 87, 90
Great Yarmouth 57
Greenwood A 197, 202

Harrogate 60
Hawkins, John (Co.) 187
Health services 16, 46, 50, 129, 135, 167,
    173, 200, 203, 207–209
Heysham 31, 43
Highland Fabricators (Co.) 108–109, 114
Horrocks (Co.) 187, 189, 210
Households, 81, 91, 123, 147, 196, and
    passim
    civil society and 83–84
    deindustrialisation and 22–24
    gender divisions and 22, 147, 151, 153
    'household work strategies' 23–24
Howard Davis Combine (Co.) 111
Hunstanton 4

Immingham 43
Imperial Chemicals Industry (Co.) 43
Ince Marshes 43
'Industrial base thesis' 19–20
Informal economy 22–23, 123, 196
Insurance and banking services 33
Invergordon 108
Inverness 106
Ipswich 57
Ireland, 92–94
    Northern 40, 69
Isle of Sheppey 24
Isle of Skye 112
Italy 23

Japan 16

Kirkaldy 42

Labour markets, passim
    local 4, 26, 31, 54, 63–67, 98,
        184–186
    men in 34–35, 47–49, 122, 211–212
    sex segregation in 8–9, 10, 12, 47–49,
        122, 128–129, 131–142, 152–160,
        167–175, 210–214
    types of 99–101, 132, 154–155
    women in 8, 101, 124–143, 147,
        151–160, 163, 181–182, 184–186,
        210–214

Labour movement 12, 26, 50, 52, 90, 94,
    201–209
    (see also trade unions, Labour Party)
Labour Party 3, 24, 61–63, 198,
    201–209, 211–215
Labour process 17, 90, 131, 177–194
Lake District 31
Lancashire, 59
    Mid 37, 69
    North 195–215
    North East 37, 69
    South 37
Lancaster 6, 12, 24, 30–53, 55, 59, 65,
    66, 68, 70, 72–73, 90, 201, 204, 206,
    208, 209, 210–211
Lansils (Co.) 39, 43–44, 51
Leeds 64
Leicester 65
Liberal Party 3, 62–63, 202, 211
Lincoln 57
Liverpool 31, 187
Local authorities 59–63, 73
Locality, 1, 6–7, 13, 20, 24, 82
    comparability of 7, 54–76
    comparative trajectories of 7, 58, 62,
        70, 76
    politics and 24–29, 83–84, 195–215
Loch Carron 111
Loch Kishorn 111–112, 114
London 5, 19, 26, 38, 41, 54, 64, 70, 82,
    136
Longridge 185
Lonsdale 60
Luton 54
Luxemburg 16

Manpower Services Commission 112
Manufacturing, 2, 3, 13, 45, 58, and
    passim
    differences from services 17–20
    distribution of 67–70
    employment changes in 6, 14, 15–16,
        32–38
    gender divisions in 6, 47, 129, 138,
        158, 175–195, 209–213
Marxism 13, 77, 145, 146, 159, 178, 195
Melton Mowbray 65
Merchant navy 22
Merseyside 5, 26
Mexborough 65
Middle East 106
Modernisation theory 54, 77
Moray 106–108

Morecambe 31, 60, 65, 72, 90
Mowlem-Taylor-Woodrow (Co.) 111

Nelson 12, 183, 195, 197, 200, 202-209, 211-212
Nelson, Amos (Co.) 209
'New international division of labour' 5, 30, 74
Nigg 109, 111, 112, 114
Northampton 57, 64
Northwich 31
Norwich 57

Oil industry 7-8, 69, 77, 89-91, 96, 106-120

Parliamentary constituencies 60-63
Paternalism 51, 210-211
Patriarchy, 10, 92-93, 147, 148, 150, 161
    capitalist relations and 10, 148-162
    definition of 92, 178
    in the workplace 11, 90, 177-194
Peasants 79, 85-89, 92-94
Pennines 31
Periphery 5, 7, 74, 77-95
Peterborough 57
Planning, 1, 4, 8, 20, 96-120
    definition of 104-106
Planning theory 97-106
Plastics industry 40
Plymouth 57
Portsmouth 57
'Postindustrial society' 13, 14
Preston 11, 12, 31, 177-194, 199-203, 206, 208-213
Production 27-29, 52, 81, 83-84, 98, 99
Professional services 2, 33, 45-46, 129
Public administration 33-34

Railways 22, 34, 211
Reading 57
Realist philosophy 7, 8, 80-84, 88, 95, 97
Region, 1, 3, 13, 25-26, 30-31, 50-51, 78-79, 163-164, 175-176
    definition of 31-32
Regional policy 4-5, 38, 40-41, 72, 75
Reproduction 98-99, 101
Rigby E 206
Rossendale 31
Rotherham 65

Scarborough 60

Scotland, 7-8, 40, 50, 214
    North 8, 77, 85-91, 96, 106-120
Scottish Nationalist Party 117
Services, 2, 16-21, 58
    consumer 17, 20
    definition of 6, 15, 196-197
    distribution of 6, 15
    employment changes in 6, 14-16, 32-38, 173
    gender divisions in 9, 17, 19, 45-49, 132-133, 137-142, 195-215
    producer 2, 17
    "self-servicing" 6, 15, 22-24
    state and 18, 47, 196-197, 207-209
Service workers 2, 122, 129, 131, 135, 167
Shaw T 192, 201
Sheffield 65
Shell (Co.) 43
Shetland Islands 90, 114-117, 120
Shipbuilding industry 2, 22
Skelmersdale 44
Skill 127, 155, 181
    deskilling 131, 133, 151, 177-178, 184, 193-194
Social class, passim
    struggles of 8, 24, 29, 51-52, 79-80, 195-215
Social Democratic Party 3
South Africa 51
Southampton 57, 64
Southport 31
Staffordshire 69
State, 8, 24, 88, 96, 98-105, 112, 117, 120
    civil society and 91
    employment and 13, 14, 47, 49
    local 50, 59, 90, 98, 110, 199-200, 207-209
    nation 79, 98, 117-120
    regional 112, 117-120
    struggles and 27-29, 98-99, 101-105, 117-120, 195-215
    welfare and 12, 95, 101, 204-209
    women and 9, 168, 174, 198
Status 125, 131, 140
Steel industry 22, 24
Storey, T (Co.) 204
Structuralist theory 80, 87, 95
Sussex 68

Textile industry 2, 11-12, 33, 40, 43-45, 51, 69, 90, 167-168, 177-194, 200, 211-214

Tokyo 26
Tourist industry 46
Trades unions 25, 51–52, 110, 133–135,
    153, 155–156, 174, 183–184,
    190–192, 201–202, 204–206, 208,
    212–213
"Tradition" 7, 75, 86, 167
Tynemouth 61
Tyneside 54, 60

Unemployment, 3, 31, 34–35, 40, 51,
    112, 185–186, 191
    changes in 14, 21
    women and 9, 145, 161–176
Uneven development 3, 30, 77, 78, 99,
    101
United Kingdom 7–9, 13–29, 31–32, 55,
    100, 145, 154, 155, 158, 161, 164,
    165, 196, 213
    East Anglia 2, 3, 4, 54, 68, 171, 173
    East Midlands 3
    North 40
    North East 2, 43, 50
    North West 2, 7, 12, 31–32, 45, 49,
        55, 167, 169, 171

United Kingdom (continued)
    South East 2, 3, 19, 169
    South West 3, 133
    West Midlands 69
United States of America 15, 23, 80, 140,
    146, 148, 155–156, 157–158, 160, 165

Wales 2, 40, 173, 214
    North 59, 60, 68
    South 2, 25, 26, 50, 69, 168
Warboys (Essex) 43
Warrington 31
Wester Ross 110–112, 119
Women, passim
    labour market and 8, 34, 47–49,
        124–143
    part-time work and 19, 34–35, 174
Women's Cooperative Guild 204–205
Women's movement 53, 204–209
Worcester 57

York 57
Yorkshire, South 69
    West 37, 69